COMMISSIONING THE PAST

COMMISSIONING THE PAST

*Understanding South Africa's
Truth and Reconciliation Commission*

WITWATERSRAND UNIVERSITY PRESS

Witwatersrand University Press
1 Jan Smuts Avenue
Johannesburg
2001
South Africa

© Witwatersrand University Press 2002

First published 2002

Reprinted 2003

ISBN 1-86814-358-9

All rights reserved. No part of this publication may be reproduced, stored in a retrieval system, or transmitted in any form or by any means, electronic, mechanical, photocopying, recording or otherwise, without the prior permission of the copyright owners.

Funded by the European Union through the CWCI Fund

Cover art: Penelope Siopis

Cover Design and Typesetting by Crazy Cat Designs,
Johannesburg, South Africa
Printed and bound by Interpak Books,
Pietermaritzburg, South Africa

CONTENTS

Introduction

The Power of Truth: South Africa's Truth and Reconciliation
Commission in Context
Deborah Posel and Graeme Simpson   1

Part One
Insider Accounts

1 Researching the 'Truth': A View from Inside the Truth and
Reconciliation Commission
Janet Cherry, John Daniel and Madeleine Fullard   17

2 False Promises and Wasted Opportunities?: Inside South Africa's
Truth and Reconciliation Commission
Piers Pigou   37

3 Monumental Historical Memory: Managing Truth in the Everyday
Work of the South African Truth and Reconciliation Commission
Lars Buur   66

Part Two
Victims' Stories

4 The Murder of Sicelo Dlomo
Piers Pigou   97

5 The Story of Thandi Shezi
Pamela Sethunya Dube   117

6 Nothing But the Truth: The Ordeal of Duma Khumalo
Mtutuzeli Matshoba   131

Part Three
Outsider Assessments

7 The TRC Report: What Kind of History? What Kind of Truth?
  Deborah Posel   147

8 The Truth and Reconciliation Commission and the Pursuit of 'Social Truth': The Case of Kathorus
  Philip Bonner and Noor Nieftagodien   173

9 National Narrative versus Local Truths: The Truth and Reconciliation Commission's Engagement with Duduza
  Hugo van der Merwe   204

10 'Tell No Lies, Claim No Easy Victories': A Brief Evaluation of South Africa's Truth and Reconciliation Commission
  Graeme Simpson   220

PREFACE

This book evaluates the complex and contradictory processes of 'truth recovery' embodied in the practices of the South African Truth and Reconciliation Commission. The various papers emerged from a conference entitled 'Commissioning the Past – An Evaluation of the South African TRC', which took place in June 1999 and aimed to create a multidisciplinary forum for evaluating the TRC. This conference, jointly organised by the Centre for the Study of Violence and Reconciliation and the University of the Witwatersrand's History Workshop, brought together academics, researchers, community workers, historians, NGO activists, victims of human rights abuses, members of survivor organisations, and staff and functionaries of the TRC itself. The conference paid particularly close attention to the opportunities and obstacles associated with the official commissioning of 'truth' about South Africa's recent past, in relation to strategies of nation-building, reconciliation and restorative justice.

Like the conference, this book aims to provide a multifaceted evaluation of the TRC's truth-production enterprise. It poses key questions about whether a necessarily selective and haphazard process of truth recovery could ever satisfy local and individual needs, as opposed to national political ones. The book sets out a series of evaluations of TRC processes and the 'truth' they delivered. These evaluations are concerned with national politics, but also take into account the specific, local implications of the TRC's hearings and findings, as well as the uncensored voices of some of the survivors of human rights abuses, who testified before the Commission and in whose name the entire exercise was ostensibly undertaken.

The conference aired the views of three groups with different perspectives on the TRC: academic scholars; Commissioners and researchers who worked with the TRC; and people who told the Commission stories of victimisation, on behalf of themselves or a family member. The emerging dialogues between 'outsiders' and 'insiders', and between national, local and individual experiences, were a distinguishing feature of the conference, and have shaped the way the book is structured.

We gratefully acknowledge the financial support of the European Union's CWIC Fund, which subsidised the conference and the printing of this book. Without this support, it would not have been possible to present to an international audience some of the lessons of the South African experience.

Introduction

THE POWER OF TRUTH
South Africa's Truth and Reconciliation Commission in Context

Deborah Posel and Graeme Simpson

The concept of truth, always cause for controversy, became the object of newly vitriolic and sceptical contestation during the late twentieth century. Embracing postmodern theories widely in the ascendancy, many scholars abandoned the pursuit of truth altogether, as an entirely fruitless and impossible project. Others, less persuaded by the relativist case, regrouped in defence of modest – and often lingeringly uncertain – claims to truth with a small 't'. These academic ructions had ripples more widely, too, in popular currents of debate. In his book *Truth: A History and a Guide for the Perplexed*, Felipe Fernandez-Armesto laments that 'trapped between fundamentalists who believe they have found truth, and relativists who refuse to pin it down, the bewildered majority in between continues to hope there is a truth worth looking for, without knowing how to go about it or how to answer the voices from either extreme'.[1]

Yet, in one of the striking historical ironies of the late twentieth century, this philosophical angst about the pursuit of truth has been accompanied by a new-found political confidence in exactly this project. The growing global enthusiasm for truth commissions represents a reassertion not merely of the possibility of the idea of objective historical truth, but of its profound political importance. Indeed, widely promoted as appropriate and effective vehicles of conflict resolution or restorative justice in countries trying to break away from authoritarian and violent pasts,[2] truth commissions evoke high expectations of the power of truth. By retrieving typically veiled and traumatic histories of atrocity and violation, truth commissions are seen as serving critical functions of historical acknowledgement in lieu of denial, memorialisation (particularly in respect of those whose experiences of suffering were denied and trivialised), and moral redress.

In the midst of postmodern scepticisms, truth commissions can seldom be wholly naive about their task. Indeed, their setting, typically in the context of a politically negotiated transition from authoritarian rule, may produce contentious debates about the robustness of truth-telling standards, themselves often shaped by the politics of compromise. Nonetheless, the aggregated truth that is recovered is seen as the basis on which to pass informed, objective judgements on the past, in ways that can help to transcend the legacies of past conflict and prevent their recurrence. Any obvious traces of bias or distortion, any signs of a desultory or timid engagement with the task at hand, would scupper such a project from the start.

In the pursuit of 'truth', a truth commission also has to confront daunting political challenges, alongside the more familiar scholarly difficulties of truth-telling. Truth commissions are political interventions, usually under highly charged and volatile conditions, in countries marked by histories of extreme violence and conflict. Institutions of law and governance may themselves be unstable, making it untenable to prosecute human rights violators, but also rendering the fate of an official commission precarious and uncertain. The authorised confrontation with the past may be strongly resisted, with the commission having to coax participation, woo testimonies and shape versions of events so as to avoid exacerbating existing tensions and ruptures. The greater the power of truth, the more contested it is likely to be.

South Africa's Truth and Reconciliation Commission (TRC), the twenty-first of its kind, was arguably the most ambitious to date, and has been hailed in many parts of the world as a new model for confronting a troubled and divisive history. With the violent overthrow of the apartheid regime averted and the institutional matrix of the state largely intact, the TRC took shape within the politics of negotiated compromise between the outgoing exponents of white minority rule and the incoming champions of constitutional democracy. Here, the pursuit of truth was construed as a multi-purpose exercise. The official confrontation with the past was seen not only as a means of setting a distorted and contested historical record straight, important and central though this was. Truth itself was also to foster individual and national reconciliation, through the catharsis of confession and forgiveness undergone by the perpetrators of human rights abuses and their victims, and an ensuing national consensus about the need to preserve a culture of human rights in the future. The production of a shared national history and of public memories in respect of landmark historical events and struggles was understood to be an integral part of the new nation-building project. Going further still: unveiling the truth was envisaged as a constitutionally defensible alternative to criminal prosecution, by enabling the granting of amnesty to perpetrators who made full disclosure.

This book looks at how the problem of truth arose in the case of South Africa's TRC, the modalities of truth that it delivered, and their effects. In explicit and sometimes very searching ways, the TRC took the sorts of questions familiar to scholars of the past – questions about the nature of truth, evidence, orality and representation – into a much more heated public and political domain. Our aim in this volume is to capture the complexities inherent in the TRC's truth-finding, understood as an active, productive and contested enterprise, embedded as much in the political drama of South Africa's transition from apartheid and the new state's aspirations to nation-building, as in the less visible, more humdrum daily life of the Commission's bureaucracies.

Given its multiple imperatives, the TRC's truth-finding mission was wide-ranging and demanding. The enabling legislation required the Commission to establish as full and reliable as possible a record of gross human rights violations in the country from 1960 to 1993 (subsequently extended to May 1994), both by examining individual cases and by producing aggregated data showing local and national patterns of violence and violation. In addition to this descriptive record, the Commission was required to establish the 'antecedents' and 'causes' for gross human rights violations, as well as the 'motives and perspectives' of victims and perpetrators. Understanding why gross human rights violations had taken place was seen as crucial to the future of democracy in the country: 'It is only by accounting for the past that we can become accountable for the future.'[3] Furthermore, truth was to be told from a variety of perspectives, giving both victims and perpetrators opportunities to tell their own stories. As far as possible, these stories were to have a national airing, in public hearings that would be widely broadcast. By inserting these declarations into the public domain, the veiled, distorted version of the past propagated under apartheid would be widely and openly debunked, while more 'authentic' accounts would be heard and acknowledged across the nation, and more globally. (In fact, only some ten per cent of the nearly 22 000 victim testimonies were aired in public hearings, while the rest were gathered in the form of written statements, and a large proportion of amnesty applications were decided in chambers rather than in public hearings.)

A sizeable and variegated institutional structure was established in a bid to meet these diverse and ambitious goals. TRC Commissioners presided at a series of public hearings around the country, intended to authenticate the stories of selected individual victims of gross human rights violations and confront the perpetrators who came forward to confess their deeds publicly. These hearings – particularly those of the Human Rights Violations Committee – were imagined as creating a 'safe space' for 'giving voice' to the once voiceless victims of South Africa's violent past.[4] This Human Rights Violations Committee researched the veracity of individual narratives of violation, and compiled quantitative national data in respect of types and patterns of gross human rights violations. An Amnesty Committee (in fact, several amnesty committees) investigated and adjudicated perpetrators' claims to amnesty, according to the accuracy and exhaustiveness of their disclosures and their compliance with a set of criteria, including the ability to demonstrate that they had been acting with a political motive and in the name of a known political organisation.

Along with these differentiated institutional functions went different techniques of truth-finding, with distinct genealogies and epistemological underpinnings. A large part of the TRC's enterprise was 'forensic', involving the pursuit of objective 'facts' about the country's past. This was primarily the work of the TRC's research and investigative bureaucracies, which gathered, classified and stored tens of thousands of applications for amnesty and claims of gross human rights violations.

This 'fact-finding' mission itself drew on dual traditions of evidence and registers of meaning, part 'science' and part 'law'. In some respects, the TRC closely resembled the quasi-judicial official commission of inquiry, a well-established formation in the repertoire of the South African state. Invoking the semiotics of science, the model commission of inquiry was headed by respected experts or judges, trusted for their capacities for sober, rational deliberation and reflection, who gathered all relevant data, heard all pertinent sides of the story, and then ostensibly extracted the reliable, objective truth. Seemingly elevating its activities above the normative and ideological into the domain of fact, the commission of inquiry offered states a device for producing authoritative judgements in the midst of politically competing versions of how things were and how they ought to be. In the case of the TRC, the epistemological domain was unusually contested, with notions of truth, method and objectivity problematised and internally debated (Posel & Simpson, in this volume), in the light of global philosophical controversies about truth. Yet the imprints of resolutely positivist epistemology – typical of most official state commissions – remained powerful, underpinned by the assumption that the domains of fact and value were thoroughly separable.

The pursuit of relevant 'facts' was intended to be rigorous and substantial, drawing on appropriate expertise and experience, in the interests of 'scientifically' objective and robust findings. The Commission's Research Department was given serious powers of search, seizure and subpoena, and was significantly larger and better resourced than most other truth commissions.[5] In prospect was a serious engagement with South Africa's recent past, in which an analysis of the 'antecedents and causes' of violence, 'motives' of perpetrators, and chains of command and responsibility could become the object of systematic research.

Yet the promise was richer than the practice. The TRC's capacity to verify the evidence and information placed before it was severely impaired (Pigou, in this volume). This significantly compromised the quality of the empirical data necessary to sustain the sorts of positivist outcomes anticipated in the TRC's legislative and political mandate. Indeed, Pigou implies that there was a self-conscious retreat from any such positivist evidentiary burden when he hints at the working notion of 'sufficiently verifiable information' employed in the TRC. This contradictory notion is a highly significant echo of the term 'sufficient consensus', which was so central to the politically negotiated settlement that gave rise to South Africa's interim constitution, paved the way for the 1994 election, and underpinned the establishment of the TRC in the first place.

If recourse to 'science' created one set of expectations and practices in the pursuit of 'the facts', the idea of 'law' created another. Many signifiers of the TRC process invoked the sobriety, formality and discipline of the law, in ways that complemented and confirmed the aura of 'scientific' expertise and objectivity. However, the legal paradigm within which the Commission operated also invoked conflicting benchmarks of evidence and therefore of 'truth' itself. In some respects, the TRC was presented explicitly as an alternative to the option of putting the perpetrators of gross human rights violations on trial; it would be a speedier and more reconciliatory process, requiring less exacting standards of evidence and providing opportunities for victims and survivors to testify that were conventionally precluded in criminal justice proceedings. Yet for all this, the TRC represented the claim to an alternative (albeit non-punitive) system of justice, which had been shaped by the vagaries of a politically negotiated settlement but was inextricably intertwined with the law – and this had an important influence on the parameters of the Commission's truth.

First, the TRC's mandate, frame of reference and methodology were largely defined by legislation enacted by Parliament. The Commissioners frequently had recourse to 'the Act' in order to determine what matters fell within the purview of the Commission's various committees, and this substantially and selectively shaped the kind of truth about apartheid that the TRC was capable of recovering. In particular, the legislative framework could only accommodate patterns of violence and social conflict that were narrowly defined as 'political'. This narrow definition precluded an examination of more widely experienced structural violence, or violence based on race and gender, and could not deal with the hazy boundaries between the political and the criminal, which actually characterised lived experience under apartheid.

Second, as a statutory institution able to make legally enforceable decisions, the Commission was subject to the rules of administrative fairness, and had to respect the constitutional rights of those who testified or were implicated during its various hearings. Indeed, on the basis of the *audi alteram partem* rule, which states that both sides must have the opportunity to be heard, much of the TRC's administrative and legal 'firepower' was consumed in trying (often unsuccessfully) to ensure that victims were informed of amnesty hearings related to their cases or that alleged perpetrators were represented when they were implicated during a victim's testimony. Pigou makes the point that the quality of TRC investigations into specific cases was also heavily dependent on the quality of the legal representation that particular victims or perpetrators could afford. He implies that the TRC's truth-recovery processes largely fell foul of the ordinary problems of access to justice that disproportionately afflict the poor within the criminal justice system more generally. Either way, this enormous, legally-enforced bureaucratic responsibility clearly limited the 'quantity' and 'quality' of truth accessible to the TRC.

Even more striking were the all-consuming legal challenges to the Commission, which tied it up in court proceedings for much of its life. More often than not, these were initiated by former violators of human rights, who now invoked the new constitution to protect themselves and their reputations from the scrutiny of the Commission or the allegations of their former victims. At the outset, the families of victims launched a constitutional challenge to the amnesty provisions of the Promotion of National Unity and Reconciliation Act. There were intricate legal battles over the refusal of former state president P.W. Botha to testify before the Commission, even when subpoenaed, and ultimately the legal challenges brought by F.W. de Klerk and others successfully prevented the Commission from printing their names in its final report.

The Commission employed a large contingent of lawyers, with particular styles of investigation and expectations of forensic evidence, generally more attuned to describing individual acts of abuse than to reading these within a broader historical context. Indeed, there is little room in legal proceedings for structural explanations of wrongdoing; from the perspective of the law, agency is first and foremost a question of individual accountability. Yet there was an irresolvable tension between these uncritical, jurisprudential notions of forensic truth, and the commitment to a psychologically sensitive and empirically uncritical 'healing process' associated with the victim's testimony or the perpetrator's confession (Simpson, in this volume).

The TRC's engagement with truth was also significantly shaped by its role as a powerful media spectacle in South Africa's reconciliation enterprise. As one of the Commission's researchers put it, 'the TRC's direct impact on the process of national reconciliation [was] powerfully mediated by the mass media. The public domain in which this "major social and political drama" unfolded [was] increasingly a "mediazised" arena.'[6] The most familiar and influential global face of the TRC was the public hearing – a novel feature of the South African Commission. These hearings were the primary means for constructing collective memories of oppression and struggle, shaped by powerful epistemological myths about the primacy and authenticity of direct experience – 'seeing' – in recounting truth. The hearings were construed as opportunities to 'uncover' pristine, uncorrupted truths about a past previously 'hidden from history', by creating safe public spaces in which victims and survivors (or their spokespersons) could tell their stories directly and openly. Memory was rendered as merely a passive recollection of the past, rather than as a more active, selective remaking of it.

The opportunity for public audiences to witness these accounts and the emotional anguish associated with their retrieval directly became, in all their intensity, became the basis for their collective authentication.[7] The televising of the hearings supported this epistemology of 'seeing' as self-evidently authentic. Television viewers worldwide witnessed the TRC as a compelling drama of exposé, confession and, at times, repentance, broadcast live or in snippets on national television, as well as on global networks such as CNN and the BBC. In the words of Max du Preez, a local journalist who covered the TRC extensively, 'South Africans sat spellbound as we broadcast seven hours a day of hearings. The Truth Commission hearings were perfect for television journalism. It was not a story about politicians – it was about the way ordinary men, women and children felt about the horrors of apartheid. The TV cameras could rake the close-ups of these feelings into every living room in the country, and beyond[8] – as though bringing television cameras close-up confirmed the immediacy and veracity of the truths being told.

In other ways too the medium was powerfully part of the message. It was implicitly selective about who spoke and who was heard in the public hearings. This selection was determined partly by sensitivities to the demography of race and gender, and partly by the historical magnitude and profile of the cases themselves. In determining what truth was commodified within the global market, the performative priorities of the electronic media were more important than either the facts of particular cases or their deeper resonance with more widespread experiences of violence under apartheid. Equally significant was the way in which the chosen cases were projected into the living rooms of selective memory. The sheer power of the public testimonies of victims and perpetrators, coupled as they were with the drama of catharsis and the rhetoric of forgiveness, created neat, emotionally charged 'sound bites' of truth, and seemed to remove the need to penetrate the background or look beyond the specific testimony. In the media arena, the truth delivered by the TRC was truncated and carved up into consumable information and drama, from which an aggregated impression was selectively extracted. Indeed, even the vagaries of what was and wasn't newsworthy, or the extent to which the public became saturated with these media images as time passed, meant that those who testified towards the end of the TRC process were not 'heard' as clearly as those at the beginning.

If the disciplines of science and law ground 'truth' in careful attention to the details of particular cases, the televised hearings tended to extract more general, 'universal' truths about experience, truths about suffering and victimisation, remorse and reconciliation, which undergirded the TRC as a strongly moral performance. The televised confessional, which is what the public hearings became, created space for the telling of individual stories, but with an overriding sense of their more global, 'human' messages.

This universalising impulse was especially conspicuous in international media coverage of the TRC. The Commission found a devoted television audience outside the country. But global television, which pitches its messages in limited sound bites across widely divergent cultures and contexts, is not well suited to the communication of complexity. The truths about South Africa's violent past told on television, those facets of the country's history that are now widely known as a result of this coverage, were thus moulded in a global discourse of violence and suffering. What happened in South Africa under apartheid, as depicted on CNN, for example, looked essentially similar to what happened under authoritarian Eastern European regimes: both were instances of a globally comprehensible tale of wrongdoing, of 'man's inhumanity to man'. Details about the historical context, or the particular motivations and preconditions that explained the circumstances under which a particular victim was murdered, were less relevant than the fact of the violation, captured under the broad rubric of apartheid's injustices. In this way, the televised drama of the TRC told many powerful truths about South Africa's past, but in a discourse that would make the experiences of a rural black insurgent, for example, comprehensible and accessible to an urban American or Iranian.

This pursuit of the general and representative was reinforced by other communicative repertoires of global television. For instance, the TRC's media-friendly modes of truth-telling were shaped by some of the conventions of televangelism: the medium was used to portray and affirm the religious intimacies of confession, faith and repentance. Overseen by the charismatic figure of Archbishop Tutu, whose appearance on television was compelling, the public hearings became a vehicle for the sort of healing and redemption that, in Tutu's view, would help cement the new nation morally. The reconciliation that might be effected by truth-telling was regarded as more important than the details of the stories being told, not just because this made for more gripping television, but because the promotion of reconciliation was one of the powerful rationales for the TRC. Once again, the 'truths' of suffering and injustice were universalised, in this case within a Christian framework of compassion and forgiveness.

Another critical notion that shaped the truth-recovery process was the vital contribution the TRC was meant to make to the reconstruction of nationhood, with voluntary confessions leading to forgiveness on the part of victims and repentance on the part of perpetrators. Nowhere was this perspective more graphically represented than in the title of Desmond Tutu's book reflecting on the Commission and his role as its head, *No Reconciliation Without Forgiveness*.[9] The TRC was one of the earliest sites for the enactment of the idea of the 'rainbow nation', with the Commission seen as a means of putting a divided and conflictual past behind the nation through acknowledgement, rather than amnesia. Indeed, this project was rooted in the oft-quoted postscript to the interim constitution, which was framed in the final hours of the negotiation process at Kempton Park and provided the bedrock for the eventual establishment and constitutional defence of the TRC. This text is unequivocal: 'The pursuit of national unity, the well-being of all South African citizens and peace require reconciliation between the people of South Africa and the reconstruction of society.'[10]

This script of nationhood, which supplied the dominant themes of Nelson Mandela's presidency, represented South Africa as a collection of different peoples, different cultures, competing political affiliations, and therefore different perspectives on the past – all of which merited acknowledgement. South Africa's unity as a nation would derive from its heterogeneity as a 'rainbow' and its respect for diversity. Building a nation depended fundamentally on virtues of mutual respect and tolerance. Closely linked to the politics of compromise that shaped the transition from apartheid to a constitutional democracy, 'rainbowism' required the TRC to demonstrate its sensitivity to divergent viewpoints on the past, its capacity to recognise and affirm diversity, yet produce a moral framework and historical narrative that combined these differences into a harmonious larger whole. For this purpose, it was necessary to excavate the horrors of the past, and confront them openly and honestly in the present, so as to produce a national consensus on the 'truth' as the ground for moral unity in the future.

This framework for passing judgement on the past was essentially moral: the aim was to identify the perpetrators of morally reprehensible actions and the victims whom they had harmed. From a nation-building perspective, many details of the thousands of individual narratives were unimportant (Posel, in this volume). The task was rather to produce an account of the past sufficient to portray the moral fact of gross human rights violations. The 'truth' would be told in terms of simple moral binaries of 'victim' and 'perpetrator', associated with unambiguous judgements of right and wrong. There was no place here to explore moral ambiguities born of the politics of complicity or collaboration under apartheid; nor to explore the complexities of social causation, where individuals are caught up in structural processes that both motivate and constrain their actions, in ways that may not be intelligible to the actors themselves (Bonner & Nieftagodien, in this volume).

If the moral binary of 'victim' and 'perpetrator' imposed one set of constraints on the 'truth', the prism of nation-building restricted the focus further to a relatively narrow band of gross human rights violations deemed to be 'political'. With regard to the 'full disclosure' required for amnesty, the TRC relied on a clear-cut distinction between politically motivated violence and crime. Tacitly, the hallmark of 'political' action was that it derived from association with one or other known political party (or with the liberation movements that were their predecessors in the apartheid era). Although the TRC did contemplate the roles of criminal gangs in political assassinations, and turned down a significant number of amnesty applications specifically on the basis that they had been brought by convicted violent criminals who could not prove a political motive, the Commission's contribution to nation-building could only be sustained at the party-political level, and by denying the blurred dividing line between party-political and other forms of violence. It is only through a somewhat sanitised version of the past that it is possible to cultivate such a clear distinction between political and criminal violence, with 27 April 1994 (the date of South Africa's first democratic election) standing like an unbreachable wall between the era of political violence and the era of antisocial, criminal violence. In the process, the TRC arguably did more to mask than to reveal some of the most deeply rooted and sustained patterns of social conflict under apartheid.

The conception of the TRC as a nation-building endeavour, rooted in a restorative justice model, had implications not just for the past but for the future. Although the 'victim-centred' restorative justice model was based on the idea of reparation for victims and survivors, it omitted to confront the consequences of the failure of reparative measures in the wake of the Commission. Even more striking was the assumption that restorative justice would contribute to the re-establishment of the rule of law in South Africa, as if the post-apartheid thief or carjacker would somehow come to respect the legitimacy of the law, despite the fact that the political assassin was literally getting away with murder.

In short, the TRC's truth-telling mission was a complex, multi-pronged set of engagements with the past, drawing on multiple sites of confession, narrative accounts, processes of investigation and sets of data, in the hands of discrete committees, Commissioners and researchers. Science, law, global news, documentary drama, religious confessional and the rhetoric of nation-building were all distinct discursive domains implicated in the production of the TRC's 'truth'. Each had its own internal norms for selecting, shaping and adjudicating evidence; each entailed particular sets of priorities and interests in making sense of these data. How then did they fit together? To what extent did they cohere, in the production of a consistent – if multifaceted – body of truth about the past? The papers in this book take stock of the various dimensions of this exercise, the different versions of truth associated with it, and their composite effects.

In the final analysis, on the evidence of its own discourse and mandate, the TRC could only render up a range of fractured, incomplete and selective truths. In its quest for forensic truth, as argued by Simpson later in this volume, the TRC set up a standard that is not even sustained within the criminal justice system, which seeks proof beyond a reasonable doubt. Indeed, in yielding to the propensity for criminal law to define a narrow universe of facts designed only to reach conclusions about individual liability, it cultivated a standard of proof that simply could not creatively engage the contradictions that complicate sociological or historical truth at the structural level. Yet, at the same time, the TRC sought to span these levels of individual, local and national truth recovery.

In evaluating the TRC as bureaucratic practice, Cherry et al., Buur and Pigou map these tensions in its daily functioning. Their papers all examine the fractured and largely uncoordinated component parts of the Commission, and draw conclusions about the limited verifiability of much of what the TRC dealt with – at least at the individual and local levels. They show that in the investigation of the various cases before it and in the writing of the final report, the TRC failed to grasp adequately the relationship between individual experience, collective action, and the national or structural elements of apartheid's human rights violations.

Bonner and Nieftagodien, and Van der Merwe are similarly critical of the TRC's ability to reach conclusive truths about local experiences of violence and human rights violations under apartheid, or to extract the necessarily more selective interpretations that would allow for the drawing of national or macro-historical conclusions. Furthermore, they raise critical questions about the failure to penetrate the veil of subterfuge and deceit that masks complex relationships at the local level, and about how the failure to transform these relationships might affect the goals of nation-building and reconciliation.

Posel's paper explores in detail the tensions that inhered in the TRC's mandate and made the simultaneous accomplishment of all its objectives impossible. She explores the strategies developed by the researchers and authors of the report to manage these tensions, and their consequences for the truth-telling enterprise. One of the results, she argues, was an uneven and at times surprisingly scant concern with the bigger canvas: the system of apartheid itself, the higher chains of command in the apartheid state, and the allocation of responsibility for the moral harms done.

Finally, those papers in which we hear the voices of victims and survivors themselves (Pigou, Matshoba, and Dube) question some of the core assumptions about the cathartic effects of storytelling, assumptions that lie at the heart of the TRC's restorative justice and reconciliation enterprises. These papers critically examine the nature and effect of individual truth recovery, pointing to the fact that individual expectations change over time, are themselves contradictory and 'unreliable', and may have outcomes with unpredictable psychological consequences. The relationship between individual truth recovery and personal healing is not straightforward, and the TRC was not always able to let complex, contradictory stories speak for themselves. These papers challenge the notion embodied in the slogan on the posters and banners that adorned the walls at TRC hearings: 'Healing is Revealing'.

The commissioning of the 'truth' under the auspices of the TRC was framed by a mandate that was essentially impossible to fulfil. The process produced no integrated, comprehensive or internally consistent body of 'truth'. To some extent, the obstacles to such a goal could have been overcome with fuller planning and foresight, more effective research in certain areas, closer organisational synchrony between the different institutions and functions of the Commission, more time and greater political will. Yet the tensions among different genres of evidence, argument and 'truth' also inhered in the process and contributed to – rather than wholly detracted from – the scope and impact of the Commission. The idea of 'truth' is variegated, as we have argued, and so it is appropriate to view the TRC as a set of disparate processes with distinct accomplishments as well as limitations. Ultimately, the politics of 'truth' may render the unevenness and incompleteness of the TRC's 'truth-finding' as a strength rather than a weakness. If 'the past is an argument',[11] as Michael Ignatieff asserts, then we should welcome the fact that the TRC did not settle the matter, close the debate, and put paid to lingering questions and controversies about South Africa's troubled history.

Notes

1. F. Fernandez-Armesto, *Truth: A History and a Guide for the Perplexed* (London, Black Swan, 1998), p. 3.
2. P.B. Hayner, *Unspeakable Truths: Confronting State Terror and Atrocity* (New York, Routledge, 2001)
3. Truth and Reconciliation Commission, *Truth and Reconciliation Commission of South Africa Report*, 5 vols (Cape Town, Juta & Co., 1998), vol. 1, ch. 1, para. 28.
4. B. Harris, 'History, the TRC and the "Essential Truth" of Experience', paper presented to the 'Commissioning the Past' Conference, University of the Witwatersrand, June 1999.
5. Hayner, *op. cit.*
6. W. Verwoerd, 'Continuing the Discussion: Reflections from within the Truth and Reconciliation Commission', *Current Writing*, 8:2 (1996), p. 70.
7. Harris, *op. cit.*, p. 16.
8. J. Thloloe, 'Showing Faces, Hearing Voices, Tugging at Emotions: Televising the Truth and Reconciliation Commission', *Nieman Reports*, 52:4 (1998), pp. 53-6.
9. D. Tutu, *No Reconciliation Without Forgiveness* (New York, Doubleday, 1999).
10. Section 251, Constitution of the Republic of South Africa Act, No. 200 of 1993.
11. M. Ignatieff, untitled, in *Index on Censorship*, 5/96, www.oneworld.org/index_oc/issue596/ignatieff.

PART ONE

Insider Accounts

1

RESEARCHING THE 'TRUTH'
A View from Inside the Truth and Reconciliation Commission

Janet Cherry, John Daniel and Madeleine Fullard

> I would like to draw the distinction between revealing the truth about secret crimes and interpreting the political processes that led to such situations ... The distinction between fact and interpretation has become very important in the working of truth commissions. They should concentrate largely on facts, which may be proved, whereas differences about historical interpretations will always exist ... The report can make recommendations by pointing to the immediate context of the atrocities, but not to the remote context. This is not the place for an historical analysis of class struggles.
>
> *José Zalaquett, member of the Chilean Truth Commission*[1]

Introduction

This paper contains some reflections from 'inside' the Research Department of the South African Truth and Reconciliation Commission (TRC) by some of its members. It expresses their views, and not those of the Department as a whole, on the possibilities and limitations, the successes and failures, the extraordinary opportunities and terrible frustrations that working for the TRC offered.

The problems raised here fall into two broad categories: methodology and organisation. These categories overlap considerably, but it is worth bearing them in mind when trying to assess the TRC's work as reflected in the final report.[2] When considering a weakness or omission in the report, one needs to ask whether it was the result of an organisational problem, for instance, a lack of capacity among staff; or whether it arose from methodological concerns, for instance, an ethical debate or the perception of a potentially serious legal difficulty. Was the acknowledged lack of coherence in the report a result of the conflicting methodologies employed, or of the different and contested conclusions reached by the various contributors, or of hasty editing within strict constraints of time and space? Or was it some combination of these factors?

In addition to exploring these questions, the paper flags some of the silences or gaps which we as researchers perceive in the final report, those places where it fails to present 'as complete a picture as possible' of human rights violations by all parties to the conflicts in the mandate period.

Problems of Methodology and Interpretation
The Challenge of the Mandate

More than any other truth commission to date, the TRC had a multidimensional mandate. In pursuing this mandate, as set out in the Promotion of National Unity and Reconciliation Act,[3] the TRC was required to answer different kinds of questions and seek different kinds of evidence, both legal and historical, factual and evaluative, and it therefore had to undertake a number of different tasks. These included historical scholarship (in providing 'as complete a picture as possible' of violations); political analysis (in reflecting 'the perspectives of the victims and the motives and perspectives of the persons responsible'); police-type investigation (in 'establishing and making known the fate or whereabouts of victims'); legal findings pertaining to individuals, organisations and institutions (in determining 'accountability, political or otherwise, for any such violation'); judicial decisions on amnesty for perpetrators; and psychological and other types of decisions on reparations for their victims. Each of these tasks, in turn, was meant to serve the overarching goal of promoting national unity and reconciliation.

The various sectors of the Commission differed in their approach to this extensive and ambitious mandate. Different approaches emerged between the researchers, most of whom were academically trained social scientists, and the investigators and amnesty personnel, most of whom were seconded police officials, lawyers and judges. The two groupings developed distinct methodological approaches to their tasks and different conceptions of the kind of report they believed the Commission was expected to produce.

These differences were compounded by the fact that among the Commissioners themselves, that is, at the policy-making level of the TRC, there was no initial consensus on the approach and no clear interpretation of the mandate. There was a general lack of clarity about how truth commissions were supposed to function. Few in the Commission had experience even of judicial commissions of inquiry, and none had experience of truth commissions and their unique demands. What methodology, language and approach were appropriate for such an enterprise? Which disciplines should shape it? At what audience should its report be pitched? There were no ready answers to these questions. As a result, each division of the Commission was largely left to find its own way forward.

For the Research Department,[4] the starting point was the Act's stipulation that the Commission prepare as comprehensive an account as possible 'of the causes, nature and extent of the gross violations of human rights' committed during the mandate period, 'including the antecedents, circumstances, factors and contexts of such violations, as well as the perspectives of the victims and the motives of the persons responsible'. To the researchers, this suggested the production of a new history of the years since 1960, a revisionist text largely reflecting the views and experiences of the victims, the oppressed underclass of the late apartheid period. They envisaged volumes in which those who were hitherto voiceless would be heard to speak.

When the Commission began its work in April 1996, the Research Department set its sights on these goals. Detailed national and regional chronologies of key historical moments were constructed, secondary sources were scoured for background information, and links were established with bodies in Europe that had extensive collections of anti-apartheid material. A researcher was sent to England and the Netherlands to examine these documents, and research was commissioned from bodies such as Amnesty International, Africa Watch, the Dutch and British Anti-Apartheid Movements, and the Dutch-based church group, Kairos. Unsolicited submissions were received from groups in Ireland, the Netherlands, and Scandinavia.

About six months into the process, however, the dream of producing a radical new history began to falter in the face of a consensus that was then developing within the Commission, and the day-to-day demands of the work. Largely as a result of the many legal requirements built into the Act regarding evidence – prior-warning notices, the making of findings, and the granting of amnesty, the TRC gradually came to assume the position that it was essentially a state-directed investigative commission rather than an exercise in writing or rewriting history. For the researchers, the 'historical analysis' approach began to give way to a more empirical one, to the notion that 'the facts' should be reported, and readers left to draw their own conclusions. There was a growing recognition that the operations of commissions of inquiry intersect with the disciplines of history and law in ways that are utilitarian and functional rather than definitive, episodic rather than framing. Reluctantly, the researchers accepted the view that the reports of such commissions generally do not contain fine historical or legal analysis and do not satisfy the academic eye, which judges them to be poor history or poor law, or both. The subsequent complaint from some academic quarters that the report was lacking in legal, sociological or historical analysis was not unexpected.

The Reactive Nature of the Research Agenda

As the hearings on human rights violations commenced, the Research Department slipped into reactive rather than proactive mode. One urgent ad hoc task after another demanded attention. The staff of the Commission, including the researchers, became absorbed in practical matters, such as hunting for birth and death certificates or the addresses of perpetrators, tracing newspaper reports, handling angry lawyers, typing thousands of letters, making tens of thousands of phone calls, meeting with communities to prepare for hearings, trying to find translators, booking venues, driving vast distances in search of witnesses, and last, but by no means least, dealing with the scores of foreign researchers and media people who descended on the Commission to do their Ph.D.s or make their documentaries.

The pace was relentless, the research tasks both microscopic (such as locating a single date) and immense (such as tracing a chain of command). Weeks were spent locating complete sets of the Institute of Race Relations annual surveys for each office, or providing Commissioners with an urgent executive summary of the classified Steyn Report into allegations of security force involvement in illegal operations. Sudden deployments had to be made, as when documents relating to the chemical and biological warfare programme were discovered in trunks in Dr Wouter Basson's garage. The number and variety of tasks did not make for a serene workplace, where staff could burrow away quietly on independent research and pursue a predetermined agenda. Instead, the maelstrom generated its own research demands and constantly thrust new issues into view.

The hearings on human rights violations, which went on almost continuously, dominated the life of the Commission and the work of the researchers. These hearings generated tremendous workloads for all the staff and absorbed the Commission's energy decisively for the first eighteen months. Nevertheless, time continued to be spent on some of the tasks that had been set initially, and which in retrospect turned out to be largely fruitless. A certain obsession from the top with chronologies manifested itself in the laborious assembling of lists, which ultimately contributed little to developing insights or preparing the report.

Much time was spent on the arduous process of developing definitions. There were lengthy debates on developing a common language and approach, particularly a vocabulary for the database. Did a slap in custody constitute torture? Should arson attacks on people's homes be considered a gross human rights violation? Could buildings be said to have rights, such as in the bombings of the African National Congress (ANC) office in London or COSATU House, headquarters of the Congress of South African Trade Unions? Was a 'stone-thrower' a combatant? What was 'severe ill-treatment'? Weeks were spent trying to define categories for groupings of perpetrators. A protracted debate was needed to convince data processors that petrol bombs should not be coded as explosives. This was important because petrol bombs and formal explosives were generally used by different perpetrator groupings.

This work was important but vastly time-consuming. In retrospect, it should have been done during a foundation phase before the Commission was launched. The TRC should have devoted months to closed-door discussions and essential infrastructural preparations before going public. As it was, the clock started ticking on the life of the Commission before support staff had been hired and offices properly furnished. Several months passed before a fully functional database was available.

Some of the historians who presented papers at the 'Commissioning the Past' Conference[5] were dismissive of what they called the 'quantitative research exercise'. We consider it incorrect to regard the 'information management process', which included the taking of statements, coding, and developing database summaries, as purely quantitative. It was actually a deeply interpretative process, in which decisions of categorisation and meaning were made and assigned to each statement. The sorting and coding were a significant beginning in the analysis of each statement, and formed part of a search for patterns. It was precisely this coding that alerted the Commission to a pattern of sexual torture in the Southern Cape, for example, and brought to light the torture patterns and techniques of certain Special Branch perpetrators or certain police stations, such as Reddersburg in the Free State.

The statement form, known as the protocol, gave rise to many time-consuming tussles within the Commission, especially regarding the 'narrative' section, which was a space left open for victims to tell their stories in the terms of their choice. While the original document assigned a number of pages to this individual narrative, a subsequent version eliminated this section entirely, reducing the form to a series of questions to be answered and boxes to be ticked. After a long struggle, a limited space for the narrative section was reinstated.[6]

A further debate took place over secondary source material. How should one deal with an event or violation for which no TRC statements were taken, but which was nevertheless of historical significance? The Johannesburg office argued that researchers should confine themselves strictly to TRC-generated materials and engage with outside sources only minimally, whereas the Cape Town and Durban offices felt otherwise. Different sections of the final report reflect these largely unresolved differences.

The Language Issue: Riots or Uprisings?

The question of appropriate language and terminology was hotly contested in almost every forum of the TRC's work – the database, the hearings, the drafting of the report – and was particularly important for the researchers. For example, how should a clash between protesters and security forces be described? As a riot? An uprising? A revolt? While politically conscious Commission personnel shied away from the term 'riot', it was very widely used by ordinary deponents, who would often say, 'There were riots that day'.

As the work of the Commission gained momentum, researchers began to adopt a neutral phraseology appropriate to the conventionally dispassionate nature of an investigative inquiry. There was a gradual move away from terms that might reflect an individual researcher's biases, such as referring to certain local political figures as 'warlords' rather than 'leaders', or describing them as 'notorious' rather than 'popular'. Eventually, a fairly subdued and 'cold' language predominated. Thus, the term 'operative' came to triumph over 'freedom fighter', 'terrorist' or 'guerrilla', and 'former government' over 'regime' or 'apartheid state'. The Commission spoke of 'killings' rather than 'murders'.

This was apparently consistent with the experience of other truth commissions. José Zalaquett, a key figure in the work of the Chilean Commission, noted that their commissioners were encouraged 'to write the report in a very flat language. For example, the commission should report that 200 people were killed, not that a brutal massacre took place. People should formulate their own emotional responses. The facts speak loudly by themselves.'[7]

History versus Law

The relationship of research to the legal dimensions of the Commission's work was complicated, reflecting a tension between the 'historical analysis' approach favoured by the Research Department and especially the historians within it, and the positivist or more empirical approach favoured by the lawyers. This tension was noted by both Deborah Posel[8] and André du Toit[9] in their papers at the 'Commissioning the Past' Conference, where they suggested that the structure of the report, built as it was around 'window cases' and 'human rights violations findings', led to the omission of analysis.

It could be argued that the outcome of this tension was that neither approach was followed satisfactorily in the report. The lawyers, or those social scientists who adopted a more positivist methodology, argued that the TRC did not 'test the evidence' sufficiently, did not make findings on the basis of sufficient evidence, did not do sufficient empirical research or make use of existing statistics adequately. However, the historians and researchers argued that the complexity and specificity of particular acts, and the details of particular contexts and historical debates were lost through the imperative of 'making findings' that had to be quasi-legal. Both the lawyers and the historians shuddered at some of the sections of the report written by the opposite camp.

On occasion, researchers were devastated when the legal department required them to omit an important case because the evidence was shaky, or because the department had forgotten or failed to notify the perpetrator, or because the perpetrator's lawyers were demanding the documents. More than one serious perpetrator avoided being named for these reasons. In certain instances, the lawyers dug in their heels over inconclusive evidence. The very process of making findings did not easily accommodate difference, debate or complexity. The 'Guguletu Seven' incident is a case in point. The TRC's investigation revealed an extraordinary tale, deserving of a chapter on its own, yet the description in the report is shorn of detail and fails to do it justice.

Researchers schooled in disciplines such as history, sociology or philosophy found themselves in a difficult situation. Ultimately, they had to develop a unique language and methodology, straddling the quasi-legal, the psychological 'case study' and the historical. It was a 'pastiche' methodology that arose at the difficult intersection between diverse disciplines, the tasks required and the nature of the evidence. We readily admit that the solutions were not always adequate.

How Much 'History'?

As indicated above, one of the central complaints that historians made about the report concerned the lack of both broader analysis and contextual detail. Simply put, there was a cry for 'more history'. Posel states that 'the report reads as an often bland, largely descriptive account of what happened, when and how. One of the striking features of these narratives is that they convey almost nothing of "social networks and contingent cultural meanings".'[10] We have tried to explain how it was that the descriptive came to prevail over the analytical and historical. But the question needs to be asked: Was it really the task of the TRC to embed all violations in specific and detailed historical backgrounds?

Any violation in Katlehong or Oudtshoorn or KwaMashu certainly took place in the context of localised experiences, struggles and conflicts, with their own antecedents of forced removals, racial divisions and legal controls. Each violation involved specific encounters with power brokers, in the form of security forces, community councillors, rival political organisations, and so on. Yet the violations also took place in extraordinarily similar conditions, being marked by broad symmetries with wider regional and national events. Hugo van der Merwe points to this intersection of local detail and the larger picture in his study of Duduza township. 'While the conflict in Duduza can be located directly within the struggle over apartheid, the way it plays out in the local community is not simply as a racial or class struggle. Local struggles for resources and power are superimposed on the conflict.'[11]

The second and third volumes of the report pay some attention to these national symmetries, patterns and differences, but given that hundreds of towns and townships were represented in statements to the Commission, it would not have been feasible to sketch the local backdrops to all violations. Not only towns and regions, but virtually all social and political groupings referred to in the report (whether victims or perpetrators), had historically relevant and interesting origins and features. Every self-defence unit, every regional unit of the security police, indeed every crowd that ever materialised and attacked the home of a policeman (such as 'Jetta' Sethwale in Upington, to name but one) had a remarkable tale to tell of its origins and networks. If the research capacity had existed, would it have been desirable to explore each instance? How could such a report be constructed in any meaningful way for a reader?

Other truth commissions have grappled with the question of historical interpretation. With reference to Chile, José Zalaquett, quoted in the epigraph to this paper, recommended a flatly descriptive approach. Fateh Azzam, a member of the Palestinian Commission for Citizens' Rights, argued during an international discussion on truth commissions at the Harvard Law School that 'it is very important for these commissions to focus on factual details in order to avoid getting stuck in an interpretive framework. We Palestinians and Israelis exacerbate our conflict by arguing in terms of interpreting history. This involves the denial of factual truth.'[12]

Henry Steiner, Director of the Human Rights Program at the Harvard Law School, took a similar position:

> Perhaps truth commissions should have this same attitude, holding to the role of truth-tellers in the flat sense of doing their best to record who did what to whom and when, period. Were they characteristically to engage in social analysis, by identifying structural phenomena underlying violations, and by proposing deep changes in a society's socio-economic organisation, they [would] risk being viewed as but another voice in a world of disputed opinions and theories about justice, development, whatever. Their reports might lose distinctiveness and a sense of objectivity by being absorbed into the broad play of political ideas and historical debate.[13]

Views like these were taken into account by the report writers. At times, we deliberately tried to sidestep historical debate and opted for a flat narrative. The simple statement of an incontrovertible fact – the name of the victim, the date of the killing, the name of the person who pulled the trigger – can have enormous power. However, as we have already made clear, we do not subscribe to simple empiricism, and incline rather towards historical analysis, the need for which is expressed in the very Act that brought the TRC into existence. The final report falls somewhere between these two approaches.

Does all this mean that the report is fundamentally inadequate? In the strict terms of academic sociology and history, this might be so. But from other equally significant perspectives, the report does make an important contribution. It casts light on political violence at the immediate, experiential level. It records the diverse experiences of absolutely ordinary South Africans. Those who came to the Commission – and they came in their thousands – had tales to tell of a kind that had barely been acknowledged or examined in the apartheid era. They spoke, as SABC journalist Anneliese Burgess put it, 'to a nation whose time it was to listen'.[14] This was perhaps the unique and most worthy contribution of the Commission, and it is what differentiates the report from a conventional history.

There is no easy solution to the problem of balancing factual description and historical analysis. Although in certain specific instances one approach may be favoured over the other, the two approaches are complementary and need to be reconciled somehow. While truth commissions have to operate within certain legal parameters, this should not mean that the historical context is ignored.

The Conflicting Imperatives of Truth and Reconciliation

Initially, few members of the Research Department, if any, gave much attention to the notion of reconciliation. Their priority was to find the truth, to lift the veil on a hidden past and expose abuse. Reconciliation was seen largely as a sop to the right wing, an attempt to sweeten the pill for those opposed to the very creation of the Commission.

As time passed, however, it became clear that to certain Commissioners, and most notably the Chairperson, reconciliation was not only a meaningful concept but a priority. Clothed in Christian theology, it rapidly assumed primacy as the Commission began to deal with thorny issues that seemed to pit the imperatives of uncovering the truth against the demands of furthering reconciliation. While both the Investigation Unit and the Research Department clung to the notion that there could be no reconciliation without truth, some of the Commissioners seemed to think there were times when too much truth could imperil the goals of national unity and reconciliation.

In two notable cases, truth-seeking was subordinated to what a majority of Commissioners saw as the greater national interest of reconciliation. The first involved the serving of a subpoena on Chief Mangosuthu Buthelezi, leader of the Inkatha Freedom Party (IFP), to appear before the Commission. This was as controversial an issue as any confronted by the Commission. The argument that prevailed was that forcing Chief Buthelezi to appear might threaten the fragile relationship between the IFP and the ANC, and lead to conflict in which lives would be lost. Ultimately, the report conceded that the wrong decision was probably taken.[15] It is absurd that the leader of a grouping central to the perpetration of political violence was not questioned in any significant detail, aside from an appearance at the hearing on political parties.

The second case in which the Commission proved unwilling to rock the institutional boat involved access to documents. The South African National Defence Force (SANDF) was the repository of vast collections of documents relating to its predecessor, the South African Defence Force (SADF), and these were potentially of great use to the Commission. Although the Commission was empowered by the Act to access any documents it saw fit, by force if necessary, it gained little access to these papers. In frustration, the Investigation Unit asked the Commissioners to authorise search-and-seizure operations. Early in the life of the TRC, such a raid was conducted, in the full glare of media publicity, on a military facility in the Western Cape. The SANDF was outraged and, it is widely believed, made its unhappiness known to the government. Similar actions directed against the military were never repeated.

The Commission also gained only very limited access to the ANC's documents. It was never established exactly what holdings the ANC had in its possession at its head office in Johannesburg or elsewhere. However, hundreds of requests for information sent to Shell House went unanswered. While this was as likely the result of disorganisation as political obduracy, the point is that the Commission failed to use the powers it had to acquire information and documentation which it badly needed and to which it had a legal right.

Organisational Problems

Time Pressures

Without excusing the weaknesses of the final report, it is worth clarifying the actual circumstances in which it was produced. The production process played a significant role in determining the content and structure of the report.

The original intention was that the report would be written after the Commission finished its work in mid-1997. However, as is well known, that work did not end then, but kept being extended in fits and starts. So, while the actual writing of the report began in early 1998, the process was continually sidetracked by other events: the trial of P.W. Botha in George in May 1998; the crucial hearing on the chemical and biological warfare programme in June; an in camera appearance by a senior operative of the Civil Cooperation Bureau (CCB) in the same month; and the United Democratic Front (UDF) submission in July. These events covered topics of great importance to the Commission and the report, raising new questions and opening new lines of inquiry. But the scheduled handover of the report was just four or five months away, and routine TRC work, such as the serving of prior-warning notices, went on without pause. In the writing phase, there was therefore no time for reflection, no opportunity to gain an overview, precious little chance even for the writers to undertake a collective review of each other's work.

Further complicating the process was the fact that the bulk of the amnesty hearings – and crucially some that involved former cabinet ministers (Adriaan Vlok), and senior security officials of the state (Eugene de Kock and Craig Williamson), and the liberation movements (Siphiwe Nyanda and Aboobaker Ismail) – had not taken place by the second half of 1998. In addition to having to extract information very carefully, without threatening the Amnesty Committee's fiercely guarded independence, the report writers were also denied access to the potentially useful information those hearings were expected to generate (and subsequently did).

Instead of the measured integration that the writing of the report demanded, large parts of the last few months were spent in the tortuous legal process of attempting to serve prior-warning notices on persons named to their detriment in the report. Hours and days were devoted to locating a 'Sergeant Coetzee' from the early 1980s, or a torturer known only by a nickname ('Hello, is that the

Mossel Bay police station? I am trying to find a policeman known as "Bak Ore" …'), or a squatter leader identified only by a clan name.

By the beginning of October, and with the handover date of 29 October apparently cast in stone, the writers were labouring eighteen hours a day to finish the report. Yet the work of the Amnesty Committee was only just getting into full swing. Pieces submitted by diverse authors at the eleventh hour, to the despair of the Research Director, were rushed straight into editing and layout, which were often done simultaneously. Certain sections were virtually done overnight by outsiders brought in at the last minute to edit work with which they were not familiar. There was never time to conduct integrated analyses of various chapters, such as the regional reports, and no overall content management could take place. An objective reading of the report reveals the absence of a guiding eye providing integration, flow and coherent argument. The report is patchy and the organisation of text sometimes incomprehensible. The organisation of the material into volumes and sections is fairly haphazard. The first volume, for example, contains the most philosophical sections of the report and the most prosaic, jostling side by side. Posel is correct to describe the report as 'a rather disconnected compilation of discrete chunks of information … What the report lacks is an attempt to integrate and synthesise these into a unified analysis.'[16] It is little wonder that the final product is no model of technical perfection either.

As many of us in the Research Department argued until the end, the handover of the report in October 1998 was premature in almost every respect. Politically, it may have been appropriate to complete the report, but from the point of view of the researchers, the analysis was far from finished; indeed, some would suggest that in late 1998 it was only just beginning.

Space Constraints

Early in 1998, the Commissioners endorsed a particular format for the report, namely, five volumes of a specified size. This decision was taken before anyone had a meaningful sense of what length the content would require. A subsequent decision to use double spacing in the layout complicated things. As a result of these decisions, space considerations became paramount. For Volumes 2 and 3, in which the bulk of violations are dealt with, space ultimately became the central determinant of what was included or excluded. The frustration this created for the writers can scarcely be overstated. A concern with nuance and complexity became impossible.

In these circumstances, the sections that were sacrificed tended to be those that dealt with context and analysis. Most savagely cut were the Natal and Transvaal regional profiles. This was particularly upsetting in regard to the Natal profile, perhaps the most eagerly awaited section of the report. For years, international groups such as Amnesty International and Africa Watch had alleged that there was high-level political complicity in the civil war which swept the province between 1984 and 1994, and they looked to the Commission for conclusive evidence to support these claims. What they got was little more than a bare-bones listing of incidents, shorn of detail and context. Overall, the 600-page profile was cut to 175 pages. The section on the 'Seven Day War', a searing and conclusive indictment of the police's complicity with Inkatha in a murderous campaign to cleanse Edendale of ANC supporters, was cut from thirty pages to ten. The Transvaal profile was cut by more than a third. While a certain amount of cutting and reworking was clearly necessary, the cuts that were made virtually obliterated whole sections. For example, the section on the self-defence units in the 1990s was cut by more than a third to eight pages.

Other crucial sections that were severely cut included those on the ANC, on the security forces as perpetrators, and on gross human rights violations perpetrated by the state outside South Africa (cross-border raids). What made these cuts particularly irksome was the insistence by the TRC management structures that the report include portfolio and regional office reports on the TRC itself. While these may be of great interest to researchers, many in the Commission argued that they had no place in the report and should have been submitted directly to Parliament in a separate document. Some 200 pages were given over to these descriptions of the Commission's inner workings. In our view, this space would have been better used for content related more directly to the TRC's mandate.

The Archives

One of the main regrets of the researchers is that the pressures of time and the need to maintain a narrow focus did not permit a more detailed examination of state records. The researchers and some of the investigators did peruse the remaining records of the State Security Council and its substructures, a substantial body of documentation despite the massive destruction of records detailed in one of the report's most substantial chapters.[17] However, as the Commission was concerned purely with gross human rights violations, these examinations tended to be in the service of particular cases, and thus concerned themselves with the development of security policies and structures. The examination of these records was also painfully abbreviated. A full appreciation of the evidence they contain regarding the exercise of state power would have required a team of people working for a year. In retrospect, it is clear to us that such a dedicated team of archival researchers should have been created. But this was not done and the opportunity is unlikely to come again.

Neither were the full records of the liberation movements available for perusal. While some limited holdings of the ANC's archives at Fort Hare University and the Mayibuye Centre were studied, the bulk of the ANC's records were untouched. Though the ANC established a TRC desk within its documentary collection at Shell House, it was generally uncooperative. As stated earlier, most requests went unanswered, including those for critical files on such high-level cases as the assassination of ANC national executive member, Joe Gqabi.

It seemed to us that the SANDF, whose holdings are separate from those of the state, quite consciously blocked access to the records of its SADF predecessor. More than a year was wasted in painstaking negotiations with the military for the right to access its collections in Pretoria. It was not until well into 1998, when the deadline for finishing the report was only months away, that members of the Research Department were given access to some SADF files.

But this was not free access. The Commission could only submit motivated requests for files, and when these were produced, they had been sanitised by defence force lawyers. Where researchers were told that files were not available or did not exist, there was no way of verifying these assertions independently. While it is true that boxes of files were made available on certain SADF operations, such as the raid on Kassinga and Operation Protea in Angola, time prevented a rigorous and comprehensive inspection of them. Nevertheless, even a brief inspection was enough to change the perspective of the researchers in the Kassinga case, and their account of the raid differs from the established one presented by the United Nations and the South West African People's Organisation (SWAPO). This may indicate that the defence force's obduracy was short-sighted in some respects. Or it may be that the former SADF was manipulating the Commission by releasing or withholding particular files.

The wholesale destruction of records investigated by the Commission and reported on in Volume 1 also had a negative impact on the work of the Research Department, especially when it came to documenting human rights violations outside South Africa. Among the records lost to the shredders were those of the Directorate of Special Tasks (DST), the arm of Military Intelligence that orchestrated the SADF's surrogate force activities in Angola, Mozambique, Lesotho and Zimbabwe, as well as inside South Africa in the case of the Inkatha squads trained in Caprivi; those of the CCB; and, with the exception of some documents seized by the Goldstone Commission, those of the Directorate of Covert Collection (DCC), that body which seems to us to have been at the very centre of apartheid's 'dirty war'.

The Octopus Effect

The poor system of organising and sharing information within the Commission was a fundamental weakness. Information was gathered and processed by several 'arms' – statement-takers, data processors, investigators, researchers; and through a multiplicity of routes – hearings, meetings, submissions, interviews, telephone calls, letters, statements, in camera (or 'section 29') hearings. A great deal of this information remained in the heads of individual staff members.

The Commission was required to assemble and integrate literally hundreds of thousands of fragments of information. Searching for one of these fragments frequently reduced staff members to tears. A significant staff turnover exacerbated the problems. So did the fact that the various arms of the TRC tended to operate separately. On the whole, there was poor communication between the researchers and investigators. There was also ongoing tension around their roles in the 'information gathering' process. Naturally this varied from office to office. The East London and Durban offices integrated the work of researchers and investigators more effectively, whereas the Cape Town and Johannesburg offices did not, except in specific investigations, such as those into the KTC squatter camp and the *witdoeke*, or into the chemical and biological warfare programme (also known as Project Coast).

At times, the tension between researchers and investigators mirrored the tension between a more historical or analytical approach and a legal, 'case-building' one. Yet the roles of the two groupings were often blurred. The Investigation Unit had an 'analysis unit', which was meant to draw out trends from the data it had accumulated. At the same time, the Investigation Unit sometimes called on the Research Department to help with particular cases. The cooperation necessitated by this overlap did not often occur. Thus it was that work done by the Research Department on ANC cases and passed on to the Investigation Unit was never followed up. It was highly frustrating, for researchers and investigators alike, to develop a deep interest in an individual case, only to see it fade back into near oblivion as the focus shifted elsewhere.

Of course, some cases were solved satisfactorily. The case of Robert Beech, David Berry and Albert Wessels, who were killed in an operation in Zimbabwe in 1982, comes to mind. The SADF contention that they had been involved in an unauthorised 'private trespassing mission' was shown to be false. The killers of Petros and Jabulile Nyawose in a car bombing in Swaziland, and the killers of Theophilus Dlodlo (Comrade Viva), were uncovered without the benefit of amnesty applications. So too were the circumstances in which Phila Portia Ndwandwe was abducted and killed. The allegation that Anton Lubowski had been an informer was found to be unproven.

The Silences

There are two very important gaps in the report's coverage: the documentation of gross human rights violations outside South Africa; and the neglect of the rural areas, notably the northern homelands of Lebowa, Venda, Gazankulu, Qwa Qwa and KwaNdebele.

The scale of the atrocities perpetrated in South Africa's neighbouring countries, especially from the mid-seventies to the early nineties, is certainly recognised in the report. In fact, Volume 2, which focuses on the state as perpetrator, gives primacy to the external theatre. This section of the report presents the telling finding – one which fell largely on deaf ears inside South Africa – that most of the victims of the government's attempts to cling to power lived outside the country. It contrasts the hundreds of thousands of Southern Africans who died as a direct or indirect result of South Africa's calculated destabilisation of the region with the twenty to twenty-five thousand South Africans who died in political violence within the country's borders during the mandate period.

For all that, the external section is inadequate. Based primarily on secondary sources, it lacks the human dimension, the dramatic testimony of the participant or the eyewitness account of the observer, except in regard to the theatres of lesser action – the inner-periphery states of Botswana, Lesotho and Swaziland. The greater dramas of the wars in Angola and Mozambique and the frequent incursions into Zambia and Zimbabwe are related largely from afar, relying on other published accounts.

An extraordinary conspiracy of silence enveloped those who had served in these wars and campaigns. Only one amnesty application was received from a participant in the Kassinga raid, the single worst massacre of the entire apartheid era. Incredibly, the Amnesty Committee decided that this application did not merit a public hearing, and instead dealt with it in chambers. Apart from that application, and a few pertaining to incidents in Namibia, no other serving permanent force member of the SANDF submitted an application regarding SADF operations outside South Africa. In all, only a handful of former soldiers – fewer than ten – made statements to the Commission, and all of them were conscripts. No mention was made of horrifying incidents, such as that in which SWAPO combatants were dumped in the sea and left to drown. In part, this reflected the prevailing scornful attitude of the former SADF towards the Commission, but it was also a product of the perhaps more understandable notion that soldiers obey orders and do their duty, and that it is up to their political superiors to come clean – which, in the South African case, very few did.

The exception, as far as the dearth of rich primary material in this part of the report is concerned, involves Botswana, Lesotho and Swaziland. The operations here were mostly by police hit squads, such as the Vlakplaas unit headed by Eugene de Kock. De Kock's trial and subsequent amnesty application opened the floodgates and led to a rush of other police operatives to the Commission. It is no coincidence that a number of the breakthrough findings about the responsibility for killings concerned people who died in Botswana, Lesotho and Swaziland. As the Commission noted in its report, the huge gap in its knowledge of SADF actions stems from the fact that a whistle-blower in the De Kock mould never emerged from the ranks of the SADF.

Other factors hindered the Commission's reportage on violations outside South Africa. There were insufficient resources to send investigators into the region. Furthermore, most, if not all, of the governments of the region did not want investigators ferreting around for information in their backyards. They had secrets of their own, of witting or unwitting collaboration, for example, which they preferred to keep hidden. Some governments seemed downright hostile to the Commission. The Zimbabwe government, for example, was uncooperative in the face of the Commission's desire to gain access to a CCB member imprisoned in Zimbabwe, who had applied for amnesty for an operation against the ANC in which a Zimbabwean citizen was killed. He was an important potential source of information on the external workings of this clandestine murder unit, but the Commission was never able to speak to him.

Some of the worst atrocities of the mandate period were committed in the homelands. KwaZulu was the worst of these, and the report documents events there well, if incompletely. The conflicts in the Transkei and Ciskei receive some attention. But accounts of similar struggles in the northern homelands are significantly absent. The so-called witchcraft killings in Venda are under-reported; so too are the violations committed in Lebowa in the 1980s by youths operating in the name of the UDF. The vicious internecine struggles around 'independence' in KwaNdebele are also inadequately reflected. All this has issued in what is probably the largest gap in the story of human rights abuse inside South Africa.

Conclusion

This paper has pointed to some of the practical factors as well as the more complex debates that both facilitated and constrained the work of the TRC, its capacity to fulfil its mandate and write its report. It would be dishonest to claim that these issues were debated explicitly within the Commission at the time, but in retrospect they can be identified as important underlying currents.

In our view, the somewhat shaky methodological foundation of the report in a blend of history, law, psychology and philosophy precisely reflects the absence of a prior definition of what a truth commission actually is. The growing literature on truth commissions does not really grapple with this issue, although there are some pointers. Priscilla Hayner comments that 'truth commissions are of a fundamentally different nature from courtroom trials, and function with different goals in mind. It is also clear that many methodological questions that are central to truth commissions cannot be answered by turning to any established legal norms or general principles, nor can they be well addressed by universal guidelines.'[18] However, 'methodology' is often taken to refer simply to a commission's information management systems or practical activities (for instance, whether hearings are public or private), as opposed to its conceptual framework.

For as long as the nature of truth commissions remains undefined at this deeper level, the reports they produce are likely to be problematic. Drawing on a variety of models and methodologies – the commission of inquiry, the courtroom, the archive, the psychological counselling room, the statistical graph, even the theatre – the South African TRC and its report satisfy neither lawyer, historian, psychologist nor statistician. However, they open up a range of possibilities for important work in all these fields. To demand that a truth commission relate only to a single discipline would disable its work and prevent it from serving its multidimensional mandate. While there is a long way to go in developing a nuanced and integrated approach, we believe that the South African TRC has done innovative, principled work that future commissions can build on.

Finally, while the report was the necessary legislated conclusion to the work of the Commission, it should be seen as only one of the mechanisms through which the task of uncovering truth and promoting reconciliation was pursued. The public processes of the Commission – the victim hearings where families recounted their bitter experiences, the amnesty hearings where perpetrators confessed to their ghastly deeds, the sector hearings that pointed clearly to wider social involvement – were highly effective means for publicising its work. So too were the daily and weekly reports carried by the media, perhaps none more so than the weekly television programme, the *TRC Special Report*.

The reality is that the testimony of a single victim relayed to the country by the media will ultimately have had more of an impact upon the national consciousness than any number of volumes of the report. The enduring memory of the Commission will be the images of pain, grief and regret conveyed relentlessly, week after week, month after month, to a public that generally remained spellbound by what it was witnessing.

For other truth commissions, their final reports may have represented the crowning achievement of their work. We feel that our report takes its place humbly in a wider range of achievements, and should not be the only or final measure of the Commission's success.

Notes

1. H. Steiner (ed.), *Truth Commissions: A Comparative Assessment* (Cambridge, Mass., World Peace Foundation, 1997), p. 15.
2. Truth and Reconciliation Commission, *Truth and Reconciliation Commission of South Africa Report*, 5 vols (Cape Town, Juta & Co., 1998).
3. Promotion of National Unity and Reconciliation Act, No. 34 of 1995.
4. The Research Department was made up of twelve researchers – three each in the Johannesburg and Durban offices, two in East London, and four in Cape Town. The department was smaller than its 'sister structure', the Investigation Unit, which had some sixty investigators, and it was oriented primarily towards producing the Commission's report.
5. 'Commissioning the Past: An Evaluation of the South African TRC', Conference hosted by the Wits History Workshop and the Centre for the Study of Violence and Reconciliation, University of the Witwatersrand, June 1999.
6. Commissioner Wynand Malan was one of the prime movers behind the narrow questionnaire-type protocol. It is thus ironic and not a little disingenuous that he should suggest in his Minority Position that a 'qualitative analysis of the data that has been collected, especially from victim statements and testimonies or through the amnesty process, would have made a very valuable contribution to a better understanding of our society ...' (*TRC Report*, vol. 5, Minority Position Submitted by Commissioner Wynand Malan, para. 86).
7. Steiner, *op. cit.*, p. 61.
8. D. Posel, 'The TRC Report: What Kind of History? What Kind of Truth?', in this volume.

9. A. du Toit, 'Perpetrator Findings as Artificial Even-handedness? The TRC's Contested Judgements of Moral and Political Accountability for Gross Human Rights Violations', paper presented to the 'Commissioning the Past' Conference, University of the Witwatersrand, June 1999.
10. Posel, in this volume, p. 160.
11. H. van der Merwe, 'National Narrative versus Local Truths: The TRC's Engagement with Duduza', in this volume, p. 216.
12. Steiner, *op. cit.*, p. 17.
13. Steiner, *op. cit.*, p. 16.
14. *TRC Special Report*, South African Broadcasting Corporation (SABC 3) television programme, screened July 1998. This half-hour programme reviewed the activities of the TRC over an eighteen-month period.
15. *TRC Report*, vol. 5, ch. 6, para. 55.
16. Posel, in this volume, p. 160.
17. *TRC Report*, vol. 1, ch. 8.
18. P.B. Hayner, *Unspeakable Truths: Confronting State Terror and Atrocity* (New York, Routledge, 2001), p. 7.

2

FALSE PROMISES AND WASTED OPPORTUNITIES?
Inside South Africa's Truth and Reconciliation Commission

Piers Pigou

Introduction

Debate about the truths that emerged from the Truth and Reconciliation Commission (TRC) will continue for some time. Much of it will focus on the nature and quality of the data collected by the Commission, and how they were interpreted and analysed. This paper explores some of the issues that affected the Commission's efforts to develop and effectively exploit a range of potential sources of data.

In September 1998, I gave a talk in Denmark on the progress of the TRC. I stated that probably over 90 per cent of the people who had appeared before the Commission had not been provided with meaningful new information about their cases, because of the methodologies employed and the failure to capitalise on opportunities. The TRC had only scratched the surface of past conflict, I argued, and should be regarded as no more than the first, formal step in the process of looking back into South Africa's past.

A senior member of the South African diplomatic mission in Copenhagen, who had seen the remains of one of his close relatives disinterred during the well-publicised exhumations undertaken by the TRC, strongly disagreed. He argued that continued retrospection and investigation would be counter-productive. For him, the end of the Commission's work signalled the end of a chapter in South Africa's history.

Given the enormity of past abuses and the limited scope of revelations made before the TRC, the political expediency of making a clean break with the past is perhaps understandable. But we are constantly reminded that reconciliation remains fragile, particularly in the context of continuing inequality and a lack of material improvement in many people's lives, and such a break with the past may be neither possible nor desirable.

For over two years, I was involved in the workings of the regional Investigation Unit of the TRC based in Johannesburg. This paper provides an insider's perspective on the successes and failures of the Commission. It looks specifically at the work of investigators, the extent and limitations of their contributions, the difficulties they faced in exacting the truth, and some of the missed opportunities.

Background

South Africa's TRC is increasingly held up as a model of how to address past abuses and conflicts in countries changing from authoritarian to democratic rule. It is regarded as a key component of South Africa's miraculous political transition, and has many advocates and admirers, especially abroad. Visiting delegations from as far afield as Nigeria and Indonesia have come to South Africa to learn lessons for their own truth-recovery processes.

Much of what the TRC achieved is laudable. For the first time, without fear or prejudice, the marginalised and oppressed were given a public platform to tell the world what had happened to them and their loved ones under apartheid. In addition, the amnesty process confirmed the involvement of individual perpetrators in a range of abuses that had been vehemently denied in the past. For the most part, the process was transparent and open. A huge resource of documentary and other material has been left for future analysis, as little analysis could be done in the rush to produce the Commission's final report.

Perhaps inevitably, though, the Commission was controversial from its inception. Political parties, academics and commentators have criticised the TRC for many different reasons, accusing it of being politically biased, or perpetrator-friendly, or selective and blinkered in its focus on victims of gross human rights violations. Direct allegations were made against the Chairperson and some individual Commissioners.[1] Serious questions were raised about the final report, including the fact that it contained factual errors in the dates and details of incidents.[2] Some of these inaccuracies were probably simple typing errors,[3] while others were taken up elsewhere and used as the basis for drawing critical conclusions[4].

There were also inconsistencies in the way in which some TRC decisions were made, in regard to findings as well as the granting of amnesty, and this raised legitimate concerns that conclusions were reached on the basis of inadequate information and inquiry. Indefensible decisions, such as the 'blanket amnesty' given to a section of the African National Congress (ANC) leadership (subsequently challenged and overturned), gave considerable ammunition to those who claimed that the TRC was a tool of the ANC. However, one could argue that the Commission favoured most parties in the political spectrum by exempting them from serious examination.[5]

Many unfounded generalisations were also made about the legitimacy of the data collected and the specific interpretations made. Often such comments were rooted in subjective perception, rumour and political bias. Some critics were guilty of precisely the inaccurate and rash judgements they denounced in the Commission.[6]

Underlying much of this criticism was disagreement about whether the truth had been told or not, and whether it should be pursued further (if at all). The Commission argued that reconciliation could only be built on a foundation of truth. While the truth by itself would not automatically ensure reconciliation, the absence of truth would effectively prevent it.

The relationship between truth and reconciliation is complex. Yet many people assumed that the TRC itself would somehow 'create' reconciliation or be the vehicle for 'delivering' it. On occasion, the opposite appeared to happen, and the attempt to establish the truth led to greater enmity. Having heard the testimony of amnesty applicants, many victims were unprepared to forgive, especially if they felt that the truth had still not been told. Sylvia Dlomo-Jele, the mother of murdered activist Sicelo Dlomo, for example, refused to speak to the young men who executed her son. She was convinced they had been selective about the truths they disclosed, to ensure that their applications complied with the amnesty criteria. Many other families felt similarly. The situation was complicated further by Amnesty Committee decisions that supported the applicants' versions of events. Families were unlikely to want to reconcile with those they believed had told half-truths, especially when there was little or no investigation of the applicant's version.

Difficulties such as these have given some critics an excuse to argue that all truth-recovery processes are counter-productive and potentially dangerous. For some, including advocates of blanket amnesty, the discrepancies in the amnesty process indicate that the TRC was not the required solution. Interrogating the past, they argue, endangers reconciliation instead of fostering it, and we should rather pursue a policy of 'forgiving and forgetting'. Although this line may be politically expedient, it fails to acknowledge that 'knowing' the truth is a requirement for 'understanding' the past, which itself underpins reconciliation. Even the 'forgive and forget' approach must rest on an understanding of what actually happened. Of course, many who criticised the TRC's findings offered no alternative explanations of past events or how they should be dealt with.[7]

Although certain deponents may have come to the TRC expecting a material gain, for the most part this was subordinate to the broader objective of finding out what happened and why. 'Reconciliation' appears to have been of secondary importance for many people. 'People wanted "the truth", they wanted to know why, they wanted the remains of their dead sons, daughters and husbands, and closure from the trauma with which they have lived.'[8]

The Commission's founding legislation gave it a broad and exhaustive mandate. At the centre were provisions to investigate and establish 'as complete a picture as possible of the causes, nature and extent of the gross violations of human rights'[9] committed during the period under review. Accordingly, a Human Rights Violations Committee and an Amnesty Committee were set up to afford victims 'an opportunity to relate their own accounts of the violations of which they are the victims' and to grant amnesty to persons who 'make a full disclosure of all the relevant facts' relating to acts associated with a political objective committed during the course of conflicts of the past.[10]

The human rights violations process would allow people to report the names of perpetrators known to them. They could provide contextual information based on perceptions and prejudices. The process encouraged the use of hearsay evidence and did not allow for cross-examination by implicated persons. By contrast, the amnesty process was narrower, and generally did not allow for a broader examination of the context, motivations, and other aspects relating to the 'nature' and 'causes' of the violations. Those who applied for amnesty had to fulfil certain criteria, such as full disclosure, as set out in the Act, in order to qualify.[11] Failure to apply or the refusal of amnesty could result in criminal or civil prosecution.

In theory, the two processes were complementary, and it was envisaged that material would flow between the two Committees, facilitated by investigations and the checking of facts. In reality, as discussed below, the Committees worked in isolation, and vital opportunities to conduct further investigations based on amnesty applications and testimonies were missed.

Generally, the criticisms considered thus far stemmed from difficulties inherent in the evolving structures and processes of the Commission. Other problems must also be taken into account.

Constitutional and Judicial Problems

The Commission faced various legal challenges, from the left and the right of the political spectrum. The Biko, Mxenge and Ribeiro families, under the mantle of the Azanian People's Organisation (AZAPO), took the TRC to the Constitutional Court in April 1996, in an effort to have the amnesty provisions in the Act declared unconstitutional. This challenge was not about the objective of uncovering the truth, but about the means of doing so. The applicants wished to seek redress before the ordinary courts, and they argued that the amnesty provisions violated their constitutional rights in this regard. The Court rejected their application.[12]

In another case, the Supreme Court upheld on appeal the applications of two former Eastern Cape security policemen to prevent the mother of murdered Eastern Cape activist, Siphiwe Mthimkulu, from testifying before the Human Rights Violations Committee. They claimed that she was going to name them as the men responsible for killing her son, and argued that they were entitled to know what they were accused of well in advance of a public hearing, so that they had time to respond to the allegations. The court agreed. In a twisted irony, both policemen subsequently applied for amnesty in connection with Mthimkulu's killing.

This ruling had a tremendous impact on the subsequent functioning of the Commission, as energy and resources now had to be diverted into locating any person who might be adversely named in a public process and warning the person that he or she had the right of reply.

The Time-frame

Initially, the enabling legislation gave the TRC an eighteen-month time-frame, with an optional six-month extension, and an additional three-month period to complete the final report. The cut-off date for human rights violations and amnesty cases that would be considered by the TRC was originally set at December 1993. This was later extended to May 1994. The deadline for the receipt of amnesty applications was also extended from December 1996 to May 1997. In mid-1997, the Commission requested the six-month extension, which would allow it to complete its final report by the middle of March 1998. Later in 1997, it again became clear that more time was needed, and a further extension was sought and granted, which allowed the Human Rights Violations Committee to complete its public hearings in March 1998. Investigations continued until the end of July, when the TRC closed its doors for the three-month report-writing period. An interim 'final report', based on the information then available, was published in October 1998.

The Amnesty Committee continued its work, wrapping up the public hearings in May 2001 and amnesty decisions in November. The Commission formally closed on 30 November, with only the revised version of the final report to be completed by April 2002. Informal discussions with TRC researchers indicate that a considerable amount of information gathered during the amnesty process has not been incorporated into this report.

It is evident that the original operational time-frame of thirty months was unrealistic and had a negative bearing on the Commission's ability to establish 'as complete a picture as possible' of the mandate period. It is unclear why the drafters of the legislation miscalculated the time required so badly.

Resources

The TRC did not have enough skilled personnel or resources to sift properly through the huge amount of documentation and other evidence gathered by investigation and research. The task demanded targeted recruitment and considerably more funding. Of course, it must be acknowledged that the constraints on the government budget were tightening during this period, and there were many other equally pressing claims on the limited resources available. The TRC has been criticised for being too expensive, with an average annual budget of R75 million. But expenditure was relatively modest, if one considers what was at stake. By way of comparison, R100 million was spent on the retrenchment packages of 850 police officers between 1994 and 1996.[13] While the resource allocation was unprecedented for a truth commission, other international comparisons are telling: for instance, more money was spent during the Starr investigation into President Clinton's personal dalliances. An evaluation of exactly how the TRC spent its money, and what proportion went towards effective truth-recovery activities, has yet to be undertaken.

The Definition of a Violation

The scope of the TRC was severely curtailed by the Act's definition of a 'gross human rights violation' as:

> (a) the killing, abduction, torture or severe ill-treatment of any person; or (b) any attempt, conspiracy, incitement, instigation, command or procurement to commit an act referred to in paragraph (a), which emanated from conflicts of the past and which was committed during the period 1 March 1960 to 10 May 1994 within or outside the Republic, and the commission of which was advised, planned, directed, commanded or ordered, by any person acting with a political motive.[14]

This definition excluded tens of thousands of other serious human rights violations that occurred during the same period. One could mention socio-economic violations related to discriminatory legislation (such as forced removals and pass laws) and non-political violations (such as the torture and killing of criminal suspects). This clearly narrowed the parameters of truth-seeking. As one commentator put it, 'the TRC's version of truth was established through narrow lenses' and 'obscured what was distinctive about apartheid'. The 'limited definition of the beneficiaries of apartheid' allowed most whites to distance themselves from the violations addressed by the Commission.[15]

The Definition of a Political Act

The Act prescribed that only actions emanating from political conflict could be considered by the Commission. Understandably, the Commission wanted to place realistic limits on its mandate, even if this meant neglecting a host of gross human rights violations that could be linked, albeit indirectly, to the political situation. The abuse of criminal suspects by the security forces stands out in this regard. But in defining the TRC's parameters, there may have been a superficial interpretation of what past conflicts could be construed 'officially' as 'political'. Thorny issues such as racism were dealt with in an apparently contradictory way.[16]

The vast majority of amnesty applications came from convicted prisoners, and most of these were refused because they did not meet the criteria set out in the Act. It is possible that some prisoners were simply 'trying their luck' by placing their crimes in a political context. But during the 1980s and 1990s, the lines between political and criminal activity had become increasingly blurred in South Africa, and it was not always easy to distinguish between the two. Economic and social dynamics had a direct effect on the political arena, resulting in a widespread overlap of criminal and political objectives, on both sides of the political spectrum. This situation was compounded by the fact that the apartheid state dealt with ostensibly political actions as if they were ordinary criminal matters.

The Amnesty Committee has refused to hear a large number of cases on the grounds that the acts described were not politically motivated. Of the 5 392 applications refused thus far,[17] the bulk fall into this category, and have therefore never been investigated. It could be argued that we need a more thorough exploration of the murky world where politics and crime overlap.

Access to Legal Representation

The TRC was empowered to facilitate legal representation at state expense for victims, perpetrators, and anyone adversely named in its processes. However, proceedings had been under way for several months before an agreement was reached with the Legal Aid Board to process applications and ensure representation. This arrangement placed strict limits on financial disbursements, which affected the time, and presumably the effort, that legal representatives devoted to a given case.

It is unclear how many amnesty applicants were aware of this facility. Over 77 per cent of applications came from prisoners,[18] and most were submitted without the benefit of legal assistance, and probably without the knowledge that it was available. This is in stark contrast to other groups, including some in the security forces and the liberation movements, who had top-flight legal representation, bankrolled, at great expense, through the State Attorney's office, or by special arrangement with the TRC.[19] The quality of prison applications was woeful, and this raises serious concerns about what might have been missed.

Human Rights Violations Committee

The work of the Human Rights Violations Committee dominated the daily functioning of the Commission, especially between 1996 and 1999. The Committee's task was to obtain and evaluate a range of submissions from individuals and groups in relation to the past conflict.

The initial victim hearings involved the complete panel of fifteen Commissioners. Thereafter, the Committee split up, additional members were appointed, and a series of victim and event hearings was conducted in the jurisdictions of each of the four regional offices, namely, Cape Town, Durban, East London and Johannesburg.

Various factors limited the TRC's ability to access the truth through these hearings. Some were purely logistical. The limited human and financial resources available meant that selections had to be made. More than 21 000 submissions were received by the Committee over a two-year period.[20] Over 2 000 of these were examined in more than 80 public hearings around the country. Most of the hearings dealt with specific cases from particular areas. In addition, several institutional hearings were held, dealing with specific groupings, such as the legal, business and faith communities; and several special hearings explored specific themes, such as women, youth or conscription. Only a small fraction of those who made submissions could be heard publicly.

The Committee tried to ensure that a cross-section of cases were heard in each area. Often, the attempt to be even-handed, to be representative and show diversity, actually had the effect of distorting the picture, as high-profile cases and cases involving minority groups were sought out specifically. 'In consequence the demographics of human rights abuse in South Africa, as well as the historical context thereof, often became subsumed or obfuscated.'[21] Ironically, indigent black victims were under-represented and white victims over-represented in the name of impartiality.

Given the sheer scale of the abuse committed during the mandate period, the extent to which various constituencies would engage with the process was pivotal. In early 1996, senior staff members made informal projections that as many as 120 000 submissions would be made, but this was clearly unrealistic, as only eight statement-takers had been allocated to each of the four TRC offices for this purpose. Even if each statement-taker had been able to manage five statements a day, which was asking too much, the capacity would have been grossly insufficient. As it was, most statement-takers had little experience of this kind of work, with the result that many statements were insubstantial, making the subsequent investigative and other work more difficult.[22]

By April 1997, a year after the first hearings, the Commission had received only 9 000 statements. Access had proved problematic, especially outside the cities, and the Commission needed to reach more people in the peri-urban and rural areas to avoid a skewed geographical emphasis. It therefore launched the designated statement-taking programme, in conjunction with non-governmental and community-based organisations around the country, and engaged 300 community-based statement-takers.[23]

Despite these efforts, and the subsequent increase in the number of statements received, it is clear that many thousands of violations were not reported to the TRC. This is evident from the limited correlation between cases registered on the TRC's own database and those registered on the database of an independent NGO.[24] The extent to which these missing cases might complement or challenge the versions of events already recorded remains to be seen.

Among those who did come forward, there appeared to be a preponderance of middle-aged black women, many of whom could be depicted as 'reporters of abuse', telling what happened to their loved ones rather than themselves. This led inevitably to criticism that the truths obtained were selective, not based on facts, and unhealthily reliant on hearsay evidence.[25]

The Commission was unable to secure a representative cross-section of submissions. Disappointingly, many political activists, community leaders, parliamentarians and cabinet ministers did not submit statements. In addition, most of the more significant former members of the civil service, National Security Management System, judiciary or magistracy did not appear before the Commission, or were not asked to submit relevant information.

Inevitably, perhaps, there were biases in the number and type of submissions received from supporters of different political parties. The Inkatha Freedom Party (IFP), for example, which consistently refused to cooperate with the TRC, told its members at the last moment to submit statements, to avoid losing out on possible financial reparations. The TRC's Durban office was inundated, as close to 5 000 people submitted their statements over a period of eight weeks.[26] This rush affected the quality of the information gathered. In total, the Durban office received over 9 700 submissions,[27] an impressive number which nevertheless represents only a fraction of the violations in KwaZulu-Natal, the country's most conflict-ridden province.

Only a handful of statements were received from some of the best-known epicentres of violence, such as the Soweto uprising (1976) and the Vaal Triangle uprising (mid-1980s). Some minority groups, notably whites in general and coloureds in the Western Cape, largely stayed away, prompting concerns about their lack of commitment to finding a common understanding of the past and to building reconciliation. It may be that these communities perceived the TRC as an ANC entity,[28] or decided not to engage with a process that would expose how they had benefited under apartheid. The extent to which activists and others boycotted the TRC because they did not support it or did not feel the need to participate remains unclear.

The TRC itself took conscious and controversial decisions not to engage with certain constituencies. For instance, it decided not to subpoena IFP leaders such as Mangosuthu Buthelezi about their party's role in the violence,[29] nor to question members of the judiciary and magistracy about their role in implementing apartheid laws. Given the significance of these two groupings and the subsequent findings made against them, the decision not to engage with them undermined the Commission's credibility, and severely hindered its ability to assess conflicts in which they had been involved. This shortcoming was recognised by the Commission itself.[30]

The processes of the Human Rights Violations Committee generated an enormous amount of valuable primary data. The quality of the information gathered was not always good, and the versions presented often could not be tested thoroughly. But these are not sufficient grounds for concluding, as some commentators have done, that these versions are unreliable. While this might be true in certain cases, the Committee did not pluck its findings out of thin air. There was a process, albeit an imperfect one, and findings were based on relatively consistent procedures, using corroborative information (discussed in more detail below), secondary documentation, and similar factual evidence. For example, where the Commission was unable to find evidence of torture relating to a specific submission, it could make a finding on the basis of contextual corroboration, if other cases of a similar nature had been reported. This diminished the reliance on 'hard' factual truth, and allowed for the emergence of a range of truths, as outlined in the report.[31] Some could not make this leap of faith. Time and again, they opposed the TRC's findings on the basis of the old adage: 'If you can't prove it in a court of law, it didn't happen.' The Commission, however, was more inclined to give the benefit of the doubt to those who claimed they had been victims of abuse, not only for the purpose of establishing that the version provided was essentially truthful, but also to restore the dignity of those who came forward to testify.

Amnesty Committee

The Amnesty Committee was completely unprepared for the 7 060 applications it received by the cut-off date in May 1997.[32] Without adequate administrative support or its own investigative component, the Committee struggled to cope with its workload. Initially, there was a single Committee with just five members, which slowed down the process of hearings and decision-making. Unlike the human rights violations hearings, the amnesty hearings were quasi-judicial, allowing for legal representation and cross-examination, and placing a higher premium on factual evidence. In the beginning, at least, the Amnesty Committee also moved without any apparent sense of urgency or regard to the Human Rights Violations Committee.

By the end of 1996 – the original cut-off date for receipt of applications – the Amnesty Committee had dealt with only a handful of cases. This prompted a series of parliamentary amendments to the Promotion of National Unity and Reconciliation Act during 1997 and early 1998, extending the cut-off date for receipt of applications and increasing the size of the Committee from five to seven members. The Committee was subsequently expanded to twelve members, and finally to nineteen. To expedite the process, the Committee was split into six smaller committees, which operated simultaneously. The Committee was also provided with additional administrative staff, evidence analysts and evidence leaders (who presented cases during the public hearings). This made it possible to deal with up to six matters at any one time.[33] The process therefore accelerated, although the period needed to conclude all outstanding matters had to be extended several times.

Amnesty applications involving 'gross human rights violations', as defined in the Act, were required to be heard in public. The Commission estimated that this type of application accounted for about 20 per cent of the total.[34] These applications would consume the most time and resources, whereas the remaining 80 per cent could be dealt with administratively in chambers. By August 1998, some months past the end point originally envisaged, the Committee had dealt with only two thirds of the total number of applications. Of these, over 4 500 had been dealt with administratively, and all but 50 had been refused.[35] However, only 136 of the 1 400 cases that had to be dealt with publicly had been heard.[36] This public hearing process was eventually completed in May 2001. Outstanding decisions were finalised in November 2001.

Two previous indemnity laws, passed under the last National Party government, afforded immunity from prosecution or release from custody on the basis of public provision of minimal information.[37] Specifically designed around the negotiation process, neither Act sought to elicit detailed truths about past violations. Although the Indemnity Act required that violations and their motivations be considered and investigated, the Further Indemnity Act dropped both of these requirements and extended amnesty to anyone who believed they were fighting for a political objective.[38] Although the validity of these indemnities was upheld by the TRC, it made no attempt to examine the information contained in indemnity applications or to use it as a basis for further inquiry. This was despite the fact that in several cases before the Human Rights Violations Committee, where perpetrators were unknown, persons had applied for and received indemnity in relation to the same incidents.[39] Nothing prevented the TRC from questioning those who had benefited from indemnity. In a handful of matters, previously indemnified persons applied for amnesty, presumably in an attempt to avoid possible civil litigation.[40]

The TRC's amnesty arrangement differed considerably from the previous indemnities, although it was also the product of negotiation between the country's main political players. Under the shadow of possible criminal prosecutions, the amnesty provisions aimed to give perpetrators a 'way out', which would lead to the acknowledgement and comprehensive understanding of past violations, yet avert the witch-hunt the security forces feared and claimed would transpire. Amnesty was conditional, and an application would be rejected if it failed to meet the stipulated criteria.

Significantly, and unlike prior truth commissions, the TRC legislation did not allow for a general amnesty, and required detailed disclosure of specific events. 'We are not dealing with generalities,' Dumisa Ntsebeza, the head of the Investigation Unit, told the media at the outset, 'we are dealing with what actually happened.'[41] However, 'full disclosure' necessarily referred only to those matters for which the individual was applying, allowing the applicant to disclose selectively with regard to related or similar incidents. Furthermore, while the Act required the disclosure of 'all relevant facts',[42] interpretations of relevancy varied, with the Amnesty Committee leaning towards a narrower definition. Not surprisingly, the disclosures made tended to be limited, adding to the frustrations of victims and their families.

The murder of Stanza Bopape is a case in point. This Mamelodi activist disappeared while in police custody in June 1988. In the only case of its kind, ten former security policemen, ranging from a constable to the head of the security police, applied for amnesty in connection with the torture and murder of Bopape, and the illegal disposal of his body. Despite clear evidence before the TRC that others had been involved, at least in the cover-up, there was no further investigation, and amnesty was subsequently granted. The Bopape family understandably felt cheated. A number of victims' families have felt similarly, and many have opposed the amnesty applications.

Amnesty hearings were often frustrated by legal argument. Attorneys argued passionately for the exclusion of certain testimony, for rulings against certain lines of questioning, for the recusal of Commissioners, and so on. There were interminable delays as legal representatives manoeuvred to protect their clients' interests, instead of assisting the Commission to get to the truth. Often applicants revealed the bare minimum required to secure amnesty, effectively preventing the TRC from establishing 'as complete a picture as possible'.

A handful of attorneys and advocates represented most of the security force members and politicians. Tightly interlocking submissions and testimonies reinforced the perception that their versions of events were contrived, and designed to minimise fallout. On several occasions, leaders of evidence raised concerns about collusion between witnesses, and ethical misconduct by lawyers.[43] In addition, some of the legal representatives themselves, such as Ernst Penzhorn, the attorney who represented P.W. Botha and Magnus Malan, appeared to have dubious backgrounds.[44] Some families felt that applicants or their legal representatives were acting in bad faith.

Perhaps the greatest obstacle to determining whether the truth had been disclosed or not was the lack of an effective investigative capacity. The investigative component of the Amnesty Committee was only developed in the second half of 1997, and was drawn from the Human Rights Violations Committee. Amnesty applications sometimes contained the barest detail, and the Amnesty Committee frequently corresponded with applicants, requesting further information. But the capacity to verify information or pursue leads was extremely limited, and the gathering of evidence focused on official documents and other secondary sources, as opposed to statement-taking or other primary research. Given the questionable reliability and limited content of some of this documentation, such 'investigation' was similar to the 'corroboration' undertaken by the Human Rights Violations Committee (discussed below), which helped to confirm that an incident had occurred, but did little to explain how or why.

Counsel for victims and the Committee therefore relied heavily on cross-examination to test the versions presented. The discretion allowed in this regard varied greatly, with some committees immediately shutting down any line of inquiry they felt was not directly relevant, and others allowing lengthy cross-examination. Even where victims were competently represented, carefully crafted amnesty applications that neatly dovetailed with one another were effectively immune from contradiction, as alternative hypotheses were simply denied and held no weight in the absence of additional evidence.[45]

Some applications in which the evidence was blatantly contradictory, poorly constructed and generally unbelievable also seem to have been immune.[46] Although a comprehensive analysis of amnesty decisions has yet to be undertaken, preliminary research indicates that a number of these decisions are contradictory and that there is a lack of consistency in the emphasis given to particular criteria.[47] Many victims and survivors can feel justifiably aggrieved by this situation, which is a direct consequence of the Amnesty Committee's limited investigative and analytical capacity.

The Investigation Unit

Initially, it was envisaged that the Investigation Unit, the largest single component of the TRC, would be central to all its work. But it soon became evident that it would be impossible to investigate all the reports made to the Amnesty Committee, let alone the Human Rights Violations Committee. With regard to the latter, Commissioner Ntsebeza indicated that the Investigation Unit, of which he was the head, would instead 'look for themes in the history of abuses ... such as the incidence of torture, train attacks and cross-border raids'.[48] The plan was to investigate a selection of cases that would hopefully shed light on the broader picture of violations. This immediately raised questions about how the mass of individual cases would be handled, and highlighted the tension between the demand for individual investigation and the practical necessity of thematic investigation. What were the implications for the kind of truth that could be determined? Even with a narrower focus, the Unit had too much to do and too few resources. And there was still no clarity on how the Amnesty Committee would investigate applications for amnesty.

The Investigation Unit only became operational in mid-1996, and in some areas did not have its full complement of investigators until the end of the year.

For some months, virtually no investigation was done at all. In the Johannesburg office, several investigators were tasked with summarising human rights violations statements to facilitate the choice of matters to be heard in public. Administrative support was virtually non-existent, and was only developed during the course of 1997, after repeated efforts to secure it.

The Unit's capabilities were circumscribed by the skills and expertise of its sixty members, who were drawn from a range of backgrounds, including the law, NGOs and the South African police. Lawyers with varying degrees of expertise in investigation and management filled four of the six senior investigative positions. Most investigators, however, had limited or no experience of human rights investigations. Twelve members of the team were seconded from various European police forces, and most had little or no experience of South Africa. Controversially, members of the intelligence services were also employed, including a former operative of the Bureau of State Security (BOSS), and individuals connected to the ANC's Department of Intelligence and Security. Recruitment was painfully slow at times, and staff turnover undermined productivity and continuity. A number of investigations were abandoned because the original investigator left the Unit.

The Unit was divided into four regional offices – Cape Town, Durban, East London and Johannesburg – and a national office based in Cape Town, each with twelve members. Each regional office was allocated the same number of investigators, despite the fact that Durban and Johannesburg had heavier workloads. Ineffective channels of communication, and attempts to centralise investigations in Cape Town, the region with the fewest cases, compounded the logistical and administrative problems. For much of the first year, those in charge of the Unit actively resisted proposals to decentralise, thereby perpetuating the inertia this approach created. Recommendations on decentralisation, made by members of the Johannesburg office in August 1996, were embargoed, but the approach was finally adopted early in 1997. These problems and tensions further hindered the Unit's work and reflected ongoing disagreements about its precise role and its relationship to other components of the Commission.

The Investigation Unit had to sift through a mountain of documentation in order to service both the human rights violations and the amnesty processes. Initially, when investigations were centralised, certain classifications of information had to be sent to the Unit's analytical department based in the TRC's national office. The theory was that this unit would map out violations and provide the other units with connections between cases and personalities, thereby facilitating more detailed and complex inquiries. High-profile cases involving hit squads and other abuses were to be dealt with by the national unit. These systems were largely unworkable. Logistical problems and related expenses rendered a number of investigations unviable. Various cases that the Johannesburg office had referred to Cape Town during 1996 were returned in 1997. But limited capacity meant that most of these matters could not then be dealt with by the regional office.

As the final report points out, '[t]he structure and functioning of the Investigation Unit altered as the institutional priorities of the Commission changed'.[49] This meant that limited attention and resources could be allocated specifically to proactive investigations into a range of pressing matters.

In-depth Investigations

The Investigation Unit was plagued by organisational, managerial and bureaucratic difficulties. Priorities and strategic objectives were not set, and there was a lack of direction and integration of activities. It was evident, given the size and limited experience of the Unit, that even when cases had been selected for in-depth probes, no more than cursory 'investigations' would be conducted. Indeed, there were very few independent investigative breakthroughs, and many investigations were focused on the time-consuming task of gathering information.

From the regional offices, it was difficult to see what the Unit's strategic plans were. The selection of cases for focused investigation seemed arbitrary. A number of individual cases, where there were good prospects for detailed investigation, were not probed in any depth. Even though there were no limits to the number of times a person could be subpoenaed, no efforts were made to solicit information by this means until the end of the first year.

The investigation into the State Security Council (SSC) is a study in missed opportunities. The SSC, at the apex of the National Security Management System (NSMS) and believed by many to be more important than Cabinet, required in-depth examination. The TRC needed to establish how decision-making in this high-level structure filtered down through regional and local Joint Management Centres (JMCs) and affected operations on the ground. This was essential if it was to hold political decision-makers responsible for gross human rights violations.

Senior members of the Investigation Unit and the TRC began to interview politicians and security officials who had been attached to the SSC. A number of amnesty applications had already been received providing details of murders and assassinations. Not surprisingly, those subpoenaed to the SSC hearings denied that any decisions had been taken to murder political opponents, even though the available SSC documents referred to 'eliminating' and 'wiping out' terrorists and other opponents.

Then a vital opportunity presented itself. Towards the end of 1996, facing arrest and prosecution by the same unit responsible for the Eugene de Kock trial, Brigadier Jack Cronje, a former police hit squad commander who chaired the Northern Transvaal JMC, and four of his colleagues confessed to the killing of over sixty people during the 1980s. The attacks had taken place in the former Northern Transvaal, the 'independent' homeland of Bophuthatswana and the self-governing territories of KwaNdebele and Lebowa. These applications prompted others from Northern Transvaal security policemen and, significantly, from former SADF Special Forces members and their commanding officer, Brigadier Joep Joubert. Apart from those concerning the KwaMakhutha massacre in KwaZulu-Natal, these were the only admissions before the TRC of hit squad activity undertaken jointly by the police and the defence force.

The TRC now had a range of amnesty applicants who had been involved in operations across the territory, many of whom faced prosecution and imprisonment if they were not granted amnesty. A full set of JMC minutes was available, and the former chairperson of this body had stated publicly that 'a secret counter-revolutionary intelligence target centre was set up in 1985 as another cog in the NP government's elaborate security apparatus'.[50] Although it was clearly impossible to investigate the NSMS in its entirety, this combination of JMC documentation and information provided by amnesty applicants opened the door for an in-depth inquiry at local and provincial level.

A proposal to do just this was drafted by members of the Investigation Unit in Johannesburg and submitted to an ad hoc committee of the TRC dealing with strategic investigations in early 1997. There was no response. Subsequent investigations into Cronje's allegations about the 'target centre' were cursory and unsatisfactory, which raises questions about the credibility of the Commission's findings in this regard.[51] The TRC undertook no further detailed probes of the NSMS or related security and intelligence committees, and was left to draw conclusions from its national probe and details contained in untested amnesty applications. The opportunity for an extensive probe was lost.

Similar concerns could be raised about the Investigation Unit's failure to probe the apparent inadequacies of internal investigations conducted by the ANC into abuses committed in its own facilities during the 1980s.[52] Names and details of perpetrators and offences were available, yet the Unit chose not to pursue these matters, except for three in camera hearings with senior MK commanders, put together hastily towards the end of the process. It is regrettable that important issues like these were not addressed adequately.

Corroboration

Despite undertakings, often made at public hearings by members of the Human Rights Violations Committee, that individual cases would be referred to the Investigation Unit, this generally did not happen. In the Johannesburg office, for example, there was no referral mechanism, and the Unit was largely in the dark about the Committee's undertakings.

It was only towards the end of 1996 that a decision was taken on how the bulk of submissions to the Human Rights Violations Committee would be handled. Earlier that year, the Johannesburg Investigation Unit had circulated a document arguing that the first step in any investigation was to corroborate certain facts. It came as a surprise when this idea subsequently emerged as the TRC's central methodology for handling submissions and making findings.

Corroboration mainly involved accessing and assessing official and unofficial documentation that could support the allegations made in a particular submission. For example, if someone claimed that a relative had been killed in a demonstration, the Investigation Unit would try to verify that this person had indeed died there. It would establish the basic facts, but it would not investigate the circumstances of the violation or call alleged perpetrators to a hearing. However, many people had approached the TRC specifically to find out more about what had happened and why. Although corroboration helped to establish patterns of allegations and corroborative detail, it did not provide the individual truths that many were seeking, and it could not be construed as primary investigation.

In many offices, staff members were reassigned to corroboration, and additional staff were employed to assist with this. The Investigation Unit devoted most of its time and resources to the human rights violations process, with only a handful of members conducting more detailed investigations or working on behalf of the Amnesty Committee. The main transfer of members to amnesty investigations took place towards the end of 1997. All remaining members were transferred to amnesty work at the end of July 1998.

Relationship with the Attorney-General's Office

It is unclear whether a significant number of amnesty applications were prompted by the Investigation Unit's activities, or whether they came about almost entirely because of actual or potential prosecutions. The De Kock trial caused a number of former operatives to turn state witness, in order to avoid prosecution, and subsequent investigations in KwaZulu-Natal, the Eastern Cape and the former Transvaal reached quite an advanced stage and prompted further amnesty applications. Brigadier Cronje and his colleagues, for example, applied for amnesty in the same week in which they were arrested and charged, thereby stalling the criminal prosecution, pending the outcome of their application.

The relationship between the TRC and the Attorney-General's office held enormous potential for the broader truth-recovery process. The Transvaal Attorney-General had its own special investigation unit, set up following revelations before the Goldstone Commission in 1994. They had also been responsible for investigating the allegations in the Steyn Report, a preliminary inquiry into illegal covert military operations, conducted by SADF General Pierre Steyn in December 1992.

In spite of public announcements that a positive working relationship had been established between the Attorney-General and the Commission,[53] it is unclear to what extent the Commission was able to access witnesses or use information available to the Attorney-General's unit. Certainly, very little of the Attorney-General's information reached the Johannesburg office of the Investigation Unit, although the Unit was dealing with cases that had already been under investigation by the Attorney-General. In at least one meeting between members of this Investigation Unit and police investigators working for the Attorney-General, it was stated that the latter office had a negative attitude towards the Commission and would not go out of its way to be of assistance.

The threat of prosecution was meant to prompt the public disclosure of illegal actions by amnesty applicants, and this happened in a number of cases involving the security forces. There is a clear correlation between the amnesty applications of many former security policemen and ongoing criminal investigations by the Transvaal Attorney-General and other prosecuting authorities.

The pressure to apply for amnesty grew with the conviction of former Vlakplaas commander Eugene de Kock in October 1996, two months before the first cut-off date for amnesty applications. And the pressure intensified when damning information was disclosed during De Kock's evidence in mitigation of sentence, and when he subsequently decided to testify in the case against other security policemen for the 1989 killings at Motherwell in the Eastern Cape. The successful prosecution of these men challenged the myth that former policemen were immune from legal action, and indicated that the Attorney-General's criminal investigations were progressing. Before the December 1996 deadline, the TRC received a rash of applications from former security force members.

Information in the possession of the Attorney-General was therefore central to investigations involving both amnesty and human rights violations. As far as the latter are concerned, there was generally no interaction with former security operatives who decided to turn state witness, and many statements or other documents were either not made available or were not requested by the TRC. However, a number of these operatives did apply for amnesty, and the details of their involvement have been interrogated to some extent during the amnesty process. One notable exception is the former askari and Vlakplaas operative, Joe Mamasela, who refused to apply for amnesty, but was questioned by the Investigation Unit at an in camera hearing.

The Attorney-General's office had only a limited capacity to investigate and prosecute apartheid-era crimes. It is unlikely that all the information in the possession of this office could have been used in criminal prosecutions, but fuller access to this information might have enabled more detailed questioning of applicants and others subpoenaed before the Commission's investigative hearings. This in turn might have prompted more amnesty applications, or at least more detail on both specific and generic issues. Once again, important opportunities may have been lost.

The Attorney-General's special investigation unit, now operating as a specialised unit of the Department of Public Prosecutions, has spent over six years investigating a host of apartheid-era crimes, mostly relating to the activities of former security force members. The apparent focus on prosecuting middle-ranking apartheid operatives may undermine the long-term possibilities of successfully prosecuting their generals and political leaders. The allegations against police generals in the Goldstone Report have yet to result in any prosecutions. However, all three of them, Lieutenant Generals Basie Smit and Johan le Roux, and Major General Krappies Engelbrecht, have appeared before in camera investigative hearings of the TRC. Smit and Le Roux applied for amnesty in certain matters, while Engelbrecht did not, denying all cases in which he had been implicated.

Neither military leaders nor a number of senior IFP members implicated in gross human rights violations and other politically related crimes have applied for amnesty. Although investigations have continued and, in the case of the military, have resulted in the prosecution of Dr Wouter Basson, the government has made public its intention to address the issue of special amnesties. This will only be done after the revised version of the final report is released later in 2002.

Access to Information

The effectiveness of any investigation depends on access to information. Most of the important information on security force involvement in violence came from amnesty applications. Much of this was not available until past the cut-off dates for applications in December 1996 and May 1997. A comprehensive amnesty database was not available until the second half of 1997, and even then regional investigators did not have direct access to this resource.

Access to state-controlled information was blocked in several ways. In 1996, largely ineffective agreements were made between the TRC and the South African National Defence Force, the South African Police Service and the National Intelligence Agency to establish 'nodal points' through which the Commission would access official documentation. At one point, it was even suggested that all requests for police documents should be channelled through a single office in Pretoria, but this was clearly unrealistic. Although the situation eventually improved, for over eighteen months the Investigation Unit was effectively prevented from going to specific police stations to obtain dockets or other information, and was instead obliged to go through police liaison officers.

Access to National Intelligence Agency documents was equally problematic. Security clearance requirements immediately excluded all foreign members of the Investigation Unit. In at least one regional office, not a single staff member received clearance. Controlled access to security information also gave people within these structures the opportunity to vet whatever information was requested and handed over. The TRC did not challenge these arrangements.[54]

Many official records were simply unavailable. Minister for Safety and Security, Sydney Mufamadi, informed the Commission that thousands of police files had been destroyed. According to one report, the files of 314 000 individuals and 9 500 organisations were burnt or shredded.[55] In October 1996, hundreds of documents relating to Eugene de Kock's allegations of fraudulent claims made by senior policemen were stolen from police archives.[56] Major General B. Mortimer testified during the first SADF submission to the TRC that he was unable to find any other documents relating to the Civil Cooperation Bureau (CCB) and that any available information on the CCB had already been handed to the Harms Commission in 1990. He was unable to explain why there were no other documents, especially as it was later discovered that the CCB was only 'put out of existence' formally in 1991, after the Harms Commission had finished its work.

Former military, police and intelligence personnel played down the suggestion of a cover-up in these cases, but it is almost certain that incriminating documents were involved. The TRC undertook to find out why documents had been destroyed and who was responsible, but the Investigation Unit made no detailed investigations in this regard. A promised 'comprehensive hearing' into missing Military Intelligence files did not materialise.[57]

The Investigation Unit was also empowered to conduct searches. With one or two exceptions, these powers were never exercised, although there were opportunities to do so. The Commission also failed to examine documentation that was available. Valuable resources that were virtually overlooked included the thousands of personal files relating to all restricted, banned and detained persons contained in the archives of the Justice Department's Directorate of Security Legislation, which 'serviced' the security police until mid-1986.

Fortunately, former operatives retained a certain amount of documentation, some of which was handed over to the Commission. It also received important SSC documentation uncovered during police investigations in KwaZulu-Natal and used in the prosecution of former Minister of Defence, Magnus Malan, and others.

Although the Investigation Unit collected a considerable amount of information in this process, the development of a centralised database and access to the material it contained were largely restricted to the analytical department and a handful of investigators. Consequently, most staff members remained unaware of the possibilities of this resource.

Amnesty Investigations

Since amnesty applicants had to tell the truth in order to qualify, the quality and accuracy of information contained in their applications were obviously crucial. Yet the nature and extent of investigations in the amnesty process were cause for concern.

It is evident that very little investigation was done in some instances, and many 'investigators' were tasked only with logistical functions, such as delivering subpoenas, or locating witnesses and documentation. Interestingly, in the final edition of the TRC magazine *Truth Talk*, the terminology of 'corroboration' cropped up: it was reported that amnesty investigators were being 'sent out to conduct investigations so as to corroborate information contained in the application'.[58] Although the bulk of applications were not investigated in detail, there were some exceptions.[59]

After the 'investigation' phase, evidence analysts based in Cape Town assessed the available information and directed requests to Investigation Unit members based at the various regional offices. These analysts were responsible for compiling briefs for the evidence leaders who represented the Commission at amnesty hearings. There was concern about the general quality of the analysis, and the fact that the analysts had little or no experience with the issues. They were largely dependent on the information presented to them, and had limited power to initiate further inquiries.

The narrow 'case-by-case' approach adopted by the Amnesty Committee and the limited examination of contextual information were problematic. The amnesty applications from members of self-defence units in Katlehong and Thokoza, of which more than a hundred were received, best illustrate this.[60] Several committees were established to look at groups of these applicants. But where one committee accepted the need for a thorough examination of the context, in order to understand the nature and cause of the specific violation for which amnesty was sought, another did not. Such inconsistencies were probably exacerbated by the creation of additional amnesty committees.

The performance of evidence leaders was also inconsistent, and sometimes most unsatisfactory. At several hearings, evidence leaders were woefully under-prepared, and failed to ask questions. It seemed that some were simply going through the motions, rather than interrogating issues professionally. During the amnesty application of the murderers of Sicelo Dlomo, for example, the evidence leader asked no more than a handful of questions, and failed to challenge massive contradictions in the applicants' testimony. The evidence analyst also failed to provide any details of the investigation conducted by the Investigation Unit for the Human Rights Violations Committee, which had apparently resulted in the applicants coming forward. These proceedings did not help to establish the truth for the Dlomo family, and the granting of amnesty simply added insult to injury.

Conclusion

Any evaluation of the TRC's successes and failures requires an examination of both the Human Rights Violations Committee and the Amnesty Committee. Investigations were pivotal in facilitating both processes. The Investigation Unit, to its credit, managed to secure a considerable amount of very useful information, in difficult circumstances, and in conjunction with the Research Department provided backbone to the TRC's findings. However, more time was spent on collecting than on using information, and most cases were not explored sufficiently.

Although the human rights violations and amnesty processes both sought to establish the truth, the former leant towards narrative and social truths, and the latter towards forensic or factual truth. The work of both Committees was not properly integrated, and the tensions between their different approaches undermined the Commission's ability to exploit the available or potential information and testimony fully. An opportunity to access considerably more information has apparently been lost.

The Act envisaged that the human rights violations and amnesty processes would run concurrently, and did not clarify how they would interrelate with regard to establishing the truth of past conflicts. In practice, the two processes were never synthesised successfully, as most amnesty applications were only received after the Commission had been in existence for more than a year. Recommendations to establish an amnesty database were not implemented for several months, and when regional investigators eventually gained access to this resource in 1997, it did not provide details of what information was available.

This was a critical problem, as amnesty applications were the most important investigative resource for the Human Rights Violations Committee. Even after the time-frame had been extended, the delay in receiving these applications meant that there was less than twelve months in which to investigate human rights violations. The quality and amount of relevant amnesty information made available to the Investigation Unit, and the slow pace at which this was done, made matters worse. In fact, the Human Rights Violations Committee began winding up its work just when the Investigation Unit was getting to grips with some in-depth investigations. It is clear that much more could have been achieved if these and other investigations had been allowed to continue.

Although much was achieved by the TRC, we must acknowledge that it was essentially a disjointed, uncoordinated and selective process, and this in turn has broader implications for our understanding of the past, whether from the point of view of political leaders or ordinary people. Many findings have limited credibility as far as physical evidence is concerned. How the outstanding issues are dealt with is an open and necessarily political question. Most of those who came to the Commission in search of the truth, did not receive answers to their questions. It is evident that the process of recovering the truth has only just begun.

Notes

1. See, for example, the IFP allegation that TRC Commissioner, Dr Khoza Mgojo, was involved in smuggling arms to the ANC during the 'Seven Day War'. Hansard, 5 February 1999, pp. 72, 78.
2. For example, vol. 2, ch. 7, para. 124 states that the Goldstone Commission found that Phola Park self-defence unit member, Michael Phama, was a police informer. The allegation is repeated again in vol. 3, ch. 6, para. 545. Para. 620 of the same chapter eventually provides an accurate account of what Goldstone found, namely, that Phama's commander, who had ordered the attack, was a police informer. Truth and Reconciliation Commission,

Truth and Reconciliation Commission of South Africa Report, 5 vols (Cape Town, Juta & Co., 1998).
3. A glaring example is contained in the findings on the Boipatong massacre. Despite numerous previous references that are accurate, these state that the incident occurred in 1972 rather than 1992 (vol. 3, ch. 6, findings following para. 598).
4. The allegations against Phama were used by Thabo Mbeki (then deputy president) during the parliamentary debate on the TRC. Hansard, 5 February 1999, p. 50.
5. The TRC failed to question a range of individuals from the main political parties. Many implicated members of the security establishment were also never interviewed.
6. For example, there are several inaccuracies and distortions in Anthea Jeffrey's *The Truth about the Truth Commission* (Johannesburg, South African Institute of Race Relations, 1999). On pp. 38-9, she writes that Sylvia Dlomo-Jele testified at the Commission that she believed the police were responsible for the death of her son, Sicelo Dlomo, whereas four ANC cadres – 'all comrades of her son and frequent guests of her home' – were actually responsible, having suspected Sicelo of being an informer. Jeffrey concludes that Sylvia's version was wrong. In fact, there are many unanswered questions about Dlomo's death, and especially about the role of the MK commander who ordered the assassination. There is no evidence that Dlomo was an informer, but more than a suggestion that the commander was. This matter was never followed up by the TRC. Even though Sylvia discovered through the TRC who pulled the trigger and gave the orders, she still believed, with reason, that the police had a hand in Sicelo's death.

Elsewhere (pp. 138-9) Jeffrey argues that a British policeman, Dr Peter Waddington, was tasked with investigating allegations of police involvement in the Boipatong massacre, and that he cleared the police in this regard. In fact, Waddington was tasked with investigating the police response to the massacre, and a senior member of the Special Branch investigated the allegations of complicity. Rather than clearing the police, he reported that his investigation had not unearthed any evidence to support the allegations, which is a different matter.
7. This is true of the IFP especially. See Hansard, 5 February 1999, pp. 68-78.
8. J. Grobbelaar, 'The South African Truth and Reconciliation Commission: Some Reflections from Inside', paper presented to the Annual Conference of the South African Sociological Association, July 1999, p. 11.
9. Promotion of National Unity and Reconciliation Act, No. 34 of 1995, Preamble.

10. *Ibid.*
11. Grobbelaar, *op. cit.*, p. 2.
12. Constitutional Court Judgement 17/96, 25 July 1996.
13. *Star*, 10 December 1996.
14. Promotion of National Unity and Reconciliation Act, No. 34 of 1995 (see www.truth.org.za).
15. M. Mamdani, 'The TRC and Justice', in R. Dorsman, H. Hartman and L. Noteboom-Kroenmeijer (eds), *Truth and Reconciliation in South Africa and the Netherlands* (Utrecht, Netherlands Institute of Human Rights, 1999), p. 35.
16. For instance, the Amnesty Committee accepted racist motivations in a number of APLA and Pan Africanist Congress applications, but rejected them in the case of the Van Straaten brothers (see www.truth.org.za/decisions/1996/961206VanStraaten).
17. Summary of amnesty decisions as at 1 November 2000 (see www.truth.org.za/amntrans/index).
18. Briefing by Advocate Denzil Potgieter, 7 August 1998.
19. 'Lawyers feast at the body of truth', *Mail & Guardian*, 17 October 1997.
20. Briefing by Adv. Potgieter, 7 August 1998.
21. Grobbelaar, *op. cit.*, p. 6.
22. There was tension between investigative and psychological needs with regard to what should be included in the statement protocol. In the end, the former received precedence, although the quality of data collected was often poor. As far as psychological assessments are concerned, the TRC was later forced to develop another protocol, which has been used with limited success to facilitate reparations.
23. TRC press release, 1 April 1997, Statement by Archbishop Desmond Tutu on the launch of the TRC's designated statement-taking programme.
24. HURIDOCS database compiled in 1994-5 by the Centre for the Study of Violence and Reconciliation (for the now defunct Justice in Transition NGO) from the records of the Human Rights Committee of South Africa, the Detainees' Parents Support Committee, the Independent Board of Inquiry, Peace Action, and others.
25. Jeffrey, *The Truth about the Truth Commission*. See ch. 5, 'The need for factual evidence'.
26. TRC press release, 21 January 1998.
27. *Ibid.*
28. Grobbelaar, *op. cit.*, pp. 7-8.
29. These included senior IFP officials such as Themba Khoza, Humphrey Ndlovu and Rev. Celani Mthetwa, whom the Goldstone Commission

implicated in gun smuggling and criminal collusion with members of the South African Police.
30. www.polity.org.za/govdocs/commissions/1998/trc/5chap6, see para. 55.
31. For the purposes of making its findings, the TRC adopted four notions of truth: factual or forensic truth; personal or narrative truth; social or 'dialogue' truth; and healing and restorative truth. *TRC Report*, vol. 1, ch. 5, paras 29-45.
32. www.truth.org.za/amnesty.
33. TRC press release, 12 November 1997.
34. Briefing by Adv. Potgieter, 7 August 1998.
35. By 18 June 1998, the Amnesty Committee had administratively refused amnesty to 4 510 applicants: 385 because the applicant denied guilt; 2 830 because the Committee determined that there was no political objective; 320 because the applicant had acted for personal gain; 410 because the matter fell outside the Committee's jurisdiction; and 565 because the matter fell outside the cut-off date. Information provided by Amnesty Committee, 1 August 2000.
36. Briefing by Adv. Potgieter, 7 August 1998.
37. Indemnity Act, No. 35 of 1990, and Further Indemnity Act, No. 151 of 1992.
38. For further information, see P. Parker, 'The Politics of Indemnities, Truth Telling and Reconciliation in South Africa: Ending Apartheid without Forgetting', *Human Rights Law Journal*, 17:1/2 (1996), pp. 1-13.
39. For example, Guybon Khubeka received indemnity for the attempted murder of Stompie Seipei.
40. For example, MK member Robert McBride, who had received indemnity for his part in the Magoo's Bar bombing.
41. 'Hand that steers ship of vital TRC arm', *Saturday Star*, 14 September 1996.
42. Promotion of National Unity and Reconciliation Act, No. 34 of 1995, Preamble.
43. See, for example, concerns raised by the TRC's chief legal officer, Hanif Vally, during Soweto Special Branch hearings, 28-9 January 1998: www.truth.org.za/hrvtrans/event_hearings.
44. 'Penzhorn – man in the middle', *Mail & Guardian*, 24 March 1995. Countering allegations that the military had been involved in the assassination of SWAPO leader Anton Lubowski, former Minister of Defence, Magnus Malan, claimed in Parliament that Lubowski had in fact been working for the army. Payments from Global Investments, a Military Intelligence front

company, were offered as proof that Lubowski was an informer. Ernst Penzhorn was named as the signatory to these payments. See also 'The smoke and mirrors world of PW's lawyer', *Electronic Mail & Guardian*, 9 February 1998.
45. For example, the amnesty applications and testimony of ten former security policemen in the Stanza Bopape case. See www.truth.org.za/amntrans/pta5/bopape1 and www.truth.org.za/amntrans/1998/98060109PRE/3bopape1.
46. For example, the amnesty applications and testimony of four MK members in the Sicelo Dlomo case. See www.truth.org.za/amntrans/1999/99021519JHB/990216br.
47. M. Saino, 'An Analysis of the South African Amnesty Granting Process', Centre for the Study of Violence and Reconciliation, unpublished paper (Johannesburg).
48. *Business Day*, 22 March 1996.
49. *TRC Report*, vol. 1, ch. 6, para. 42.
50. 'Former Vlakplaas operatives reveal secret unit', SAPA, 25 October 1996.
51. The 'C4' unit, known by its Afrikaans acronym Trewits (Counter-Revolutionary Intelligence Task Team) was based in Pretoria, under the same section responsible for Vlakplaas operations. Its purpose was to draw up a priority list of activists who could not be dealt with through normal legal processes. The selections took place at monthly meetings attended by representatives of Military Intelligence, the Special Forces, national intelligence and the security police. TRC investigations left many questions unanswered, as key Trewits operatives refuted Cronje's allegations that the unit was responsible for operational targeting.
52. The three main investigations undertaken by the ANC were the Stuart Commission, Motseunyane Commission and Skweyiya Commission.
53. TRC press release, 4 July 1996, Statement by Dr Alex Boraine.
54. TRC press release, 30 September 1996, Joint statement by TRC and SADF after discussions.
55. G. Evans, 'The hunting of the nark', *Leadership*, July 1998.
56. 'Key De Kock files stolen: Archives raided for evidence linking top policemen to hit-squads', *Sunday Times*, 13 October 1996.
57. 'Secrets Vanish: Search for missing documents from the apartheid era', *City Press*, 9 June 1996.
58. V. Green, 'More than 1 000 amnesty applications must still be heard in public', *Truth Talk*, July 1998, p. 9.
59. Amnesty application of J.B. Botha and eight others for the abduction and

murder of Mrs Ngcobo (née Khubeka). See www.truth.org.za/amntrans/2000/00071927DBN/200719db.

60. These applications tell one side of the story only; with one or two exceptions, there were no applications from Inkatha supporters or members of the security forces.

3

MONUMENTAL HISTORICAL MEMORY
Managing Truth in the Everyday Work of the South African Truth and Reconciliation Commission[1]

Lars Buur

Introduction

The ritualised public representations emerging from the work of the South African Truth and Reconciliation Commission (TRC), and in particular from the public hearings and the final report, are powerful performances of truth-telling by the 'new' nation-state that clearly distinguish it from the former violent and evil apartheid state, which was characterised by 'mendacity'.[2] However, this celebrated, 'on-stage' public truth-telling goes together with the invisible, 'backstage' dimensions of bureaucratic truth production.

While reconciliation was the overall aim of the TRC,[3] it is nonetheless interesting, as Mahmood Mamdani has pointed out, that the Commission was not popularly referred to as the 'Reconciliation Commission'.[4] There are good reasons for this: for the Commission, 'truth' was considered to be 'the road to reconciliation'. This presupposition about the prime importance of the truth is shared by most people studying truth commissions.

In the recent literature, the production of truth in official truth commissions, including the South African one, is generally conceptualised in positivistic terms. Conceptualisations such as 'bringing truth to light', 'ascertaining the facts', 'revealing' or 'finding the truth about the past' flourish.[5] The underlying assumption is that the categories and descriptions applied by truth commissions are in accordance with the 'real' world of human rights abuses. The relation is usually described as a simple one. Commissions 'find' their facts as though there were a body of common knowledge that just had to be 'acknowledged'.[6] That both the management of 'truth-finding' systems on the one hand, and their appropriation by staff on the other, actively shape the truth produced, is never a concern, except if 'bad planning', 'the wrong use of categories', 'incomplete statement-taking', 'the lack of technical resources', or 'political limitations' hinder the process.[7] The irony is that when such constraining or 'contaminating' factors are articulated, they are located outside the actual everyday commission work.[8]

This paper critically examines a range of everyday practices of the TRC, focusing on the 'backstage' functioning of the bureaucratic machinery of truth production. In particular, it explores the production of a form of historical memory that is closely related to national history. It shows how the positivistic human rights documentation methodology, and its associated information management system, generated statistically informed data in the form of measurable trends, and aggregations of kinds of cases and violations. The paper thus investigates those everyday aspects of information processing and corroboration that transformed victims' narrative constructions of past incidents into data about human rights violations.

First, I will outline the organisational character, bureaucratic structure and implicit rationality of the information management system, showing how the data, rather than simply being passively accumulated, were actively shaped at every stage of the 'gathering' process. Second, I will demonstrate how the conventions and categories invoked by the information management system 'flattened' and reorganised popular narratives and memories, with particular consequences for the kind of truth-telling and the construction of official memories. Here I describe an encounter in which investigators and an 'alleged' victim of gross human rights violations negotiated local, popular memories of the apartheid era. In the process, these memories were transformed to fit into the overall framework of the Commission, which itself took on a form resembling national history.

Finally, I will reflect on some of the epistemological questions raised by my analysis of the TRC's everyday work, especially in relation to relativism and the status of 'truth'. I will also discuss the extent to which this sort of epistemology is inevitable within the confines of a truth commission.

Can 'truth' in the form of measurable trends and the classification of cases and violations – that is, the forensic, objective kind of truth garnered by the information management system – be established by truth commission work without forgoing competing local influences and negotiations? Can one demarcate a space where facts about past violations can be recounted that is not constituted by power or is free of the influence of power relations? Is it possible for staff members to leave their own 'baggage' behind? Is it possible to separate official commission work from the wider political processes in which it is inscribed? These are some of the questions we will be dealing with.

This paper does not consider a range of relevant questions, such as accountability, morality, the need for justice in a transitional society, the 'South African miracle'. Instead, it focuses on the 'backstage' performance of bureaucratic micro-politics, in an attempt to discover how and to what extent such contingent processes impeded or facilitated the production of historical truth.

The Information Management System: A Global, Circulating Technique for Truth Management

The databases of the four most recent truth commissions, including the South African one, were designed and supervised by the American Association for the Advancement of Science.[9] In order to get the right information for the database, an extensive and elaborate information management system was set up. By the time the Commission's chief executive officer, Dr Biki Minyuku, was employed, the system had already been running for several months. It had outlined the staff structure, the qualifications necessary for each position, the internal organisation of the Commission, how the truth of the past should be 'collected' and how it could be represented.[10]

This particular way of seeing, of doing empirical work and representing realistic narratives about 'actual' persons, events and processes, is not innocent and neutral. As André du Toit recently pointed out, few people envisaged the extent to which the information management system would structure both the daily work of the Commission and the composition of the final report.[11]

The first thing to note is that official truth commissions are officially commissioned by governments to investigate the *large pattern of overall events* relating to human rights violations.[12] The aim is to derive factual knowledge in the form of 'global truth'. According to Hayner, '... a commission must focus on the essential, the most important, or the most relevant cases in order to *portray a global truth* [which] could include the investigation in depth of some cases that can be seen as illustrative of the perpetrators, victims or types of violence found, with summary statistics on others'.[13]

Chapman states that the only truth the TRC was mandated to *report on* was the positivistic, objective, factual kind.[14] But this claim is not as straightforward as it seems.[15] The TRC makes it clear in the final report that it worked on four kinds of truth, of which the factual, objective kind was only one. The Act states that the Commission should 'prepare a comprehensive report which sets out its activities and findings, based on factual and objective information and evidence collected or received by it or placed at its disposal'. But, at the same time, the Act does empower the Commission to 'facilitate, and initiate or coordinate, the gathering of information and the receiving of evidence from any person, including persons claiming to be victims of such violations or the representatives of such victims'.[16]

Here two levels of truth clash: global truth and local, specific truth; or, in the Commission's terms, factual, objective truth and perceptual, subjective truth. A 'global truth', informed by a statistical representation of the past, has to be fashioned from specific experiences of violence, seen from the individual perspectives of perpetrators, victims and witnesses. The two forms of 'truth', which can be compared to what I will later describe as official memory and unofficial, popular, historical memory, are interrelated. But while the Commission was mandated to reflect the global, objective truth in its report, the individual, subjective truths contained in statements, submissions and narratives at public hearings were clearly regarded as nothing more than raw material, as data to be processed.

The difference between the local and the global is interesting, because the global way of thinking and talking about human rights violations signals an understanding of truth as separate from locally embedded human beings. Human rights data are the 'representation of acts of violence which allow human rights researchers to make systematic, comparative analyses of patterns of violations in time, space and social structure'.[17] More specifically, they are the 'combination of information and classified decisions made by an organisation that together serves as the organisation's collective memory'. The benefits from such a system almost all derive from the way people in an organisation classify information. Data are only considered as real when they are collected and represented 'according to the structure defined by the organisation', and this 'structured system' is the 'controlled vocabulary'.[18]

The Cognitive Landscape of the Information Management System and the Exclusion of 'Victims'

The 'controlled vocabulary' consists of lists of different categories, such as the list of violations the particular commission has chosen to examine; or the list of organisations and units to which perpetrators belong or belonged; or the list of regions in the country according to which acts can be localised, and so on. The list of violations is, of course, the most important, because it defines which violations enter the database and come to represent the past.[19]

In South Africa, the 'controlled vocabulary' consisted, on its most abstract level, of four main categories: torture, killing, abduction, and severe ill-treatment.[20] Every victim statement captured in a 'protocol' (as the form was known) became coded according to the 'controlled vocabulary'. The processing of data in this way moves information from its 'partly-structured, partly-coded state in a questionnaire into a fully-structured, fully-coded state in which it can be entered directly into a computer'.[21] This implies that when a commission goes out and 'collects' information from people who have suffered violations, it does not collect the stories as they are told. Narratives about violations are coded from the beginning, and undergo changes so that they are framed in the same language as that of the information management system. In this sense, the 'controlled vocabulary of violations determines how a given incident in the "real world" will appear in the coded data'.[22]

Such a global, decontextualised view created problems when the Commission entered the anchoring domain of local conflicts and human rights violations. For the statement-takers, these problems were particularly severe in the rural areas. The Commission interpreted the normative definition of 'political context' so as to exclude racism. Racial attacks that led to human rights violations were *not political* if the individuals involved did not belong to a 'publicly known political organisation and ... the incident did not form part of a specific political conflict'.[23] In the rural areas, human rights violations seldom involved known political organisations as such, but they were nonetheless closely related to and informed by racism. A statement-taker working for the TRC recalled the schism in the following way:

> We rejected many, many, many cases which came to us simply because they were not falling within the [definition of a] political act ... For instance, most cases of violations in the rural areas were along racial lines. Say a person comes to you and reports that he was walking in the street in one of the 'dorpies' [country villages] and he was shot by a white man. The problem with [this case] is that there is no political connection into the violation, because it's a civilian or an individual [who] just shot someone. So there is no [direct] political motive.[24]

The dilemma described here was common. The tensions between the interpretation of the normative framework of the Act and the realities encountered by statement-takers were also prolonged, as Commissioners took considerable time to decide whether or not to change the operational interpretation of the 'political context'. Statement-takers felt that they bore the burden of turning away person after person who had clearly suffered abuse. This made them question the definition of a 'gross human rights violation' put forward by the Commission, and the very foundation of their work. They would often ask: 'What is a human rights violation, and what makes it "gross"?' The position they were placed in was difficult to manage. Statement-takers were constantly insecure about whether they were doing their work correctly, especially knowing that an alleged victim who was turned away one week as falling 'out of mandate', might be accepted the following week if there was another policy change.

Statement-takers reacted in different ways. Some followed the Commission's interpretation of racism and turned people away. Others tried to bypass this interpretation. They felt it was unfair to exclude people who were already marginalised and deprived of resources. Classifying such people as victims might at least ensure some relief. They might be given a voice in the national history and receive state funds in the form of the expected 'final reparation'.[25]

Clearly, even though a well-known 'global' information management system was implemented, its ideal functioning was interfered with by 'local' priorities and concerns. This does not mean that the system was unproductive; on the contrary, it was extremely productive, making possible the identification of 17 500 victims of apartheid.[26] There was human suffering before the TRC appeared on the scene, but afterwards a new category of people had been identified – the 'victims of gross human rights violations'. But, as the example also illustrates, the information management system in itself was closely connected to an immanent, exclusive form of power.

It is worth emphasising a point made earlier: the categories used to classify and code information about past human rights abuses come from a source outside the local environment in which the violations happened. When a commission objectifies the past through such a controlled vocabulary, we have an interface between the world and the commission, between sensation and cognition, where all knowledge that counts is constituted. As Ball hints, another reality is created, the 'human rights reality'.[27] This implies that *meaning* is inscribed upon victims' lives by commissions.

To know what really happened, then, is not a matter of sensory attunement, but of cognitive reconstruction. Such knowledge is acquired not by engaging directly, in a practical way, with the objects in one's surroundings, but rather by learning to represent them in the protocol and on the database. As such, they form a *map* of the past, a map that is a standardised, generalised model of abstract (ab)normality. A statistical understanding of (ab)normality is defined explicitly according to specified criteria of frequency and distribution, which are applicable to, but independent of, specifics.[28]

The particular relation between the specific and the general will become clearer when we explore how different genres of memory collide and merge, using a case study taken from the Investigation Unit. The case concerns the corroboration of a victim statement alleging that a person had been shot during riots in the seventies.

The Investigation Unit and the Need for Clarity

The Investigation Unit was tasked with 'analysing and corroborating' statements received by the Commission, in order to find out whether they fell within its mandate or not.[29] The Unit was one of several working together on this project, where each step was part of an ongoing, systematic cross-checking and confirmation of the 'raw data' captured by the statement-takers. The aim of this cross-checking was neutral and objective fact-finding. The work of the Investigation Unit can be seen as the third step in the process of verifying the information captured in statements by alleged victims. The end product was either the classification of the protagonists as victims of gross human rights violations, or the dismissal of the statement as being 'out of mandate'.

Striving to Settle and Verify

Two investigators from the Commission and one Danish anthropologist went on a routine expedition to a small village half an hour from Cape Town. They were to visit a Muslim man who had handed in a statement that, according to the investigators, contained 'unclear information' about what had happened to him. In the statement protocol, he described the violation he had suffered in a sparse four-line narrative. For the purposes of this study, let us call the man Achmat.

When we arrived, Achmat's parents and one of his sisters were waiting. He was out, we were told, but he would soon be back. They invited us into the living room and placed us comfortably in the best chairs. Facing the semicircle of his family and guests, the father immediately began to tell what had happened to Achmat around twenty years ago.

'One day, my son and a friend were on their way to buy meat at the butcher. It was at the time when there were riots all the time. Outside the shop my son was shot in the stomach. They [the police] took him to hospital, where he was operated on several times. We took the police to court because we wanted compensation, but lost the case.' The consequence of this incident, the father said, was that Achmat had become incapable of working during wintertime, because of 'pain in the bones'. And he asked us: 'What shall we do now, when our oldest son cannot support the family?'

When Achmat arrived twenty minutes later, one of the investigators told him: 'We have come to your house to ask additional questions and to get things right.' He asked Achmat to tell his story in greater detail. Achmat then delivered more or less the same story we had already heard from his father, the one stated in the protocol.

One of the investigators was not satisfied. 'It is a small statement that you have given to the statement-taker,' he said. 'We need to know more about what happened and when it happened.' The investigator began posing systematic questions about the times and places of the different incidents in the story, and the names of the people involved. 'When exactly did the shooting happen? Where did it happen? Who were you walking to the butcher with? Who shot you? Which hospital did they take you to? What is the name of the doctor who treated you? What is the name of the lawyer who ran your court case?'

Each question triggered a flurry of activity among the family members and some friends who had gathered by now, and all participated vigorously in giving answers, much to the annoyance of the investigators. Nobody could remember the year in which the incident had actually taken place, but 'it was the year when the neighbour who lived behind their house still lived there'. After a fairly long reconstruction, at one stage involving a consultation of the Islamic calendar, even this new clue proved fruitless. The exact year and date could not be recalled. It was also impossible to get the names of the persons involved in the story, but we were told: 'The neighbour who lived over there' – and the father pointed to the back of the house – 'had a dog which barked.' The family did not remember the name of the friend who was with Achmat that day, nor the name of the policeman who fired the shot. They had forgotten the name of the doctor who treated him, as well as the lawyer who argued his case in court.

The sparse new information the investigators received was delivered after lengthy discussions among the people in the room. The investigators asked several times for 'objective clues' such as press cuttings, files from the court or the hospital, or official letters from these institutions, which could corroborate the story, but apparently this information was not important to the family and the story they wanted to tell. Some time was spent going through the chest of drawers in the living room, looking for papers, which they assured us they had kept, somewhere. But not a single document relating to the event could be produced.

At each question, the family seemed to grow more and more impatient, as if this questioning was unimportant. Instead, they constantly repeated their version of the story, and stressed how the incident affected Achmat during wintertime. The investigators grew impatient, too, with Achmat, and with his family and friends who had gathered to tell stories about neighbours, the Islamic calendar, and long-lost relatives.

At the end of the session, Achmat exposed the scar on his body as a final proof of the story he had just told. The scar looked quite dramatic and he seemed satisfied when he had delivered this final piece of evidence. There could be no doubt that something had really happened to him.

But there was someone who had relevant information to offer: one of the investigators. He had researched the case before he came to the house. The Research Department had established for him that the incident must have taken place during the September riots in 1976, which could be related to the Soweto uprising. He had found the name of the doctor who treated the young man at the hospital, and he had talked to the lawyer who argued his case in court.

Then something strange happened. The 'new' information presented by the investigator just slipped into the story told by the family, slowly and without any problems or embarrassment. They agreed: 'For sure it was in 1976, yes, that was the year the neighbour moved away,' and so on. Now the story about the event in 1976 was retold, this time including the parameters the investigator had been looking for. So the afternoon slipped away, with frustrated investigators, 'victims' agitating for their case, and a few cups of coffee consumed in a friendly mood.

A year later, I asked the investigator in charge of the case what the outcome had been. He remembered it all clearly, and smiled. He had classified the case as being 'out of mandate', he said. The family were just trying to get money from the Commission, Achmat had not even been politically active. He had been shot, that was a fact, but it was an 'accident', he was simply 'in the wrong place at the wrong time'. As far as he was concerned, it was now up to the Commissioners to take the final decision, he had done his part of the work.[30]

Why bring up this story? The reason is that it is symptomatic of the encounter between the Commission and the people it needed to collect information from. If we untangle how the encounter reorganised the relation between popular memories and official history, we can isolate the following three threads, each of which runs through all the steps of the information management system: first, how the data-gathering process was actively shaped at each phase of the system; second, how conventions and categories invoked by the system 'flattened' and reorganised popular memories; and third, how the system made possible a particular kind of official history.

In the above case, we see a clash between two 'memory genres', each of which settles the relation to the past differently.

One of them structures knowledge about the past around calendar time and space, parameters that can be compared with forms of knowledge contained in medical journals, police reports, and other examples of formal discourse. The implication is that information structured around calendar time and spatial coordinates can be verified and compared with information gathered in other places and at other times.

The other draws on a different set of parameters, which are considered 'useless' outside their own environment. Such references include the neighbour who lived behind their house; the neighbour who had a dog that barked; the Islamic calendar, which measures time differently; and the scar on the body of the son. This kind of memory is embedded in what Pierre Nora calls *'milieux de mémoire'* – memory environments. These are sites where memories are socially enacted, often being embodied in particular sayings, gestures and ritualised behaviour, so that a sense of continuity persists without necessarily making reference to notions like calendar time and spatial coordinates.[31] Knowledge emerging from such environments can be difficult to compare and verify, as we saw in the encounter between Achmat's family and the investigators, except in relation to knowledge obtained from the same environment.

Official History and Unofficial Historical Memory

The clash between two 'memory genres' in the above encounter can be conceptualised as a clash between official history and unofficial historical memory.

Official history is formed and conveyed in a variety of different official settings and texts, such as school books or reports of commissions. Like the TRC's final report, official texts are based on research in official archives, court records, and other places where information and data are stored publicly. This kind of history is officially sanctioned and legitimated. This does not mean that official history is not contested; only that it is considered to be official until someone from within its own domain contests it. This history, in the context of the TRC at least, is based upon the 'myth of realism'.[32]

Alongside this we find *unofficial historical memory*, which exists as an implicit knowledge of the past. People bring this kind of memory to bear on their everyday interactions with, and understanding of, the present. It is variable and relative to context and, as we saw above, sensitive to the social and collective environment and its particular history. Unofficial historical memory is mainly conveyed orally and is embedded in local stories, myths, freedom songs, rumours and hypotheses about the relation between past and present. It is often captured in everyday conversations or recollections, which can be materialised in storytelling sessions.

Often this kind of knowledge is difficult to verify. It is generally unofficial and non-legitimate, and in a society stained by violence, like South Africa, it can easily be turned to dangerous use. For example, it can be used by 'people's courts' to legitimise alternative forms of justice.[33] Or, as Steffen Jensen has shown with great virtuosity, it can be used to guide people about where it is safe to go and where not, or to reinforce the circulating stereotypes about gender, race and class in a range of everyday practices.[34] The memories that flourish in South Africa, where many people live with experiences that have not been acknowledged, are often fluid and extremely fragmented.[35] They are popular memories of a violent past, structured around stories in which the anchoring domain of individual and social reality is characterised by open conflict, betrayal, killings and differences.

It is exactly in the interface between official history and unofficial historical memory that the symbolic impact of the TRC can be located. The everyday work of official commissions lies in the codification of popular memories, so that they can become official and acknowledged (for instance, in the final report), and thus serve as the foundation for the new nationhood. For while official histories normally present a fixed chronological scheme, in which each important incident begets the next, unofficial historical memory or popular memory cuts across established official categories and schemes.

The first phase of the TRC's work, which focused on the victims and involved statement-taking and public hearings, sought to acknowledge unofficial popular memory through storytelling. The main 'subtextual statement', as formulated by Wilson, was 'how previous victims of the state are now having their story documented in an official setting, demonstrating how the balance of power has shifted away from the perpetrators to the victims'.[36] The making of official history through the telling of personal narratives was orchestrated in order to create a sense of common destiny. As people listened together to similar stories, and felt connected across former and present boundaries, a shared sense of the past would ideally be formed. This potential resided as much in the public statement-taking sessions and hearings, and in the multifaceted, public distribution of these stories in new forms by the various media, as in the official history, that is, the final report.

So, besides the differences between the two genres of memory, there is also an intricate relationship between official history and unofficial historical memory. Official history, as produced by the TRC, 'feeds on' popular memories recollected in the form of testimonies in various settings. The act of recollection is not simple. The memories of Achmat's family, which unfolded as oral discourse, became *declarative memories* by being told, first to a statement-taker and later to the investigators, with the aim of having them written down.[37] They thereby assumed the shape of a piece of documentary material for the Commission's archive, becoming subject to the rules and schemes governing this domain.

Storytelling, or testifying in a setting like the TRC, frames memories in particular ways, as we saw with Achmat. Of course, stories always reflect the storyteller's mood, aspirations and desire to impress upon the listener a specific image of the past.[38] This is not a trivial point: it implies that the stories told by victims and the stories told by the Commission are of different historical veracity.[39] Declarative memories, as Ricoeur has illustrated, are 'the first stage of history'.[40] It is exactly the veracity of memories recalled and framed as stories that official history struggles to assess, in its attempt to make a true representation of the absent past. We generally affirm that a historical text is a true representation of events '… whose traces had been stored in our archives and which have been questioned in terms of *why?* and *because*. The ultimate test is the corroboration of this basic claim of any historical piece of literature, by opposition to fictional literature, the claim to tell the truth about past events.'[41]

For the Investigation Unit, the important thing was to access the event behind the recollection of memories told as stories. This was important because the traces left behind in the form of testimonies, preserved in statement protocols and transcripts of hearings, and kept in the Commission's archives, were the basis on which the official history would be reconstructed. These stories had to meet the strict criteria for proper research. But, as we have seen in the account of one shooting, this mediated investigation was in no way simple.

Reframing the Victims' Narratives in Time and Space

The investigators in Achmat's case were not insensitive to his story. They had to assess whether the *trace* left behind by the memory was a true representation of the absent past. In doing so, they had to restructure the story according to a set of parameters that were applicable to but independent of its particulars. Without this reconstruction, the story could not be turned into something that could be preserved in the archives of the Commission as a statement of gross human rights violations. It is here that 'universal' parameters or 'global signs' such as calendar time and spatial coordinates were important, quite apart from the recoding related to the categorisation of violations.

The use of calendar time and spatial coordinates as 'global' signs was with the Commission from the very beginning. The memories presented in statements and public hearings were not just images occurring randomly or suddenly in the minds of victims. They were 'images which are targets of search, the search which we call recollection'.[42] Recollection, in this sense, refers to actions and practices that have their own rules, difficulties and, at times, failures. Besides the categorisation scheme, calendar time and spatial coordinates were the dominant means of framing the search for the past.

The first posters encouraging people to approach the TRC demarcated and ordered the past it was searching for. The posters displayed a range of events associated with gross human rights violations, as defined by the Commission. Besides hinting at what should be recollected, these posters began the creation of a new national time-line. For the first time, incidents such as the Sharpeville massacre, the Soweto uprising, the Church Street bomb, the Trojan Horse incident, the Bisho killings, the St James' Church massacre, and so on, were given formal acknowledgement, placed alongside each other and organised chronologically so that they covered the period of the Commission's mandate and the territory of the South African nation-state. The posters indicated what events the Commission saw as important in the 'new' national history, and encouraged people to come forward and tell stories about them.[43]

The Protocol and Statement-taking

The Commission received about 22 000 victim statements, memories in the form of mental images, transmitted orally and captured in the 'protocol'. But anyone expecting to find the pure, authentic, unmediated experiences of victims here would be very disappointed. The narratives captured in the statements, which are to be stored in the national archives as prescribed by the Act, are not unmediated.

In the protocol, which was much debated within the Commission, a certain amount of space was assigned for the narratives of victims. However, several layers of intervention occurred even before the narratives were put to paper – not to mention when they were later recaptured on the database – and these completely restructured the victims' stories.[44]

Officially, the protocol went through eight versions before it found its final form in mid-1997.⁴⁵ In the process, the whole thing grew from eight pages to more than twenty, and the narrative space shrank from six pages to one and a half – while one of the versions in between did not have a space for the victim's story at all. The differences among the various versions had a significant effect on the statement-taking process. The rather dramatic reduction of the space allowed for the narrative points to a change in the way in which the victim's story was captured. Whereas initially this story was written down word for word, eventually a statement-taking session, including the writing down of the 'narrative', conformed more or less to the following sequence.⁴⁶

First, the statement-taker would tell the alleged victim what was going to happen and what the purpose of the statement-taking was. Then the statement-taker would outline the TRC's mandate, in relation to the Act's definition of a gross human rights violation and the period under consideration.

The victim would then tell his or her story in the language preferred. This normally took twenty to thirty minutes.

After the statement-taker had asked a few questions in order to clarify time, place, the kind of violation, the people involved, and so on, they would give the protocol a reference number, insert the name of the person who had given the statement, the name of the person the statement was about, and where and when the statement had been taken.

At the end of this process, the statement-taker wrote down the narrative in English. This version was seldom read aloud afterwards for the victim's approval.

After this initial accessing of the victim's story, around one and a half hours would be spent dissecting it, so that detailed information on the victim's identity could be captured. The identity of perpetrators and witnesses would emerge in this process.

Sometimes, it was necessary to ask a whole range of additional questions; at other times, the statement-taker could fill in the information related to the four main categories of gross human rights violations, the political context, and so forth, on the basis of the initial story. In the latter case, the role of the victim changed, and he or she simply corroborated the statement-taker's interpretations.

The aim of this careful work was to cross-check the story of the alleged victim and ensure that information about 'who did what to whom' was secured.⁴⁷ But this parcelling out of information into around twelve pages of categories (in the later versions of the protocol) was also aimed at capturing data that could be fed into the TRC's database, through the intervention of the data processors, in order to generate statistically informed material (counts, ad hoc query results, lists of victims of arbitrary execution, and so on). Most of the information contained in the protocol and the database, therefore, did not have any direct 'value' for the investigators doing the actual verification of the statements.

The methodology just outlined followed a positivistic scientific model, where one step in the process is devoted to capturing the statement, another to investigating it, and yet another (ideally, at least) to making the final judgement. However, as I have demonstrated, these 'judgements' happened at each step in the information management system.

The Imagined Community of Victimhood[48]

In the above analysis of the 'backstage', everyday work of the TRC, we saw how the narratives of victims were transformed so that they could be *inscribed* in the protocol. We could go further and say that the memories of victims materialised first as narratives, and then, through a chain of translations, became *signs* of gross human rights violations under apartheid, inscribed in statement protocols, the database, investigative reports, the Commission's archives, the final report and, ultimately, the national archives.

These inscriptions had two dimensions. First, they were *superimposable*, in that each intermediate step (the different layers of intervention) reduced the broad, multifaceted narrative into more condensed signs and forms of data. These forms of data had to be structured according to the same logic in order to be compatible, so that they could be superimposed in the same database. Second, they had to be *combinable,* in that each intermediate step – from statement-taking to data processing, from there to investigation and further data processing, and finally to the making of findings – had to allow for new translations and articulations of propositions about what had happened, while yet maintaining some relation between the different inscriptions and translations.

Deconstruction and Reconstruction

The requirements of the information management system meant that the victims' narratives had first to be *deconstructed* into various discrete gross human rights violations, together with details such as the organisational membership of victims and perpetrators, in order to be captured in the protocol. As the term 'controlled vocabulary' indicates, past events were retold in a new 'language', and a new interpretive grid for giving the past meaning was thereby imposed. The narratives were reordered and reframed so that multiple local references for establishing veracity – the neighbour who lived behind their house, the neighbour who had a dog that barked, the Islamic calendar, the scar on the body of the son – were reclassified according to a new set of global references.[49]

The deconstructive process made possible a simultaneous *reconstruction* of the fate of victims in standard form on the database.[50] The captured narratives could involve multiple victims, multiple violations and multiple perpetrators, which had to be fed into the protocol and later the database. As illustrated above, they could also involve multiple parameters of local heritage that did not make sense outside the locality. This methodical 'deconstruction' and decontextualisation, which lifted each case out of its locality in accordance with the imperatives of data processing, thus had the 'positive' effect that events could be reconstructed within parameters that did not rely on local dynamics.

The classification of thousands of cases in terms of the same 'vocabulary' made incidents and people from different locations and times contemporaries of one another, in relation to the database and the information management system. The invisible became visible under this unifying gaze: every statement classified in the same language, whether 'collected' in March 1996 or September 1997, 'spoke' about the same 'thing'. This allowed the TRC to change the position of a statement, revealing the victims at one moment, exposing the perpetrators at another. It could also substitute one statement about apartheid for another, so that violations could be publicly presented to the nation (another movement along the continuum between local and global) without losing track of the overall story it wanted to tell. The many statements made to the TRC, scattered as they were through time and space, presented in public or kept in the offices, would never have met had their characteristics not been redistributed into new combinations.

National History: Bringing Everyone onto an Equal Footing

The Commission codes the past in such a way that individual experiences are turned into visible, emblematic images, allowing people to identify with a range of new collective identities.

For this identification to occur, the Commission must present a kind of knowledge that is widely comprehensible and free of potential misreading, and yet can still be interpreted according to different intentions and life experiences. Unlike the conditions that it deals with, the knowledge itself has to be clear of ambiguity, and it must therefore be expressed in a shared, authorised and supra-individual code.[51] Such a code is brought about by the use of the 'controlled vocabulary', calendar time and spatial coordinates. These are seen as objective, impersonal criteria for identification, which reduce the probability of misreading. As we saw in Achmat's case, the family understood and had a language for their experiences and needs, but only the investigator knew how to translate them from a specific domain into a wider realm, so that they could be verified, evaluated and used in the construction of collective identity, or as I prefer to phrase it, identification. In this sense, the investigator's main role was the capacity to interpret and translate uncertainty.

To summarise, the use of the stable, objective parameters of calendar time and nationalised spatial coordinates is important for the construction of imagined communities and collective histories, a point made years ago by Benedict Anderson when he used the concept 'homogeneous empty time' to describe the changes in collective identification resulting from new modes of representing time.[52] Anderson's point is simple but illuminating. When the experiences of different individuals are related to calendar time and nationalised spatial coordinates, they are reduced to the same formula. Temporal and spatial *simultaneity* is a precondition for the birth of the 'imagined community' of the nation-state.[53]

Even a superficial look through the final report yields numerous examples of people, largely unknown to each other, who have experienced similar and comparable events, who are all representatives, in their simultaneous, separate existences, of the conflicts of the past and belong to the country called South Africa. One example from the report:

> The St James' Church Massacre
> At about 19h30 on Sunday 25 July 1993, two APLA [Azanian People's Liberation Army] operatives burst into the evening service at St James' Church in Kenilworth [a suburb of Cape Town]. They fired machine guns and threw two hand-grenades covered with nails at a congregation of over a thousand people. Eleven people were killed and fifty-six injured. The attackers escaped in a waiting car which had been hijacked earlier. The congregation was racially mixed and those killed included four Russian sailors.[54]

The perspective adopted in the report, more than invoking 'simultaneity' – the sense that other members of the same nation, at the same time, are doing things that are meaningfully related to one's own experiences – allows for difference. It makes possible the awareness that others, meanwhile, are going about their *separate* business at the same time.[55] To imagine a common past, in this sense, does not mean that one has to have experienced the same things.

The more positive side of the processes discussed above is that individual stories can be contained in the 'new', wider, national story about the victims of apartheid. Achmat's story could have been taken up in this way. If the investigators had used the political context of the Soweto uprising as the *interpretive grid* instead of describing the shooting as an accident, his case would have been classified under the gross human rights violations category of severe ill-treatment, experienced while riot police were exercising crowd control.[56] The incident would thereby have been given a new meaning; Achmat would have been classified as a victim; he would have become part of the same larger story to which the St James' Church Massacre contributes. Now his story is probably to be found among the 4 500 cases classified as 'out of mandate'.

Conclusion

What is the significance of this excursion into the 'backstage' workings of the Commission? What does it tell us about the relation between human rights violations documentation and national historical memory?

To begin with, the absence of analysis of the everyday dimensions of official truth commission work is crucial. Our examination of the fragile interface between norms and everyday practices, informed by the ideal of how a commission should work and what it should do, must be sensitive if we want to do justice to the public representations emerging from the TRC. The danger is that an intense focus on the 'backstage' aspects of the TRC's work will create the impression that those images which are visible and public are 'false' or have been deliberately cleansed. This is not my intention. I would argue that to analyse adequately how the TRC reconstructed the past, one first has to reject the limited depth of reified public representations. Then one is forced to take into account that not only 'backstage' acts but 'on-stage' ones, too, change character. Often, seemingly incomprehensible 'on-stage' dimensions take on new meaning. The distinction does not imply that the 'backstage' domain is more authentic or correct than the 'on-stage' one; often, the tensions and contradictions between them, which observers encounter, do not arise for people moving between the different domains.

Once the limited depth of reified public representations has been acknowledged, it becomes possible to explore the relation between 'backstage' and 'on-stage' dimensions of official commission work. This we have just done by tracing how the information management system reorganised popular memories in the course of documenting human rights violations, so that they could be accommodated within an interpretive grid resembling official national history. In this sense, the human rights violations methodology and the information management system supported the wider nation-building exercise on which South Africa, as an emerging nation, embarked after the first democratic election in 1994. We have seen that as popular memories were rendered into an official record, dimensions of human rights violations documentation, which had seemed incomprehensible or insignificant, were made visible and given new meaning. We have also seen that although most personal experiences could be accommodated within the interpretive grid of calendar time and spatial coordinates, and taken up in the national story of suffering, this did not imply that everybody could be classified as a victim of gross human rights violations.

If questions about reparations and the rehabilitation of victims are discussed solely in relation to the formally extracted numbers of statements made to the TRC (setting aside those found to be 'out of mandate'), one is dealing with a neatly controlled group of people. It was mainly from this group, by way of their testimony in the public hearings, that the nation learnt about atrocities committed during the apartheid era. Because they relived a painful past for the sake of national reconciliation, it is difficult to argue against paying them reparations. But we have seen that the identification of the formal group of victims was complex. In my view, some of the underlying reasons for the government's hesitation about paying reparations to the formally identified victims become clear when we consider the limited depth of the 'on-stage' public process.

As I have argued elsewhere, knowledge generated by the information management system is based on the official and hegemonic grammar of representative samples.[57] It is the task of institutions like the TRC to define representative samples, but problems arise when they are used to distribute or allocate rights and entitlements. On a symbolic level, it is sufficient for the Commission to objectify a representative sample, which indicates a particular type of violation or person, and 'stands in' for the nation's suffering; for example, people formerly excluded from the nation may be symbolically included.[58] But in relation to material compensation, representative samples are not sufficient. To put it another way, the Commission can create symbolic reparation for everybody, even though it has objectified only a sample of the total. But the government cannot create material reparation for everybody, if the few 'stand in' for all. This would be politically unjust.

When the task of documenting human rights violations is drawn into the service of inclusive nation-building, it becomes socially unfair if symbolic, representative samples are used to distribute and allocate resources, because such samples are exclusive. There is no easy way to resolve this dilemma. Indeed, it points to the crucial fact that truth and reconciliation commissions are not an easy 'fix'. They do not work perfectly, and they do create their own, often unintended, problems. Four tactics can help us to live with the problems.

First, we can see to it that our analyses do not reproduce unrealistic representations of what commissions do, what they could do, and how they work. We can focus our critiques on those mainstream claims that too often go unchallenged, rather than writing exclusively about the 'failures' of the modern, ideal separation between politics and science. We can turn our attention to the ways in which mainstream perspectives continually reproduce, reconstruct and re-imagine commission work as homogeneous and unified.

Second, we should acknowledge that critical analyses of the 'micro-politics' of everyday work are not simply pointing out the 'failures'. The lived, active, fluid, human dimensions of the myriad ways in which norms and actions are played out in everyday encounters are as real as anything can be. My analysis has shown that the TRC staff applied and transformed the content of the information management system, making it their own according to their own logics and world-views. There is a tendency to view the problems encountered by commissions as the result of 'bad planning', 'lack of proper training', 'lack of resources' and 'inappropriately formulated mandates'. Such analyses, which imply that commissions might be 'smooth-running' and 'problem-free' if only they could rectify their 'mistakes', fail to engage with the politics and modalities of power intrinsic to official commission work. Yet the points are well taken.

Just four months into its work, the South African TRC held its first hearing. This took place only a few days after the director of the Investigation Unit was hired, at a point when the Unit had certainly done no planning. The consequences were catastrophic. People were not properly screened before this hearing or many of those that followed. It later emerged that several people who had been allowed to speak as victims of gross human rights violations could not actually be classified as such.[59] This hasty, ad hoc implementation also severely hampered the strategic planning for investigations, because investigators were tied up with screening alleged victims for the hearings.[60] In addition, the information management system was underutilised. This was partly owing to a shortage of skilled South Africans in computerised information technology, and partly to the Commission's wish to empower local researchers and data analysts instead of hiring foreign experts.[61]

Many of these 'problems' could have been avoided if the Commission had set up its units and done better strategic planning *before* jumping into the public arena, under pressure to produce results in a fairly hostile political environment. Nonetheless, it is probably impossible to come up with an all-embracing 'perfect plan', as various theorists of our modern or not-yet-modern societies, from different disciplines and theoretical vantage points, have pointed out.[62] We have to accept that the metamorphic processes highlighted in this paper are far removed from the ideal conditions of the natural science 'laboratory'. It is largely to this ideal environment that claims to 'objectivity' and Truth with a capital T appeal, since human rights violations documentation is founded on and informed by the positivistic social sciences.

At the beginning of this paper, we posed the question of whether the forensic, objective kind of truth garnered by the information management system can be established by truth commission work without forgoing competing local influences and negotiations. For ontological reasons, the answer must be a straightforward no. One cannot demarcate a space where facts about past violations of human rights can be recounted that is not constituted by power, or that is even free of the influence of power relations. Yet this does not mean that the ideal of separation between commission work and the wider society is not worth striving for, or that it is not extremely productive. Or that the work could not be executed more professionally than has so far been the case.

Third, we must learn to argue civilly about official commission work. This is crucial given the significance of such work in transitional societies. At present, one may either discuss the 'appropriate modelling' of official commission work or take the view that 'each country should follow its own patterns when setting up a commission'. What both perspectives ignore is that they are not mutually exclusive. There are continuities and discontinuities at stake, claims to both universalism and particularism. Human rights violations documentation has to be conducted in a legitimate way in order to be accepted by the wider audience of the international human rights community and democratic nation-states. This need for universalism and coherence cannot come as a surprise when one considers the claim for universalism as intrinsic to questions of human rights. But there should also be a recognition of the need to empower local actors by providing information, analysis and assistance in designing and implementing effective transitional justice programmes, based on the particular context and conflicts that led to human rights violations, and making a change in political ideology possible. A good starting point would be to recognise that truth commission work involves contradictory epistemologies, which cannot easily be reconciled.

Finally, critical evaluation is a crucial aspect of the social side of the scientific method. Concurring with Popper, I view the scientific method not as the result of each scientist's objectivity, but of scientists' inter-subjectivity, that is, the encounters and cooperation between scientists who criticise or accept one another's work.[63] In this view, 'knowledge' becomes 'stable' or 'true' when it has been developed within a particular *epistemic tradition*, with certain strict requirements concerning what counts as knowledge.[64] It is therefore important to protect the values that make an open, critical and rational investigation possible.

Official truth commission work itself should allow for open discussion and evaluation. Most commissions adhere to the same epistemic world-view, both discursively, in that they claim to follow scientific procedures for the production of knowledge; and in practice, in that they organise their work according to scientific criteria for what counts as good science. Yet too often criticism is taken personally, stifling the very possibility of open and public discussion.

Notes

1. The data discussed in this paper were collected between 1996 and 1999 during ethnographic field research conducted for the Ph.D. project 'To Establish a Truth: Victims, Perpetrators, Experts and the Work of the South African Truth and Reconciliation Commission', Department of Ethnography and Social Anthropology, Aarhus University, Denmark. I am indebted to Prof. Deborah Posel, University of the Witwatersrand; Dr Janet Cherry, University of Port Elizabeth; Dr Fiona Ross, University of Cape Town; and Alison Stent, former member of the Investigation Unit of the TRC, for their critical comments on earlier versions of this text.
2. See L. Buur, 'Institutionalising Truth: Victims, Perpetrators and Professionals in the Everyday Work of the South African Truth and Reconciliation Commission', Ph.D. thesis (Aarhus University, Denmark, 2000); and L. Buur, 'The South African Truth and Reconciliation Commission: A Technique of Nation-state Formation', in T. Hansen and F. Stepputat (eds), *States of Imagination: Ethnographic Explorations of the Postcolonial State* (Durham, NC, Duke University Press, 2001).
3. See Promotion of National Unity and Reconciliation Act, No. 34 of 1995.
4. M. Mamdani, *When Does Reconciliation Turn into a Denial of Justice?* Sam Nolutshungu Memorial Series (Pretoria, Human Sciences Research Council Publishers, 1998), p. 21.
5. There are numerous examples in the work of Hayner cited elsewhere in this paper. What this vocabulary suggests or assumes is that there is a truth out there to be found. For further comments on this subject see, for example, M. Parlevliet, 'Considering Truth: Dealing with a Legacy of Gross Human Rights Violations', *Netherlands Quarterly of Human Rights*, 16:2 (1998).
6. P.B. Hayner, 'Commissioning the Truth: Further Research Questions', *Third World Quarterly*, 17:1 (1996), pp. 21-2.
7. See in particular P.B. Hayner, 'Fifteen Truth Commissions – 1974 to 1994:

A Comparative Study', *Human Rights Quarterly*, 16:4 (1994); P. Ball, *Who Did What to Whom? Planning and Implementing a Large Scale Human Rights Data Project* (Washington, DC, American Association for the Advancement of Science, 1996); A.R. Chapman, 'How Truth Commission Processes Shape their Truth-Findings', paper presented to the 'Commissioning the Past' Conference, University of the Witwatersrand, June 1999.

8. One consequence is that in the literature and extensive public coverage of the TRC, there is literally no information about its everyday aspects. It is as if there is an *arbitrary relation* between the everyday work of the TRC (and the work of official commissions in general) and the truth produced, as if the everyday work is just a *neutral medium* for information gathering and processing, a means to an end. This is reflected in the following articles and books, to mention just some published recently: Hayner, 'Fifteen Truth Commissions'; Hayner, 'Commissioning the Truth'; P.B. Hayner, 'International Guidelines for the Creation and Operation of Truth Commissions: A Preliminary Proposal', *Law and Contemporary Problems*, 59:4 (1996), pp. 173-80; H.R. Botman and R.M. Petersen, *To Remember and to Heal: Theological and Psychological Reflections on Truth and Reconciliation* (Cape Town, Human & Rousseau, 1996); M. Osiel, *Mass Atrocities, Collective Memory and the Law* (New Brunswick, NJ, Transaction Publishers, 1997); I. Liebenberg and A. Zegeye, 'Pathway to Democracy? The Case of the South African Truth and Reconciliation Process', *Social Identities*, 4:3 (1998); K. Christie, *The South African Truth Commission* (London, Macmillan, 2000).

9. See *TRC Report*, vol. 1, ch. 6; Ball, *Who Did What to Whom?*; Chapman, 'Truth Commission Processes'.

10. See Buur, 'Institutionalising Truth'. In line with Hayner's positivistic vocabulary on truth commission work, Ball (*Who Did What to Whom?*) uses the word 'collect' to describe how information on human rights violations is generated.

11. A. du Toit, 'Perpetrator Findings as Artificial Even-handedness? The TRC's Contested Judgements of Moral and Political Accountability for Gross Human Rights Violations', extended version of paper presented to the 'Commissioning the Past' Conference, University of the Witwatersrand, June 1999.

12. See Hayner, 'Commissioning the Truth', p. 20. The specific violations dealt with in this 'large pattern' differ from commission to commission. For the Argentinian commission in 1983-4, it was the disappearance of people and what had happened to them (Nunca Mas, *Informe de la Comisión Nacional Sobre la Desaparición de Personas* (Buenos Aires, Circulo de Lectores, 1985)). For the Salvadorean commission in 1992-3, it was 'serious acts of violence

which have impacted on society or gross violations of human rights, including violations, which were part of a systemic pattern of abuse' (Hayner, *International Guidelines*, p. 174). For the South African TRC, it was 'gross violations of human rights' committed with political motives during the period from 1 March 1960 to 10 May 1994 (*TRC Report*, vol. 1, ch. 4, para. 32).
13. Hayner, 'Commissioning the Truth', p. 25, emphasis added.
14. Chapman, 'Truth Commission Processes', p. 7.
15. In retrospect, in an appendix to the final report, the TRC explicitly defined its task as scientific (vol. 1, ch. 6, Appendix 1, pp. 161-2), and the term 'positivist approach' is used in the Management and Operational Report on Information Management (vol. 1, ch. 11, para. 11). This needs to be questioned. Whereas the TRC claims that its approach was prescribed by the legislation, the Act does not refer to a positivistic scientific ideal as such, but uses terms like 'objectivity', 'even-handedness', 'independence', etc. Some staff members have stated in personal conversations that this was understood to mean that the TRC should be independent from political 'influence' and should not 'take sides'. This is supported by the phrasing in the Act: '[The] Commission, its Commissioners and every member of its staff shall function without political or other bias or interference and shall be independent and separate from any party, government, administration or any other functionary or body directly or indirectly representing the interests of any such entity' (section 36.1). Apparently, someone in the Commission chose to interpret the Act's quite general statement of 'objectivity' to mean a positivistic, scientific approach. Who actually wrote the sections in the final report referred to above is an enigma. Some staff members have suggested that people connected to the American Association for the Advancement of Science were responsible; but, at the risk of sounding tautological, the perspective might simply reflect the positivist assumptions of mainstream social science and law in South Africa (as proposed by André du Toit in a personal conversation in 1997).
16. Promotion of National Unity and Reconciliation Act, No. 34 of 1995.
17. Ball, *Who Did What to Whom?*, p. 4.
18. All quotes from Ball, *op. cit.*, p. 6.
19. Ball, *op. cit.*, pp. 22, 32.
20. See Promotion of National Unity and Reconciliation Act, No. 34 of 1995.
21. Ball, *op. cit.*, p. 32.
22. Ball, *Ibid.*, p. 33.
23. *TRC Report*, vol. 1, ch. 4, para. 127.

24. Extract from interview with a statement-taker, 1997.
25. See 'The South African Truth and Reconciliation Commission Proposal for Reparation and Rehabilitation', policy document, 1998.
26. The TRC received around 22 000 victim statements. In the end, it had to turn down 4 500 statements due to lack of evidence.
27. Ball, *op. cit.*, pp. 23-4.
28. See I. Hacking, *The Taming of Chance* (Cambridge, Cambridge University Press, 1990).
29. The initial intention was to 'investigate' each case of gross human rights violations. But by the end of 1997, when it became apparent that resources were insufficient, this was dropped in favour of a corroboration strategy. One reason for this shift was the resource-intensive public work revolving around hearings, which began in April 1996 and made it almost impossible for the Investigation Unit to deal with cases that were not going to be presented in public. A backlog of thousands of cases (around 90 per cent of the cases did not enter this public process) accumulated in the TRC offices, and had to be dealt with to fulfil the mandate. (This note is based on fieldwork material from 1997 and interviews with investigators and leaders of the different investigative units.)
30. Based on fieldwork notes from 1996-8.
31. P. Nora, 'Between Memory and History: *Les Lieux de Mémoiré*', *Representation*, 26 (Spring 1989), p. 7.
32. Elisabeth Tonkin (1990) quoted in K. Hastrup, *A Place Apart: An Anthropological Study of the Icelandic World* (Oxford, Clarendon Press, 1998), p. 24.
33. J. Ball, 'The Ritual of the Necklace', Centre for the Study of Violence and Reconciliation, occasional paper (Johannesburg, March 1994).
34. S. Jensen, 'Discourses of Violence: Coping with Violence on the Cape Flats', *Social Dynamics*, 25:2 (1999); S. Jensen, 'Hvorfor er du her egentlig...?', *Den Ny Verden, Veje til Viden, nye metoder I feltbaseret udviklingsforskning*, 3 (Copenhagen, Centre for Development Research, 1999), pp. 93-110.
35. R. Wilson, 'The Siswe Will Not Go Away: The Truth and Reconciliation Commission, Human Rights and Nation-Building in South Africa', *African Studies*, 55:2 (1996), p. 17.
36. *Ibid.*, p. 16.
37. Concurring with Ricoeur, I contend that memory is: 'A kind of mental image which claims to provide a subsidiary presence to an absent thing, more precisely to events which are no longer there, absent in that sense, but which were present to contemporaries when they occurred. Presence of absence, absence of a previous presence – such is the main paradox of

memory as representation of past events' (P. Ricoeur, 'Humanities between Science and Art', transcript of a paper presented to the 'Humanities at the Turn of the Millennium' Conference, University of Aarhus, 4 June 1999, p. 4).
38. See Hastrup, *A Place Apart*, p. 24.
39. Of course, official histories also reflect the position, aspirations and desire to make an impact of their producers. But there is a difference in that official history production is placed under particularly 'reflective' constraints related to 'objectivity', 'even-handedness', etc.
40. Ricoeur, *op. cit.*, p. 4.
41. *Ibid.*, p. 5.
42. *Ibid.*
43. This preoccupation with calendar time and nationalised spatial coordinates was apparent in nearly all interactions between the TRC and victims, and is evident in the final report, which devotes many pages to a chronology of the apartheid state and the history of the liberation movements.
44. This is part of an even wider restructuring that has happened over many years. The TRC is not the first institution to capture statements from victims of apartheid. During the apartheid era, several human rights organisations, including the Black Sash, the Human Rights Committee, and the Urban Monitoring and Awareness Campaign, took statements from victims about human rights violations.
45. In reality, there were more than eight versions; I saw more than eleven versions applied in the Cape Town offices alone. Some of the versions were used in statement-taking sessions, others in data processing and investigative activities. This metamorphosis of the categorisation schema and the protocol meant that the data processors constantly had to rewrite data already captured on the database.
46. The narrative was also called the 'statement' and, in later versions of the protocol, the 'Brief Description of the Violation of Human Rights'.
47. See Ball, *Who Did What to Whom?*
48. This section is inspired by Michael Taussig's *The Magic of the State* (New York, Routledge, 1997) and the second chapter of Bruno Latour's *Pandora's Hope: Essays on the Reality of Science Studies* (Cambridge, Mass., Harvard University Press, 1999).
49. Following Latour, it would perhaps be better not to speak about 'data' ('what is given') but about 'achievements', because data are *things,* which emerge through complicated translation processes (Latour, *Pandora's Hope*, p. 42).

50. The rationale for this double movement can be extracted from the final report. According to the report, the complex nature of victim narratives obscured what it terms 'the structural complexity of human rights violations' (vol. 1, ch. 6, Appendix 1, paras 5-7).
51. A shared, authorised and supra-individual code is not sufficient; it must also be guaranteed by an institution believed to be characterised by impartiality. Science and commissions are such institutions.
52. Anderson got this concept from Walter Benjamin (B. Anderson, *Imagined Communities* (London, Verso, 1991), p. 24).
53. Simultaneity is 'transverse, cross-time, marked not by figuring and fulfilment, but by temporal coincidence and measured by clock and calendar' (Anderson, *Imagined Communities*, p. 24).
54. *TRC Report*, vol. 3, ch. 5, para. 404.
55. See Anderson, *Imagined Communities*, p. 24.
56. Several TRC staff members suggested this when I discussed the case for the first time at the 'Commissioning the Past' Conference, University of the Witwatersrand, June 1999.
57. See Buur, 'Institutionalising Truth'; and L. Buur, ' "In the Name of the Victims": The Politics of Compensation in the Work of the South African Truth and Reconciliation Commission', in P. Gready (ed.), *Cultures of Political Transition: Memory, Identity and Voice* (London, Pluto, forthcoming).
58. It is worth remembering that the word 'victim' comes from the Latin *victima*, which means 'stand in' or 'scapegoat' (K.N. Olsen, *Offer og Objekt: En Introduktion til Michel Serres' Statuer* (Copenhagen, Danske Kunstakademi, 1993), p. 14).
59. Based on personal conversations with staff members.
60. The former director of the Investigation Unit made this point during a conference at the Centre for the Study of Violence and Reconciliation, Johannesburg, 1998.
61. This point was emphasised by Patrick Ball in personal conversations in 1997 and 1999.
62. See, for example, B. Latour, *Science in Action* (Cambridge, Mass., Harvard University Press, 1987); B. Latour, 'Postmodern? No, Simply Amodern! Steps towards an Anthropology of Science', *Studies in History and Philosophy of Science*, 21:1 (1990), pp. 145-71; B. Latour, *We Have Never Been Modern* (Cambridge, Mass., Harvard University Press, 1993); A. Giddens, *The Consequences of Modernity* (Stanford, Stanford University Press, 1992); Z. Bauman, *Modernity and Ambivalence* (Ithaca & New York, Cornell University Press, 1991).

63. K. Popper, 'Historicismens moralteori', in *Kritisk Rationalisme* (Copenhagen, Nyt Nordisk Forlag Arnold Busck, 1965), p. 111.
64. See A. Roepstorff, 'Fra det tællelige til det fortællelige: Noter fra et feltarbejde blandt hjerneskannere og videnskabsfolk', Department of Ethnography and Social Anthropology, unpublished paper (Aarhus University, Denmark, 2000), p. 8.

PART TWO

Victims' Stories

4

THE MURDER OF SICELO DLOMO[1]

Piers Pigou

Truth is not 'what is', but the understanding of 'what is' opens the door to the truth.

Krishnamurti

My wish is that all that happened should be in a history book so that the coming generations should know what has happened in the past.

Sylvia Dlomo-Jele

Introduction

For many people struggling to understand and accept the truth of South Africa's shameful past, the Truth and Reconciliation Commission (TRC) was a lifeline. Here, at last, was an opportunity to find out what had really happened in cases involving themselves and their loved ones. In the end, however, only the 'fortunate' few were to have their questions answered. In most cases, the TRC barely scratched the surface, and it now seems that many of those who came forward will remain for ever in the dark about the past.

It was not only where cases received little or no attention that the TRC's achievement was unconvincing. Some victims and survivors were indeed provided with a version of what happened, usually as a result of an amnesty application, and often this included completely new information. But on closer examination, what had been presented to and accepted by the Commission sometimes proved unacceptable to the victims themselves, who believed they had not been told the whole truth. They still did not know exactly what had happened. More importantly, they did not know why. For people like these, the TRC did not provide the balm its authors intended, but actually exacerbated their grief.

Establishing the truth about the circumstances of gross human rights violations perpetrated during the conflicts of the past was the core objective of the Commission. The truth, it was argued, was the necessary foundation upon which future reconciliation would be built. For victims and survivors, getting to the truth was a crucial part of achieving restitution, the positive complement of the immunity provided for by the amnesty process.

Given the number of violations committed during the mandate period (from 1960 to 1994), it was clearly unrealistic to expect that every case would receive the attention it deserved. But there were opportunities to examine a number of cases comprehensively. The amnesty proceedings, especially, provided a unique platform to test the versions of events put forward by perpetrators seeking release from prison or immunity from prosecution. Although there are undoubtedly victims and survivors who are satisfied with what the TRC achieved, and there are cases where comprehensive investigations were pursued, such thoroughness was not displayed consistently and was generally quite rare. In many cases, the Amnesty Committee relied on thorough cross-examination (and even investigation) undertaken by the legal representatives of victims, survivors, or other people implicated. Unfortunately, the quality of these inquiries often depended on the remuneration provided to the lawyers, which varied greatly.

Understandably, many people were opposed to the granting of amnesty. Some said they simply could not or would not forgive those who had killed or maimed their loved ones. Others felt that the applicants had failed to disclose the truth, or that the Commission had missed the opportunity to uncover it.

This is the story of one such missed opportunity. It concerns a young student activist, Sicelo Dlomo, who was assassinated on 24 January 1988, and left under a tree in a field on the outskirts of Soweto. It is also the story of Sicelo's mother, Sylvia Dlomo-Jele, and the struggles she endured in her search for the truth about her son's murder. It was a search that demonstrated an enormous and perhaps misplaced faith in the TRC.

Unlike many others, the Dlomo case gained both national and international exposure. Unlike most cases submitted to the Human Rights Violations Committee, it was probed by the national Investigation Unit. Four people subsequently applied for amnesty, and received a hearing before the Amnesty Committee. But what emerged from this entire process was not clarity but contradiction, as the applicants struggled to fulfil the key amnesty criteria of proving a political motive and presenting a full disclosure of the 'relevant facts'.

Resistance and Repression

Sylvia Dlomo and her family lived in the Soweto suburb of Emdeni. Simple economic survival, the basic struggle to put food on the table, was the family's main concern. Sylvia eked out a living as an informal trader, and her husband was in and out of work.

Born in 1969, Sicelo was exposed to the invidious policies of apartheid at an early age when his father was arrested for not having his passbook. Sylvia knew her son was perceptive, and she believed this incident had a profound effect on him. 'He was five years [old] and asked, "Ma, where is my daddy?" and I said, "He is not at home." He said, "I know that he was arrested," but I was trying not to tell him that his father was arrested. He said, "When I grow up, I'm going to kick the policemen that arrested my father." Ja, he was so brilliant, really.'

The mid- to late 1970s saw a rise in political consciousness and resistance, especially amongst urban youth. The 1976 uprisings had involved many schoolchildren and, despite the ensuing repression, even those in their preteens were now increasingly involved. In 1983, Sicelo enrolled for secondary school at the Pace Community College in Soweto. This was a period of dramatic political developments: the National Party had introduced constitutional amendments to create the tricameral parliamentary system, which was designed to give a semblance of representation to coloured and Indian minority groups. Opposition to these moves galvanised the internal resistance movements, mainly under the banner of the United Democratic Front (UDF), a loose alliance of over 600 non-governmental and community-based organisations. At the forefront were a number of student and youth organisations.

It seemed inevitable that Sicelo, a popular and articulate student, would be drawn to the protest and resistance politics of this period. Having become a member of the Soweto Students Congress (SOSCO), a UDF affiliate, in 1985, he was elected onto the college's Student Representative Council (SRC). In many educational institutions, the SRCs had become the focus of political resistance.

Like many other parents, Sylvia was not happy with these developments. Political activity brought with it the unwelcome attention of the security forces. 'All the trouble started when he was elected to the SRC. It was the time of the State of Emergency, so there was quite a lot of rioting in the location and people were being detained.' Police and soldiers came to the school looking for Sicelo and other student leaders. In addition, conflict arose between rival student organisations, creating additional danger for those involved in organisations like SOSCO.

The situation in Soweto, as in other parts of the country, became increasingly violent as the cycle of resistance and repression spun further out of control. In an attempt to break popular resistance, the security forces reacted with an iron fist. Between 1984 and 1986, over 35 000 people were detained. Of these, about 10 000 were children between the ages of seven and eighteen. In 1986 alone, children made up 40 per cent of all detentions.

Detention and Assassination

This was an extremely difficult time for Sylvia and her family. When he was sixteen, Sicelo was detained for the first time, spending five months in detention, three of them in solitary confinement, between June and November 1986. During his detention he was subjected to electric-shock torture and beatings. Sylvia and her husband were effectively powerless to protect their son. Under the emergency regulations, child detainees could be held indefinitely. Provisions of the Criminal Procedure Act also allowed for a child to be arrested, held, tried, convicted and sentenced without the knowledge of his or her parents, something that happened regularly.

Sylvia's woes were not restricted to Sicelo. During September 1986, a rival student faction attacked the Dlomos' house with petrol bombs, and Sylvia's mother was almost killed. She felt the family was increasingly vulnerable, as attacks could come from anywhere. It was also unclear whether the attackers were linked to the police. 'These things really worried me a lot, because this other organisation wanted to kill him as well. I don't know if they were influenced by the white people, because these people who were looking for him, they were riding in flashy cars but they were looking for him, and they had guns.'

During Sicelo's detention, as often happened in such cases, the police tried to pressure him into becoming an informer. His refusal led directly to a series of criminal charges being laid against him, ranging from attempted murder to public violence and arson. In December 1986, following his release from detention, he was acquitted on all counts.

Like many parents during this period, Sylvia was neither politically minded nor politically active, and felt unable to prevent her son's political engagement. 'The police used to urge me that I must tell my child to stop being involved in politics. I said to them I do not know that he is involved politically, but I do know the organisations he's involved with. I really didn't understand what was the relationship between politics and student organisations. I did try to tell my child to stop being involved in political activities, but he said that these are our rights [and] I cannot stop being involved.'

Almost inevitably, trouble returned a few months later when Sicelo was charged with being in possession of a firearm and received a five-year suspended sentence. He told Sylvia he had been with a group of youths when they were searched by the police. One of the youths had a gun, which was passed from one of his companions to the other, but was found in Sicelo's possession. The details of what happened, and why Sicelo did not receive a jail sentence, remain unclear. To be caught in possession of a weapon in these times was usually a passport to jail. Sicelo's release and suspended sentence may help to explain some of the suspicions about him that later arose.

After his detention in 1986, Sicelo became actively involved with the Detainees' Parents Support Committee (DPSC), which had offices at the headquarters of the South African Council of Churches (SACC) in Johannesburg. Sylvia had sought assistance from the DPSC during Sicelo's detention and subsequently became an active member of their Soweto branch.

Sicelo encouraged his mother's involvement in such activities, while realising that his own political activism had endangered the family. He moved out of home and, although he continued to visit, rarely slept there, preferring to stay with friends and family members elsewhere in the township. Less and less of his time was spent at school. Unbeknown to his parents, he also joined a unit of Umkhonto we Sizwe (MK), the military wing of the ANC, having been recruited by his close friend, Sipho Tshabalala.

During 1987, as a result of contacts gleaned through the DPSC, Sicelo played a major role in publicising the situation of children and youths in detention. Eloquent and forthright, he became a spokesperson for these young people, voicing their grievances, and providing some insights into why South African youth were at the forefront of the struggle for freedom.

'I just saw all my people, the masses suffering under an unjust regime. I am fighting not only for my rights, but for the rights of all the others, for my parents, who are not respected as people ... We are unhappy because of black education and the exploitation of black workers, and they must pay for school fees, textbooks and examination fees. We are unable to pay for books, I do not have a dictionary. We demand better education, better school facilities, compulsory education for all ... I am not going to retreat [after being detained]. I am going to go for it, to fight for my people and fight for my rights: for a democratic South Africa. I may die to achieve this idea. I am not going to stop or retreat. But forward I shall march.'[2]

For those who knew him, this was not just political rhetoric from the mouth of a child, but the convictions of an intelligent young man, mature beyond his years, a natural leader, and an inspiration.

Following a series of interviews with Dutch newspapers and television, Sicelo was interviewed in March 1987 for a *60 Minutes* special on CBS, entitled *Children under Apartheid*. In order to protect the participants and maximise the impact of this powerful documentary, a decision was taken to delay the broadcast, and it was eventually aired in December 1987, a few weeks before Sicelo's murder.

The DPSC, which had campaigned tirelessly to expose the extent of detentions and the brutal treatment of detainees, was increasingly successful in securing international attention. In September 1987, an international conference entitled 'Children, Repression and the Law in Apartheid South Africa' was convened in Harare. The event was a major publicity coup for the DPSC and the broader anti-apartheid lobby, and a major embarrassment for Pretoria.

Less than a month later, in early October, Sicelo was apprehended by police on his way to school. At the police station, he was severely assaulted and again put under pressure to become an informer. According to his lawyer, Ismail Ayob, Sicelo agreed to be an informer in order to stop the assault. This was not an uncommon ruse. After his release later that same day, he left Soweto and moved in with a fellow DPSC worker at his flat in the Johannesburg suburb of Hillbrow.

Once the CBS special was broadcast, the police were on the lookout for Sicelo. He had been aware of the possible ramifications of further publicity. Having told the police that he would cooperate with them, he was now telling the world exactly what they had done to him during his detention the previous year and how they had tried to coopt him. He knew they would be livid. Another young detainee, Cecila Mabiletsa, later told the DPSC that during his own interrogation at the end of December the police had said they would make an example of Sicelo. According to DPSC records, this threat seemed to have emanated from the same security policeman who was subsequently appointed as investigating officer in the murder case.

On 20 January 1988, Sicelo was arrested again, this time during a police raid on the DPSC offices. He was specifically targeted, as co-workers overheard the police involved in the raid referring to 'the kid who had been on the TV'. He was interrogated about his participation in the CBS documentary and forced to sign a statement saying that he had been 'coached' by a CBS staff member to lie on camera about bad treatment in detention. He was released the same day and immediately went home to see his parents. He was very troubled, according to Sylvia, and convinced that the police would now kill him. Despite her pleas, Sicelo refused to sleep at home and left for Johannesburg. This was the last time she saw him alive.

We do not know precisely what happened over the next four days. Sylvia told the TRC that she received a short telephone call from Sicelo on the morning of 24 January, which left her with the impression that there was something seriously wrong. Exactly what happened after that is also unclear. The police found Sicelo's body shortly after midnight the following morning. He had been shot in the head.

When the police arrived at the Dlomo house later that morning, Sylvia suspected the worst. 'I could feel it, I could just sense it that my child was gone, because the policeman came with [Sicelo's] pocketbook. I said to him, "Have you killed my son?" The policeman said, "Why are you saying such painful things? I didn't kill him. I just heard people saying there's a young boy who is dead under a tree. I went to see this boy and I found this pocketbook on him." This policeman asked me to accompany him to see where the body was. I didn't agree. I didn't want to go with this policeman. I knew they had killed him.'

Many others immediately accused the police of involvement in Sicelo's murder, and various rumours about the assassination circulated during and after the funeral. Although most people blamed the police, some suggested that youths aligned to the Azanian People's Organisation (AZAPO) might be responsible. They had been accused of attacking the Dlomo house and were sworn enemies of SOSCO. There were also rumours that members of the Mandela United Football Club were somehow involved.

Sylvia's conviction that the police were responsible was also based on a verbal threat against Sicelo that she had witnessed herself. Thirteen months earlier, following his acquittal on attempted murder charges, she was leaving the court with her son when they were stopped on the steps by a group of policemen. 'One of them [said to Sicelo], "You think you are clever, but one day we are going to shoot your brains out." ' As Sylvia later told the TRC, 'It happened exactly the way he said it would.' In her mind, there was no doubt that the police were involved, and many others in anti-apartheid circles shared this view.

In the wake of the murder, the police continued to treat Sylvia insensitively, as they took her backwards and forwards to the police station. She felt that they were gloating. At one stage, they told her she had brought this situation on herself, as she had been unable to control her child.

The police also warned her against having a mass funeral for Sicelo, although the matter was clearly out of her hands. Funerals, and especially those of fallen activists, had become a rallying point for defying the authorities and demonstrating opposition to the government. Over 3 000 people attended Sicelo's funeral in a highly charged atmosphere. 'There were lots of police, there were helicopters in different forms. They were also beating up other children at the funeral. They beat them [and they were] innocent. All those children were doing, was just to sing. But we buried my child. Even when we were in the church, the police came right inside the church and started beating up children, tearing off their T-shirts. The most painful thing, even once we have buried our child, the police followed us, they [threw] teargas at our food, I nearly also lost my niece. They threw teargas in our bedroom, and this child was foaming and suffocating from the teargas. I've never seen such a thing. It's a most painful thing. They came back again while we were sitting there. They said they didn't want to see crowds in my home and that if they see crowds coming here, they are going to arrest me …' This disdainful treatment of a grieving family only served to reinforce perceptions that the police were involved in the murder.

Not surprisingly, there was no progress in the investigation, and the police file was effectively closed. Sicelo's murder was simply another unsolved case, albeit a more famous one, in the litany of abuses committed under apartheid. Sylvia and the family could only wait, and hope that things would one day change for the better.

The TRC: Catharsis and Frustration

It was only after the 1994 elections that there was a glimmer of hope. In 1995, in response to the development of prospective legislation and with the assistance of the Centre for the Study of Violence and Reconciliation, the Khulumani Support Group was established to represent victims and survivors of the apartheid era.

Khulumani offered Sylvia a way of agitating for action on Sicelo's case. Although her priority was to see a criminal investigation conducted, the group was also a forum in which to talk about her son's murder with others who empathised. 'I went to Khulumani in order to get help. They introduced the Truth Commission to us. It is there that we are trying to put [forward] our grievances … to help us find who killed our sons, our husbands, our families.'

It was not long before Sylvia was an active member of the group and a leading advocate of victims' rights, appearing in promotional videos, on talk shows, at conferences and workshops. She also travelled abroad to promote the cause, and represented Khulumani at the parliamentary hearings on the TRC legislation.

Former minister of justice, Dullah Omar, welcomed Khulumani's role as a conduit for bringing people to the TRC. 'I hope that Khulumani will be able to reassure families, as well as communities, that this Commission represents their aspirations and their hopes, and through the Commission they will be able to get rid of the terrible things of the past and build a beautiful future. They must see it as their future. It belongs to them.'

Spurred on by the many injustices brought to the group, Sylvia also believed that Khulumani gave her and others a real chance to move forward through the TRC process. 'We have formed this group so that we can speak with one voice. When you are in the fields alone you are not heard, but when you are in a group you are easily heard. We are here to make sure our concerns are heard.'

By the time Sylvia testified before the TRC's Human Rights Violations Committee in April 1996, she had already told her story many times. Although each version differed slightly from the last and contained inconsistencies that could easily have been exploited by legal counsel, the essentials of her story remained solid. To a packed hall in the Central Methodist Church in downtown Johannesburg, she spoke of Sicelo's teenage years and her own experiences, a story of harassment and death.

Along with other members of Khulumani, Sylvia had been preparing for the big day. Although many more had wanted to speak publicly, the TRC's tight schedule meant that only certain cases were picked for the public hearings. Given the high profile of the Dlomo case, it was almost inevitable that it would receive attention. The act of testifying was extremely emotional: 'I had everything inside me. Then when I told those people [about what had happened], all the problems came back again ... it was hurting because I was crying. I felt as though my son had just died ... But on that particular day, it was as if the burden was taken from my shoulders, because other people were listening to what I was saying, and it seemed as if they were sympathising, because they were asking me questions whereby I told them.'

She was both relieved when it was over, and exhilarated that she had been able to tell everyone how she felt and what she wanted. But her positive feelings about the process were short-lived. Her work at Khulumani kept her abreast of developments at the TRC, and by early 1997 she grew very concerned that no progress had been made, and that the TRC had not even provided feedback on her son's case. It was unthinkable that nothing further would happen. 'I am worried that maybe the Truth Commission will end. It is almost a year since I testified. Now I am starting to panic and I'm having a really hard time, because I'm thinking maybe it will just end not knowing what happened.'

She was also increasingly concerned about what was happening in the amnesty process. She was personally opposed to the granting of amnesty, preferring to see prosecution and punishment. Nevertheless, she understood that there were other issues at stake, and that amnesty was perhaps a necessary, albeit distasteful product of the political compromise reached during the negotiations.

Her misgivings about amnesty were aroused again by the experiences of several other Khulumani members. They had attended the amnesty hearings concerning the murder of their children by a covert police unit operating in the Northern Transvaal, and were extremely upset by what transpired there. It was apparent that full disclosure was not taking place at hearings. The bearing and behaviour of the applicants told their own story. Sylvia felt that the absence of contrition, although not a criterion for amnesty, was tantamount to rubbing salt in the wounds of the victims. 'These people are coming forward to ask for forgiveness, just because they want to get away with it [and] not to say they are really ... sorry for what they did. It's what I see, because you can see them smiling all over the place. You can see others chewing gum right inside the court. What does that mean? And you are crying, mourning for your loved one who died in a gruesome way, but they are laughing?'

It seemed increasingly clear to Sylvia and others that the process was geared towards the perpetrators rather than the victims. The fact that the TRC was not keeping contact with the victims or communicating with them regularly made matters worse. There was no clear indication of what was happening in the cases of many Khulumani members. Sylvia believed that the opportunity to empower victims was fast disappearing, and it was more and more difficult to keep others engaged in the process as her own confidence faded. 'My interest is here – about the victims and survivors. What are the benefits from the Truth Commission? Because the Truth Commission should see that these people are well looked after, and they should be there when they promise people. I mean, they are writing up things in the papers and they are saying things on the radio. [But] they don't come to people and say, "People, we understand your problems [and] this is what we are going to do." '

She knew that her personal feelings about amnesty were not in accord with the aspirations of those who preached reconciliation and forgiveness. Her work at Khulumani left her feeling deeply conflicted in this regard. It seemed inconceivable that she could forgive her son's murderers. But she continued to grapple with the problem. 'To forgive is really a hard thing. To think that this young man was growing like a beautiful flower, but today they have decided to kill him. Then this pain that I don't think it will come off from out of my heart. It really will never come out. So forgiving and forgetting, it's a hard thing. Let's hope that if they come forward, we can change our minds. But it's hard.'

Applications for Amnesty

Painful as the loss of her son was, Sylvia had found some comfort in the knowledge that he was well regarded in the liberation movement as an anti-apartheid activist, and often depicted as a 'hero of the struggle'. She could not have imagined what would happen next.

In early 1997, one of the TRC's national investigators submitted an internal memorandum regarding the Dlomo murder. It appeared he had uncovered a bombshell: four members of an MK unit – rather than the security police – had admitted to the killing. In addition, these amnesty applicants claimed that far from being a hero, Sicelo had actually been a police informer.

Another year passed before Sylvia was made aware of the applications and the allegations they contained. When she heard the names, she was dumbstruck. Two of the applicants, Clive Makhubu and Sipho Tshabalala, had been close friends of Sicelo. On the day after Sicelo's murder, Sylvia had gone to both families' homes to warn them about the imminent danger to Clive and Sipho. Both young men had visited her house regularly after the killing, and she had fed them and given them shelter. 'Those children made me live for those days, because they were coming in and out, saying, "Our hero has died." That was something that soothed me, although my heart was broken.' Sylvia would subsequently discover that Makhubu had actually pulled the trigger, on the orders of John Dube, the main applicant and the unit's overall commander. The fourth applicant was another schoolmate, Precious Zungu.

Sylvia said she had no idea Sicelo had joined MK. Although she was aware that his sympathies lay in that direction, she saw no evidence of his involvement. This was certainly not a unique situation in those years, when many parents were unaware of the double lives their children led.

During 1986 and 1987, repression in South Africa had intensified. The army and police saturated the townships, and there was a marked increase in covert counter-insurgency operations. Clearly, detention and trial were not adequate deterrents, and every day there were reports of assassinations, disappearances, and attacks by surrogate forces who seemed to be working hand in glove with the police. Such forces appeared to operate under a veil of impunity, which allowed them to harass and terrorise local activists, as well as the general populace. What was erroneously described in some quarters as 'black-on-black' violence was in fact part and parcel of the state's internal destabilisation strategy, designed to smash popular resistance. The security forces had even taken to bombing the premises of opposition organisations.

For those actively involved in resistance politics, these were dangerous times. As resistance to apartheid grew, so the distinction between political activist and armed operative became blurred. Having changed tack during the mid-eighties, MK operatives were now recruiting among youth and other organisations inside

South Africa. Under this strategy, combat cells were established, training was conducted and ordinance secured.

According to Dube, he had returned to the country after training in 1985, and established several cells in Soweto. One of them included his three co-applicants, Makhubu, Tshabalala and Zungu, as well as Sicelo. Dube's co-applicants based their applications entirely on his written submission. In it he sketched a version of events that he would subsequently alter in several fundamental respects during oral testimony. The only consistent factor was his allegation that Sicelo was a spy.

It is not clear exactly when Sylvia was informed about the applications, and whether this was done by the ANC or the TRC. Either way, she was devastated, and wondered whether anyone would ever take her seriously again, when she had repeatedly accused the police of killing her son. Even though this now appeared to be untrue, she simply could not believe that Sicelo had been a spy or that the applicants were telling the full story. It just seemed inconceivable. If he was a spy, why had she suffered all this harassment? Why didn't the police counter allegations of their culpability by declaring that Sicelo had been one of them? Why did everything point to police involvement?

Understandably, she wanted to know a lot more. In particular, she wanted to know why the applicants had come forward, as she was aware that many applications from those not already in prison were prompted by the prospect of prosecution. In her son's case, she knew that the police investigation had not progressed at all. She had assumed that this was because they were complicit in the murder. But if they were *not* involved, on what basis were these applications being made?

Sylvia was also perplexed by the ANC's behaviour. They had sent some junior officials to 'explain' the situation to her, and she felt that this demonstrated their lack of interest in her personal grief. She refused to cooperate. She also wanted to know what the exact relationship between the applicants and the ANC had been. The ANC officials who had approached her 'on behalf' of the applicants were apparently more interested in their plight than her own. She, after all, was the aggrieved party, but it seemed that the purpose of the intervention was to secure the position of the applicants, by getting her to accept that they were sorry. Their remorse, however, did not translate into an admission that they had made a mistake, and the allegation that Sicelo was a spy still stood.

Her loyalty to the ANC was severely tested. She simply could not understand how the party could support such an atrocious allegation. She was also perturbed that the ANC had not informed her earlier that MK was involved in the execution.

Who inside the organisation had known this fact and for how long? Dube, in his written submission, claimed that he had informed both the head of MK's Special Operations, Lester Dumakude, and his immediate commander, Hein Grosskopf. Sylvia wanted to know who else in the military and political structures knew, and why they had kept it from her. In other words, how extensive was the cover-up?

Dube and one other applicant had retained their positions in official structures: Dube was a captain in the South African National Defence Force and Tshabalala had a clerical position at ANC headquarters in Johannesburg. Rightly or wrongly, Sylvia saw this as a sign that the ANC endorsed, or certainly did not condemn, their involvement in the execution.

Astounding revelations had been made and many questions remained unanswered. According to friends at Khulumani, Sylvia seemed to shut it all out, and said nothing. It was soon clear, however, that the situation was affecting her health. Although she became progressively sicker, she refused to stay at home. Her Khulumani colleagues could see she was in great pain, but she would not discuss her illness.

In January 1999, Sylvia was notified that the amnesty hearings were scheduled for the following month. The TRC also told her they would pay for her legal representation. Unlike former members of the security forces or MK, whose legal representatives were paid up to $500 per day, most people (whether victims or perpetrators) were represented at legal-aid rates of less than $100 per day. The attention lawyers gave such cases was therefore limited. Knowing that I had worked for the TRC's Investigation Unit and was in touch with several lawyers who might give proper attention to her case even at these rates, Sylvia contacted me and asked for help. Within a few minutes, Tony Richards, whom I had worked with previously on torture cases in the Vaal Triangle, agreed to take on the case.

The Amnesty Committee forwarded a bundle of papers to Tony's office in Johannesburg. Apart from the amnesty application and a transcript of Sylvia's testimony before the Human Rights Violations Committee, there was virtually no documentation. The Committee's 'evidence analysts', who had compiled the bundle, had either ignored the fact that the Investigation Unit had conducted an investigation into the case two years previously, or were unaware of it. I contacted the Committee's office and asked for this information to be made available as a matter of urgency.

In the week before the hearing, Sylvia was rushed to the Chris Hani Baragwanath Hospital in Soweto. Tony and I eventually found her in the maze of wards that make up the largest hospital in the southern hemisphere. She was pale and weak, propped up and swathed in blankets, surrounded by the sick and dying. Even from her sickbed, she was determined to fight the case and was relieved that we had come. It soon became clear, however, that much of her confidence had slipped away.

Her son, a hero of the struggle, was now accused of being an informer, of having worked for the very system she had spent the last ten years claiming had killed him. The ANC, whose former president, Oliver Tambo, had decried Sicelo's assassination as the handiwork of the apartheid security forces, was now facilitating the amnesty applicants' legal representation. Instead of being the proud mother of a murdered student activist, enjoying the gratitude and support of the liberation movement, she and her family had virtually been abandoned to fight for Sicelo's honour.

Sylvia pointed out how ironic it was that he should now be accused of being an informer. She remembered scolding her son and some of the boys who frequented her house for gossiping about others – including Dube! – whom they suspected of being informers. Although the applicants claimed MK status, she was resolute that the police had been involved. Was it possible, she asked, that the police could have got to these boys somehow and made them kill Sicelo?

In the absence of any further feedback from the Amnesty Committee, I made arrangements to meet with Pule Zwane, the former TRC investigator who had inquired into the killing. In an office in Pretoria, he provided some details of the work he had done. He felt the applicants were telling the truth, he said, although he acknowledged that many questions remained unanswered. Several sources had claimed that Dube, the key applicant, had been involved with the security police. Despite this, he had the impression that Dube was an 'important' cadre in the ANC. He had been responsible for some high-profile operations and had recruited several members who now held senior positions in the party. The implication was that he might enjoy a certain amount of protection. Zwane was not sure exactly who inside the ANC knew about the case, but many people had seemed surprised when he raised it with them. He also said that Dube had used the name 'Silver' as his *nom de guerre*.

On the advice of a former colleague from the Independent Board of Inquiry, I began looking through some of their old files containing notes of meetings with former Vlakplaas operatives, Dirk Coetzee and Joe Mamasela. And there it was: a note of Mamasela's referring to Dube, aka 'Silver', whom Mamasela had claimed was with MK, but who really worked for the police. According to Mamasela, Dube's police handler was Anton Pretorius, a notorious Soweto security policeman, who had applied for amnesty himself in a number of matters. The Soweto Special Branch had already been singled out by the TRC for its involvement in 'false flag' operations,[3] and had their own unit of askaris, as turned liberation movement guerrillas were known. It now seemed quite possible that Dube, rather than Sicelo, had been the informer.

Meanwhile, the evidence leader from the Amnesty Committee informed me that they could not find any information relating to Zwane's investigation. Either it had been lost, or no details of the actual investigation had been recorded, only the final memorandum. Tony requested that Zwane be subpoenaed to the hearing, which they immediately agreed to. I also passed on the information from Mamasela, in the hope that the Committee would see the need to probe this angle in order to establish exactly what Dube's relationship with the police had been.

As the hearing approached, I also learnt that the ANC had been unable to secure for Dube the services of the attorneys who usually represented ANC applicants. A friend at one law firm informed me that the attorneys were unwilling, because of the applicant's dubious background and the sensitivities attached to the case. In the end, it was left to an attorney working from the ANC's TRC desk to represent the applicants.

By 1999, few TRC-related stories were regarded as 'news', and the press release on the scheduled hearing of the Dlomo case barely received a mention, despite the sensational revelation that MK had been responsible for the activist's death. The empty hall at the Central Methodist Church on 16 February 1999 told its own story. Over 3 000 people had attended Sicelo's funeral in 1988. Now only a handful were present to witness what was effectively an attempted character assassination.

On the basis of the testimony, which deviated substantially from the written submission, it emerged that all the 'evidence' that Sicelo was a spy had emanated from Dube himself. He made four main allegations.

First, he claimed that he had caught Sicelo spying on him several times in the months before the killing. None of the co-applicants said that Dube had raised this issue with them, and he himself acknowledged that he had never raised it with Sicelo.

Second, Dube alleged that Sicelo had been arrested at the DPSC offices and released on the same day, despite being in possession of a hand grenade and a Makarov pistol. He said he had read about this in a newspaper. The implication was that only someone working with the police could have got away with this offence. No such incident ever occurred at the DPSC offices, or was reported in the papers. The only incident in which Sicelo was arrested with a weapon resulted in prosecution and a suspended sentence, almost a year before the murder.

Third, Dube claimed that Sicelo had 'disappeared' for three months from October 1987 to January 1988 and, as such, was acting in an undisciplined and suspicious manner. The Dlomo-Jeles' legal team located witnesses who testified that in fact Sicelo was working quite openly at the DPSC offices during this period, and that at least one of the applicants had actually visited and spoken with him there. In addition, the DPSC worker with whom Sicelo stayed in Hillbrow after his arrest in October 1987 testified that he had been an undercover MK operative himself. Sicelo was aware of this and of the fact that there were weapons in his flat. If Sicelo had been a spy, he asked, surely he would have passed this information on to his handlers? Had he done so, the operative would have been arrested. Instead, he had gone on with his work without ever being detected.

And fourth, Dube claimed that when he confronted Sicelo on the day of the murder, he discovered he was wearing a radio transmitter of the kind 'used by intelligence operatives'. Now, although the police had access to transmitter technology at this time, it was rarely used in situations like the one described by Dube. None of the other applicants were able to present any evidence to support his version. Only Makhubu had seen what was left of the device, which Dube claimed to have smashed with a rock to render it inoperable. Having described the device with its 'on/off' switch in some detail, he was unable to explain why he had not simply turned it off to stop it from working.

In his closing argument, Tony Richards made the point that Sicelo had worn a small black Walkman on his hip for years, and everyone had known about it. This was the most reasonable explanation for the device Dube claimed was a transmitter. Tshabalala, who admitted under cross-examination that he had met with Sicelo earlier on the day of the murder, confirmed that he was indeed wearing his Walkman.

Dube denied the counter-claim that he was the informer and not Sicelo. Eventually, however, he admitted that he had worked with the police, but said he had done so some time after the murder and on the express instructions of his ANC commanders. This claim was neither confirmed nor denied by the ANC, and no attempt was made by the Amnesty Committee to verify it.

Sylvia remained in hospital throughout the hearings and received daily reports on what was being said. Through her legal team, she made it clear that she opposed the applications, that she wanted nothing to do with the applicants and would not meet with them. Despite knowing her, none of them had tried to approach her in the past, and now they were trying to do so on the back of the political organisation she had wholeheartedly supported. She felt betrayed, and was bitterly disappointed and angry.

Some in the ANC clearly felt she was being uncooperative. Several attempts had been made, even at the hearings themselves, to get the family to drop its opposition to amnesty and to stop asking awkward questions 'in the spirit of reconciliation'. These people seemed quite oblivious to what this situation really meant to Sylvia and the family. Their apparent indifference heightened suspicions about what was being concealed, and strengthened the family's resolve to keep probing.

Dube's claim that he had informed MK's Special Operations chief, Lester Dumakude, and his immediate superior, Hein Grosskopf, was changed during oral testimony. Without explanation, Dube now claimed that he had not informed Dumakude, but only told Grosskopf about the murder towards the end of 1988 when visiting Lusaka. This seemed incongruous, as both Dube and Dumakude had also applied for amnesty for their involvement in a car bombing in Johannesburg in June 1988. Surely, it was put to Dube, they could have discussed the Dlomo matter at this stage? Wasn't this necessary in order to appraise the high command of what had really happened? Dube was unable to explain satisfactorily why he had mentioned the head of Special Operations in his written application. He now claimed he could not tell Dumakude about the murder, as he could only release this information to his immediate superior, Grosskopf, and to tell Dumakude would have bypassed the usual chain of command. This explanation was illogical, as Dumakude had worked directly with Dube in the car bombing. The Amnesty Committee made no attempt to clarify this, despite a request that they do so.

In addition, the TRC said they had been unable to communicate with Grosskopf, who was now based in London. As Dumakude was not called to the stand, Dube's version effectively remained untested. During 2000, however, Grosskopf returned to South Africa to testify at his own amnesty hearing. Fortuitously, Tony Richards was also representing a client in this matter and took the opportunity to ask Grosskopf whether Dube had ever informed him about the Dlomo assassination. He said he had not.

The transcripts of the four-day hearing and closing arguments are now a matter of public record, available for anyone to peruse on the TRC's website. The countless inconsistencies, contradictions and improbabilities in the applicants' versions are there for all to see.

When we met with Sylvia after the hearings, we told her we could not imagine how the applicants could be granted amnesty, as they had simply not presented their case. In addition, we had found witnesses and information that contradicted much of their limited version of events. We had also presented possible alternative motives for the murder. Everything appeared to hinge on the credibility of Dube, as the other applicants, with the possible exception of Makhubu, could not really add anything further. The fact that Dube had instructed Makhubu to pull the trigger and seen to it that the other two cell members were present to witness the execution, strongly suggested that he wanted to ensure they were accessories. All three co-applicants were reliant on the bona fides of Dube.

For Sylvia and the family several issues remained unsettled. There was the unresolved issue of Dube's own relationship with the police. There was also evidence to suggest that robbery might have been a motive. Sicelo's DPSC flatmate testified that he had given Sicelo R900 for delivery to a comrade in Soweto the day before the killing. The money was missing. In addition, an affidavit signed by Tshabalala four days after the murder was located by the Dlomo-Jeles' team, in which he claimed that on the day of the murder Sicelo had been in possession of over R800.

The Amnesty Committee had failed to deal with these and other issues sufficiently. They were keen to 'get through' the case as quickly as possible and seemed irritated that the matter was taking longer than expected.

Sylvia's condition meant that she could no longer engage actively in the fight to clear Sicelo's name. The pain of what had been alleged and her inability to protect her son's name were proving too much. On 13 March 1999, less than a month after the hearings, she died. Although the cause of death was given as a chest condition, many of her friends and colleagues believe that she had given up the will to live.

Conclusion

Eleven months after Sylvia died, the Amnesty Committee granted amnesty to all four applicants. Neither the family nor their lawyers were informed, and they first heard about the judgement when called by journalists asking for their reaction. Reading the decision, it is obvious that the Committee based their findings on the belief that the version of events presented by the applicants had not been disproved and was therefore plausible, whereas the alternative hypotheses put forward by the Dlomo-Jeles' lawyer had not been proved.

Although the Committee stated that there was 'no evidence that Sicelo was an informer and worked for the security police', they accepted that the applicants had acted 'on the information available to them which they believed to be reliable'. They also found that the applicants 'came to the decision [to execute Sicelo] honestly, and accordingly believed they had to take action to protect themselves, the MK and ANC from further police action'. This, the Committee found, established that the murder was associated with a political objective and that all the relevant facts had been disclosed. As with so many other amnesty cases, there was no clarification of what the 'relevant facts' were.[4]

The many contradictions in the applicants' testimony were dismissed as being of no material significance. No mention was made of the massive deviations between the written and oral evidence, or of many points raised in Tony Richards's closing argument against the granting of amnesty.

The fact that all the 'evidence' of Sicelo's so-called informer status emanated from Dube, who himself admitted to having worked with the police, was not even noted. Although a rebuttal or reasonable alternative to each of Dube's claims against Sicelo had been proffered, the Committee systematically ignored them. The suggestion that money had gone missing and that robbery might have been a motive was also dismissed.

Ultimately, the amnesty process in this case left many questions unanswered. This reflects a tendency that developed in the Amnesty Committee to view its mandate through a narrow lens, and to give applicants the benefit of the doubt. Although these were not court proceedings, one might have expected some acceptable standard to be maintained in regard to the quality of the evidence presented. Instead, there was an unreasonable willingness to overlook the incoherence of applicants' testimony and to grant amnesty without having formed a clear picture of the past.

For the Dlomo-Jele family, discovering the motive of the killing was crucial. But neither the Investigation Unit nor the Amnesty Committee seemed to share this concern. Having established who killed Sicelo, there was little willingness, despite the opportunity, to establish exactly why. This ran counter to the Commission's overarching mandate, which was to obtain as broad an understanding of past events as possible, and failed to address the needs of victims and survivors.

Had Sylvia lived to hear the Amnesty Committee's decision, perhaps she would not have been all that surprised. She was certainly aware that amnesty had been granted in a number of cases where families were dissatisfied with the limited, tailored versions submitted for consideration. She already knew that the process was flawed and that the Commission's investigators had failed to probe a number of cases adequately.

Despite her reservations about amnesty, Sylvia supported the TRC and fought to get others to engage with it. Ironically, she herself was betrayed by the process, which compounded her despair. She felt deceived not just by the youths she had fed and sheltered, or the ANC functionaries who had tried to placate her, but by the TRC itself, which demonstrated that it was not interested in finding out what really happened.

Notes

1. Quotations in the text are taken from a range of sources, including the testimony of Sylvia Dlomo-Jele at the Truth and Reconciliation Commission's Human Rights Violations Committee hearings in Johannesburg on 30 April 1996 (Case G0/0183), and two videos about the Khulumani Support Group made by the Centre for the Study of Violence and Reconciliation in 1995 and 1997, entitled *Khulumani* (Speak Out) and *Sisakhuluma* (We Are Still Speaking). The author, who assisted the attorney representing the Dlomo-Jele family at the amnesty hearings in February 1999, provides additional information.
2. *Children and Repression, 1987-1989*, Human Rights Commission Special Report SR-4, January 1990, p. 54.
3. Truth and Reconciliation Commission, *Truth and Reconciliation Commission of South Africa Report*, 5 vols (Cape Town, Juta & Co., 1998), vol. 5, ch. 6, para. 100b. And see www.polity.org.za/govdocs/commissions/1998/trc/5chap6.
4. www.truth.org.za/decisions/2000/ac200019.

5

THE STORY OF THANDI SHEZI[1]
Pamela Sethunya Dube

For ten years, Thandiwe Shezi, a single mother of two, lived with a terrible secret: she had been gang-raped by apartheid security policemen. With no soul to confide in, she became self-abusive, and took her anger out on those she loved the most, her children. Like thousands of other survivors of apartheid brutality, she finally told her story to the Truth and Reconciliation Commission (TRC). But it pains her that the TRC did not expose the perpetrators. And even if they had been exposed, she asks, 'What guarantee did I have that they would not be granted amnesty?'

I spent weeks with Thandi, trying to feel her pain and understand how she has managed to survive all these years. Although she has spoken publicly of the ordeal, it was no easy task to get behind the brave mask and see her true feelings. She has kept these feelings to herself for too long to part with them. She told me, 'It is like saying to me, "Rip your soul apart and lay it bare for the world to see ..."'

This is her story. It starts on the day her womanhood was taken from her, and her soul and her body ripped apart.

They came just after 1 a.m. It was mid-September 1988. I woke up to a heavy banging on the door. I opened the door, and a heavily built white policeman, pointing a gun into my face, shouted, 'Hey, wie's Tjantji?'

I stared back and found the courage to respond, 'There is no one by that name here.'

There were policemen in uniform all over. Others were on top of the roofs with guns. Outside there was a convoy of police cars. I wasn't surprised they came. I knew why they were there. They had come to pick me up, as they had been informed I was a trained 'terrorist'. I was just scared. For myself, for my mother and father. I was scared for my babies.

Earlier in the evening, I had had a premonition. It was around 8 p.m. I was doing the dishes in the kitchen, when I was suddenly gripped with fear. I called my mother over and told her I had a feeling something bad was going to happen that night. She advised me to go and hide at my aunt's place in White City. I decided against this. In the backyard, in my father's truck, I had stored boxes of ammunition. I knew that if the police came and did not find me, they would search the yard and perhaps find the boxes. That would have been bad, really bad, for my family. I knew if they came, and found me, they would not be concerned with searching the yard.

I was right. They entered the house and started ransacking the place. They found nothing, and instead went for my uncle and brother, beating them up. It was bad. My cousin, Vusi Mdaweni, used paraplegic boots and could not walk or stand without putting them on. As he had just woken up, he couldn't stand. But they still beat him up. The more he screamed, the more they kicked.

Then they commanded us all out of the house and paraded us in front of some huge lights. We were blinded by these lights. They wanted to make sure we did not see the *impimpi*, the spy, who was going to point me out. Yes, the *impimpi* singled me out. They grabbed me and beat me up, on the spot.

It was so bad, so painful for my mother, that she said to the cops, 'Do not kill her in front of me. Show me her body when you are finished.'

They shouted abuse at my mother and pushed her back into the house.

Then one asked me where Silver was. It suddenly struck me: Silver was the man they were looking for. They were not concerned with what I could have hidden in the house. They were after me to give them leads to Silver.

I told them I did not know where Silver was. I wasn't lying but, of course, they would never believe me. I had last seen Silver four weeks earlier. But I didn't tell them that.

Silver was John Dube, one of my comrades in the underground structures, in Umkhonto we Sizwe.[2] After two of our comrades had been detained a month before, Silver had come to my house and advised me to leave the township for KwaZulu. There was a problem, I knew that, trouble was brewing in the township. I left for KwaZulu, but could not stay long. I was away from home for only three weeks.

The two comrades who were in detention were Sipho Mthembu, my mentor, and Edward Mokati, the 'Prof', as we called him. They had been arrested when they were spotted by an askari[3] at Park Station in downtown Johannesburg. They were being held in connection with the bombing of the bus terminus in Vanderbijlpark. But everyone knew that Silver was the man the security police were hunting for. The word was that Sipho and the Prof had been tortured, and we feared that one of them may have succumbed to the pressure and leaked

THE STORY OF THANDI SHEZI

word about Silver and his whereabouts. Or perhaps a spy had told them I was hiding Silver in the house? How stupid that would be. To this day, nobody knows what really happened.

When the police came, I had been back from KwaZulu for only three days. Earlier that day, I had seen the woman in whose house Silver stayed. She asked me when I had come back. This made me suspicious. I had never had any real conversation with this woman before, and I thought it was strange she asked me this question. I didn't even know she knew where I stayed. I suspected that she must have given the police the information about my whereabouts. At that moment, I knew she must be the *impimpi* hiding behind the big lights.

Then I was put on the police truck, and they drove around the township collecting more people. We were five in the van by the time we reached John Vorster Square. I had never been there before, but knew of the terrible things they did there.

I was taken into a room where I was interrogated. One Andries van Heerden was in charge. In the room was also Sam, the badly burnt askari, who was doing all the dirty work. I learnt later that he was a former MK soldier who had sold out. I am told he now lives in Alexandra.

They took turns beating me up. After about thirty minutes of beating, my face swollen and my dress torn, I was told to sit on the floor. I did so, and one of them handcuffed my hands at the back. They started phoning other cops, saying, 'We have the terrorist. She is going to take us to Silver.'

Van Heerden instructed Sam, the askari, to put a sack over my head. I was then led to an underground room. Even though I could not see, I knew we were going down the stairs.

When we got there, I was asked, over and over, 'Where is Silver?' I refused to answer.

In the room, there were now four white policemen and the askari. They took acid and poured it in water. One took the acid water and poured it on the sack over my head. I could feel the acid water running down my face. I couldn't breathe. The more I tried to breathe through the wet sack, the more it got stuck to my face. My face was burning. It felt like my skin was peeling off. My eyes were burning … it was horrible. The acid got into my eyes. It was bad. Really, really bad. I was in so much pain, I couldn't scream. To this day, because of the acid, my left eye is half-blind.

With the 'acid test' over, one of them pressed hard needle-like instruments on my skin. My whole body started shaking. I was being electrocuted. The pain was unbearable. I choked. I bit my tongue and blood started pouring from my mouth. My tongue was torn.

After ten or fifteen minutes, they stopped.

Through the bleeding and the shivering, they continued to ask about Silver. I knew I had to say something, anything, to save myself. I lied. I told them, 'I am a member of the Inkatha Freedom Party.'

One said, 'You think we are stupid?' And then two were instructed by Van Heerden to take me to another room. The room was pitch-black. It was so dark, I couldn't even see my fingers. They pushed me on the cold floor and they left. With my dress torn and wet, I was so cold my body started shivering all over. I stood up.

After a few minutes, I saw the door open. Four white men came through. I could tell they were white, because even in darkness their images were clear.

> *The apartheid security forces used rape as a weapon against women in detention. The Commission received 446 statements involving sexual abuse, of which 398 specified the sex of the victim. Of these 158, or 40 per cent, were women.[4] The Commission categorised rape as 'severe ill-treatment'. The majority of rape survivors remained silent, and only a few came forward during the TRC's special hearings on women in 1997. It was at one of these hearings that Thandi Shezi spoke about her rape ordeal for the first time in ten years.*

When they entered the room, they were laughing and talking loudly in Afrikaans. One said, 'Wat moet ons maak met die kaffir terroris?' [What should we do with the kaffir terrorist?] I knew something bad was going to happen, when another said, 'Bitch, ons sal jou lekker moer.' [Bitch, we are going to give you a good beating.] But my body froze when someone said, 'My vrou is weg, ek wil haar naai.' [My wife is away, I want to fuck her.]

My body was stone-cold when they approached. One ripped off what was left of my dress. They pushed me down on the floor, and one hurriedly unzipped his pants and kneeled on me. He started raping me. When he had finished and another one was taking his turn, he said, 'Die bitch is baie lekker, nou weet ek hoekom die terroris haar liefhet.' [The bitch is very nice, now I know why the terrorist loves her.]

I was hurting so bad. They were laughing and talking as they took their turns. One by one, they entered me and ripped off what was left of me …

I found my voice and asked them, 'If you hate black people so much, why are you enjoying the body of a black woman?' And one responded, 'We must humiliate you and show you that this ANC can't do anything for you.'

My whole body was paining. My hands were still handcuffed at the back and

I could feel the cuffs eating through my skin. I was bleeding everywhere. They were humiliating me. Whoever said that raping a woman is the power men use to destroy her soul, was right. Within minutes, I was destroyed. My womanhood was taken.

It was then that I decided: I am not going to give in. I had to fight. Physically, I knew it was impossible. A small voice inside said to me: to survive, you have to remove your soul from your body.

I took control of my soul. I decided to separate my soul from my body. It was as if a supernatural power had taken control of me. On the spot, I decided that nobody is going to get control of my soul. As they huffed and puffed on top of me, I quietly separated my body from my soul. It was as if my soul was looking down on my body being abused.

> *By the time we spoke, Thandi had told this story many times, albeit in more general terms, since the TRC hearing. She had been talking freely and openly to me. But when it came to revealing the intimate details of her horror, words failed her. She admitted, 'I try to block it out all the time. I still can't take the word "rape". It is too painful.'*
>
> *Within hours of her arrest, she had been tortured and gang-raped. Further humiliation awaited her when she was taken to the doctor.*

When they were done, I was taken to a district surgeon. The doctor asked them what had happened. They lied, they told him I was a prostitute and they had found me in Hillbrow, beaten up. I could not defend myself and tell the truth. My tongue was swollen and I couldn't speak. Even if I could have spoken, I knew it would have caused more trouble.

One of my rapists had said they were going to humiliate me until I hated myself. 'You won't even look into a white man's face again.' I realised how true his words were. I was humiliated, embarrassed and ashamed. I felt very dirty, and would not even allow the doctor to touch my face.

After I had been attended to by the doctor, I was taken to Sun City.[5] I was placed in solitary confinement, under section 29.[6] I was thrown into a single cell with only one blanket. There was a hard steel bed, a basin and a toilet. The room was so small that I took one step from the bed to the basin, and one from the basin to the toilet.

I wasn't allowed to interact with fellow inmates. For the first three months, I was not even taken outside for exercise. It was bad. I wasn't allowed any visitors or any reading material. The only thing I was given was the Bible, which I would not read then, as I believed it was a weapon against us. As for visitors, in any case, my family and comrades had no idea where I was being kept. The police had lied to them about my whereabouts.

For the next four months, I had to undergo more interrogations. The security police at John Vorster Square would come in and interrogate me about the activities of the ANC. Of course, I still maintained my position: 'I don't know …'

At times, they would come and take me for a drive around Johannesburg, hoping that I would identify comrades. I learnt the art of blocking out the faces of people I knew, so that were we to come across a comrade, I wouldn't show any expression.

Sometimes, they would take me to the forests, and smear my body with butter and tie me to a tree, for ants to bite me. Then they would sit and smoke cigarettes as I twisted and screamed. Afterwards, they would take me to John Vorster Square to shower, before taking me back to prison.

Fortunately for me, the prison doctor became my saviour. He noticed the sores on my body and asked me what was the problem. I told him about my 'sightseeing' trips and what happened. He issued an instruction to the security police to stop the 'ant festivals'.

But by then, I had started enjoying the trips. Every time I felt tired of sitting in my cell, I would send a message to John Vorster that 'I remembered where we stored the ammunition …' and they would come rushing. We would then drive around and I would say stuff like, 'This place has changed since I was last here, I can't find the right spot.' Then, the following day, I would 'remember' something else, and once I was out, 'forget' it again. Once you knew them, those guys were stupid. They were prepared to buy anything to find 'terrorists'.

I also learnt how to deal with prison warders terrorising me. During my first three weeks in prison, there was this woman warder, Sergeant Schutte, who seemed intent on making my life miserable. She would come into my cell to bring me food, and start laughing and making jokes about 'the one with a torn mouth'.

One day, I decided the jokes had to come to an end. I asked other warders for an empty paint-can and soap. I claimed I needed these things to wash the floors so as to keep myself busy. They fell for my lie. I poured water in the can and soaked the bar of soap in it overnight. In the morning, the water was foamy and ready.

Schutte came as usual and continued with her arrogance and insults. Just as she was about to leave, I panel-beat her nicely, I really hit her. When the other prisoners sensed what was happening, they started banging their cups against their cell gates to drum down her screams. When I was done with her, I poured the soapy water on the floor. She slipped and hit the floor – hard. She fainted. I opened the tap to revive her. What I didn't realise was that it was hot water. As I poured the water on her face, she turned purple.

When other warders came in, I told them that she slipped in the water I was using to mop the floor.

The following day, I was taken to court. Fortunately for me, the magistrate said nothing could be done about me, because I was a 'special' prisoner and my captors had instructions that I was theirs alone to deal with. Instead, I was sentenced to two months of 'rice water'. This meant I was allowed no food except for half a cup of salty water drained from rice.

The prison doctor came to my rescue once again. After two days of the 'rice water' diet, I fell sick. The doctor ordered that I be put back on solid food.

By then, I was an 'expert' in the survival tactics in jail. We political prisoners were not allowed anything to read and could not even go to the tuck shop to buy, but I discovered the ways in which others had survived the mental torture. There were two women, in particular, who gave me the courage and the will to survive prison: Lindiwe, who had already been sentenced to ten years' imprisonment, and Sonto Masondo. They taught me how to use a sheet to exchange food for books. My cell was on the third floor, and below us were common prisoners who were allowed newspapers, books and radios. We would put food in a plastic bag and slot it between the rails until 5 p.m., when the guards disappeared from the patrols. Between then and 6 p.m., we would tie the plastic bag to a corner of a sheet and call the name of the person the parcel was intended for. Then we would swing the sheet and throw it in the direction of the recipient. She would then untie the plastic bag, attach her exchange to the sheet, and throw it back. This was an art you had to learn to survive jail.

By this time, my family were getting frantic. For months, they had been searching for me, without success. They had been to prisons, hospitals and mortuaries, hoping against hope, for a sign. Little did they know that I had started making plans to get word out.

I discovered that the doctor's rooms were the best place to let the world know your fate. As a section 29 prisoner, I was not allowed to go to the doctor's rooms at the same time as other prisoners. But I managed to befriend a prison guard called Lindi who, in the last days of my incarceration, allowed me to go to the doctor's rooms some thirty minutes before the last prisoner was attended to. There I met Thuli Mthembu, the sister of my old friend and comrade, Sipho Mthembu. Fortunately for me, she was up for release the following day. She immediately contacted my family, and they notified their lawyer, who got me out.

Then I knew God was there. I could have died in jail and nobody would have known.

But the trip home was the most difficult. When I was dropped off by the taxi, I could not walk. The distance from the bus stop to my place usually took me five minutes at the most. But on this day, my mother heard of my release from neighbours who passed me along the way. It took me an hour to get home, and still my mother could not recognise me. I was frail, I had pimples all over, and my hair was falling out. It took a lot of effort to pick my foot up for a step.

> *The trauma of rape, torture and imprisonment took its toll on Thandi and her family. From being a loving, carefree daughter, sister and mother, she had turned into a withdrawn, bitter and abusive person. Carrying the burden of rape without a soul to confide in, she saw her life turned upside down.*

How do you explain to your child that the reason you are so abusive is that you yourself were abused? It is the most difficult thing to see fear in your daughter's eyes when you approach.

After Sun City, I was not as enthusiastic as I used to be about participating in the work of the ANC. I became a loner. I avoided friends and comrades. Men couldn't even get close to me. I avoided any sexual contact. Every man I saw reminded me of the rapists. Sex became a no-no.

The worst was that I took my anger out on my children. Overnight, I had been turned into a monster. I was no longer a loving mother. I found myself shouting, screaming, throwing abusive language, and violent all the time. Anything that reminded me of the rape made me throw a tantrum. I would bang my child's head against the wall and only feel bad about it afterwards. To this day, my daughter will say, 'Please, mama, lower your voice,' when I speak. I feel bad when I think my daughter is still fearful of me.

When I was arrested, my son Ayanda was still too young to understand. But for my daughter, the picture is still clear and vivid. Mbalizethu was six years old and doing Grade 1. When I was released, I was told she wasn't performing well at school. She had changed from a jolly six-year-old child into a withdrawn, troubled soul. I knew why. She had witnessed my beating and arrest on that night. My mother told me that when I was in jail, and people used to talk and wonder about my whereabouts, my daughter would cry the moment somebody said something like, 'She could be dead.' They reached an agreement, as elders, not to mention my name. This affected her badly. And what I put her through afterwards has left her with mental scars. I know that now. At times, I wish I could turn back the clock.

> *Despite these regrets, Thandi knew why she had suffered. It was because she had dared to be part of a struggle to change the lives of oppressed South Africans.*

Up until the traumatic four months of my life that I spent in jail, I was working quietly within the ANC underground. I was an activist, a 'terrorist' to the apartheid regime. It was a family thing. My sister Busisiwe and my brother Siphiwe were in exile when I became active in the ANC.[7] I had wanted to skip the country too, but Siphiwe thought it was best for me and my other sister, Thokozile, to remain and support the family.

My mother Thakasike was always a pillar of support to all of us. She had to endure the taunting and rejection of most of the community, who called us nasty names for our role in the struggle. Once, I entered our church to find the minister and the congregation discussing 'that woman with terrorist children'. My late father, Joseph, despite his occasional cynicism – 'The Boers are never going to release Mandela,' he used to say – was a silent player. Up until the day of my arrest in September 1988, I was ready to fight to the end.

My real feeling for activism started in 1979 in KwaZulu. My parents had removed me from my school in Soweto after the 1976 uprising, and sent me away for 'protection'. I had been at Ngali High School in Vryheid for two years when I was expelled. As could be expected, life at Ngali High School became too much for a young Sowetan to accept. The school, like many others in the Kingdom of Zululand, introduced a free period for students to learn about the policies and propaganda of the Inkatha Freedom Party. Together with a few other students from Soweto, I was expelled for six months for questioning this particular programme. The following year, I was readmitted after the pleading intervention of my uncle, who was a school principal in the area at the time. But there was a condition: no political activism.

After matric, I returned home in 1982 to join the underground structures of the ANC. By the time of my arrest, I was secretary-general of the Soweto Youth Congress (SOYCO). It was through SOYCO that I was sent briefly for military training in Botswana. Those were the most fruitful years I had.

After Sun City, everything came to a standstill. I could not go back to the well-paid job I had before, because I was labelled a 'terrorist'. I did not have money to finish my studies. My plan had been to study to be a social worker, but now I could not. Rape took that away from me.

> *In 1995, Thandi and other survivors of abuse started the Khulumani Support Group. She was one of those who provided support to victims of apartheid who told their stories at the TRC. Although she became a counsellor herself, helping others to cope with their pain, she did not tell a soul about her own ordeal. A year later, she started receiving counselling from Mary Roberts at the Centre for the Study of Violence and Reconciliation. This helped her to deal with the past, but still she could not open up and talk about the rape.*

It was difficult to say, 'I was raped.' I did not know what to expect. Even my counsellor did not know I was a rape victim. It was okay to talk about the imprisonment and the torture. Everybody was talking about that, anyway.

When I started counselling sessions, I also took on a new journey. I found my spirituality. I became a born-again Christian, and this also prepared me to deal with what had happened.

Going to the TRC after almost ten years and talking about what happened was my way of trying to confront my past. It was difficult. The first person I spoke to about it was Dineo Moleko at Khulumani. She organised counselling for me with Mary Roberts. It took time, but I finally did come out.

My family, including my mother, only heard about my rape ordeal during the women's hearings. Afterwards, the only words my mother uttered were, 'Now I understand why you were so reserved and had such a rage.' We have never spoken about it since. Nobody mentions the word 'rape' in the family. It is as if they are also learning to block it out.

I suppose you could say I am fine with that. Despite the counselling, and talking about it through the play, I find that the word 'rape' still makes me shiver with anger. If I read an article about sexual abuse, it provokes bad memories.

My daughter is also attending counselling sessions. I think she needs that.

I don't know about my son. He has never said anything about it. Maybe you are right, I should get him to go to counselling. Yes, maybe he needs it.

> *Thandi is still dealing with the effects of the rape. In 1997, she participated in putting together a play entitled* The Story I Am About to Tell. *It features Thandi and two other victims of apartheid brutality – Duma Khumalo and Catherine Mlangeni[8] – playing themselves. The group have travelled to many theatres around the world to tell audiences about South Africa's traumatic past.*

Yes, I am healing – through the people around me. My family is still together to offer a cushion of support. Khulumani is there. And the play has given me the opportunity to confront my demons. There are times when I realise that I am not a victim any more. Through the play, I have been able to give a voice to thousands of women who have been raped but could not 'come out'.

It empowers me when women come to me after a show and relate their stories. Some women's stories you just cannot forget. We were in Sweden in 1999, when one woman shared her traumatic story with me. During the occupation of Namibia by apartheid South Africa, she was working as a volunteer there. She says one day, the SADF detained her, accusing her of being involved with a SWAPO man. Then about ten of the soldiers came at night and gang-raped her.

When she told me the story, we cried together. It was important for her to tell me, as she saw me as somebody who would understand the abuse and the humiliation of being raped by men in uniform. I cried because it made me realise just how bad apartheid South Africa was.

> *Dealing with her rape does not mean Thandi has forgiven and forgotten. She still does not know who her rapists are. She feels betrayed by the TRC. This feeling worsened when Andries van Heerden appeared before the Amnesty Committee for his part in the 'beating' of three women.*

Surprisingly, I was the only one of Van Heerden's victims who attended the amnesty hearings. The other two didn't pitch. Maybe they knew they would get no satisfaction.

Van Heerden sat there and looked me in the eye and said he did not know me. He said he did not recall beating and torturing me. The truth is, I don't know if he was part of the gang that raped me. I wanted to know. But the man wouldn't go even that far. He was there for 'assault' and prepared to accept that only. But for him to deny knowing me, that is impossible to swallow. I am the person he beat up, and tortured with electric shocks and acid water. Yet he stood there and denied my existence. How am I supposed to forgive and forget, when I am not recognised by my perpetrator?

I needed him to tell me who ripped off my womanhood. He wouldn't say, because he 'didn't know me'.

My pastor said that in order for me to move on, I had to walk up to Van Heerden and hug him. I froze on the spot. I could not.

But the truth now is that I don't know if I want to know my rapists. I was advised to go back to John Vorster Square, to enter the room in which I was raped. I could not. It was too painful to face. I don't know if facing my rapists will make me feel better. It may just conjure up memories. Bad memories.

As much as the play and 'coming out' have helped me confront the devils, I am still pained. I am angry and pained that I am struggling with this, while the perpetrators are walking the streets. I am not free. Their deed will be with me for the rest of my life.

> *For the victims and survivors of brutality, the TRC was a platform on which to share painful memories. But for Thandi and many others, it did not necessarily hold out the prospect of healing. In the play, Thandi says, 'I am not going near the TRC, thank you very much. Because they will talk about reconciliation and forgiveness. How can I reconcile and forgive when I am no longer a woman?' She still finds it painful to relive her appearance before the Commission.*

I am not going back there. Pray to God that I am not asked to appear before the TRC again.

Yes, going to the TRC was a victory. It was a victory in that I found the courage to confront my rape. It gave me a platform to share my grief. It made me talk. Hopefully, I will heal in time.

But going before the TRC also feels like I exposed myself to more abuse. It feels like I was abused all over again. With the TRC, it felt like all they wanted was my story. I felt used. There was no support system to help me heal. From the very day of my presentation, I cursed ever going before the TRC.

Immediately after I told my story, I was crying hysterically, when my TRC debriefer came around, patted me on the back, and asked why I was crying. I was angry. Hurt. How could this woman say such a thing? She didn't think I had a right to cry? Up until then, I had not cried over my ordeal. I needed this moment to shed my tears. My colleagues from Khulumani were angry, and it took Hlengiwe Mkhize, the Commissioner, to stop us from beating up the debriefer.

One of my major problems with the TRC is that it seems to be perpetrator-friendly. What are we, the victims, expected to feel when perpetrators are granted amnesty and we have no recourse? Worse still, the government has still not addressed the issue of reparations effectively. I have even heard some of my comrades in the ANC saying people should not expect reparations 'because the struggle was not about financial benefits'. These are the people sitting comfortably in Parliament and in government positions, taking huge cheques home to their children. They forget that apartheid denied us our basic needs. By being in the struggle, we lost the opportunity to develop as families and to continue with our studies.

Today, I am still staying in my mother's house. My children's home is my mother's home. I cannot afford to buy a house or a car for myself. And I am not alone. What is important is that the granting of reparations is not just about giving somebody a cheque to wipe out the pain. It is about addressing the needs of the communities. It is about providing the best health and education systems for the communities. It is about building monuments, and naming township streets after people who died for the liberation of South Africa. It is about land. The government needs to ensure that millions have access to land. If these issues are not addressed, South Africa could easily find itself in the same situation as Zimbabwe.

> *As much as Thandi has spoken about her rape, she has not come to terms with it fully. She still needs to reconnect her soul and her body. In the play, she explains why reconciliation and forgiveness would be difficult for her: 'I am no longer a woman. In body, I am a woman. But inside, I am dead.' As often happens, traumatic experiences led Thandi to seek a spiritual path. The last four years have been about that all-important journey.*

Yes, I have found ways to reconnect my soul to my body. I can say the process started in 1996. Becoming part of Khulumani was my way to find value in living. I had been 'dead' for a long time and Khulumani was just what I needed.

Appearing before the Commission helped. Forming the theatre group and relating my story to people I didn't know was also a process of reconnecting body to soul.

But, of course, I needed more than talking to feel whole again. I had to work hard on my spirituality. I realise now that it usually takes a traumatic experience to find oneself spiritually. I had to go back and dig into why, on that day, that very second, when I was being raped, I found courage to stay alive. I had to go back and find the small voice that told me to remove my soul from my body. It meant a lot, because it made me survive.

I started reading the Bible. I wish I'd done that in jail, but because my captors gave me the Bible, I didn't want anything to do with it. Now I needed to find out for myself. I needed the knowledge and information. The Bible guided me. I started talking to friends and colleagues. It empowered me.

I joined the Christian Revival Church Ministries and they were comfortable with my pain. They helped me to understand the struggle in the context of the church. It helped me a lot. Finding God, and in the process finding friends, meant I could work on healing the family. I reconnected with my mother. I have started the process of giving love, especially to my children. Today, I find that my children are more comfortable with me. They are in their late teens, Mbalizethu is eighteen and Ayanda is sixteen, but they still fight over who is going to sleep with me. Ayanda is even called 'mama's boy' by his friends. I find that fulfilling. I think my healing is their healing. I find happiness in their growth as persons.

But healing does not happen overnight. Thandi still struggles with one of the most important things in life, the ability to have satisfying sexual relationships. She is a beautiful woman. She is now thirty-nine years old and, unlike many women of her age, feels comfortable in jeans and a T-shirt. She is stylish and outgoing, and relationships with men should be simple. But they are a major problem.

To this day, I can't even accept sexual relations. I still shiver at the thought of a man touching my body. I am scared a man would want to abuse me the same way those policemen did. I am afraid to love. I want to be loved, I want somebody to hold me close to him and say, 'I love you.' But how do I know he won't want to abuse me? How can I tell if somebody is only with me out of sympathy, not because of who I am? I have now resigned myself to the fact that I may never find love. Maybe I am using this as an excuse, but I tell people that I can't have a sexual relationship because I am a *mzalwana*, a born-again Christian. It is difficult to know. Whatever the case, I know that those four policemen robbed me of a life. They destroyed me as a woman. I am struggling to find the woman in me.

Notes

1. This text is based on conversations between Thandi Shezi and the author, which took place in Johannesburg in January and February 2001.
2. Umkhonto we Sizwe, popularly known as MK, was the military wing of the ANC.
3. A former guerrilla, recruited or 'turned' by the security forces.
4. Truth and Reconciliation Commission, *Truth and Reconciliation Commission of South Africa Report*, 5 vols (Cape Town, Juta & Co., 1998), vol. 4, ch. 10, para. 52.
5. Diepkloof Prison.
6. Section 29 of the Internal Security Act, No. 74 of 1982, allowed for indefinite detention in solitary confinement for the purposes of interrogation. The validity of a detention order could not be challenged in court.
7. Busisiwe passed away in February 2001. Siphiwe is now a colonel in the South African National Defence Force.
8. The story of Duma Khumalo, one of the Sharpeville Six convicted under the 'common purpose' law for the murder of councillor Jacob Dlamini in 1984, is told elsewhere in this volume. Catherine Mlangeni is the mother of ANC lawyer, Bheki Mlangeni, who was killed in 1991. He was blown up by a booby-trapped cassette player that had been mailed by security policeman, Eugene de Kock.

6

NOTHING BUT THE TRUTH
The Ordeal of Duma Khumalo[1]

Mtutuzeli Matshoba

> I'm free, but I'm always haunted by people who died innocent. Their faces are with us more than those we see every day. If only people knew how those people died, they wouldn't be so irresponsible. I want to change the world, but I can't. I don't have the power.
>
> Duma Khumalo

It was 23 February 2001. In the company of some friends, I was on my way to Sebokeng to attend a 'closure ceremony' organised by the Khulumani Support Group for Mrs Makhetha of Zone 12 and Mrs Mokoena of Zone 7. The husbands of both these women had left for work as usual in 1993 – in February and August respectively – and had never come home. Their families believe that they were killed in the violence that paralysed the Vaal Triangle in the build-up to the 1994 elections.

Under South African law, missing persons may be declared dead after seven years. However, the families of these men had little recourse to the law, nor would such a declaration by a court have provided any solace. The only potential healing to their emotional wounds was the truth. If they at least knew what happened to their loved ones, they might be able to continue with their lives. But, with the assistance of Khulumani, they had exhausted all possible avenues to the truth. That is why Khulumani had organised a closure ceremony for the families at the houses of the two women, followed by a prayer meeting at the Catholic church in Zone 12.

Although we had come for the ceremony, I also had another goal: to talk to Duma Khumalo, one of the Sharpeville Six. He worked for Khulumani, which was established in 1995 to represent, counsel and support the victims of apartheid. Khulumani means 'talk', or 'speak out'.

When we arrived at MaMakhetha's in Zone 12, Duma was not there. He had gone to meet Methodist bishop Paul Verryn, who was officiating at the ceremony, to ensure his safe entry into the township.

A little, lively, bespectacled grandmother opened the ceremony by first greeting, and then saying that Khulumani had been limping along without any material support, not even from the government its members had helped to put into power. Instead of support, Khulumani was regarded as a nuisance, as evidenced by the shabby treatment they had received on Freedom Day and at the Hector Peterson Memorial on 16 December 2000, where they demonstrated to highlight their plight. 'Unfortunately for the government,' she said, 'we intend to remain a weight on its conscience, because the erstwhile perpetrators of violence against innocent and defenceless victims live in luxury while the victims are scrounging for survival.' However, she went on, they were not going to lie down and die because of that. Instead, they were going to hold hands and build Khulumani into a strong local, national, and even international voice of the innocent victim in quest of the healing truth.

Other women stood up and expressed their commitment to fighting for justice for all through Khulumani. The truth had to be told, and Khulumani seemed to be the last glimmering hope that this might happen.

There were all kinds of people present, men and women, young and old, in wheelchairs and on crutches, some still carrying bullets and shotgun pellets in their bodies. 'We took our plight to the TRC,' one woman said, 'and they told us to forgive and forget. How can we, when justice against the perpetrators has not been done?'

Duma arrived with Bishop Verryn. The warm reception given to this white 'father' assured one that the members of Khulumani harboured no racial animosity in their quest for the truth and redress. It was obvious they trusted him with their pain, and derived invaluable spiritual support from him. The closure ceremony went on, with prayers and speeches, encouraging the families to 'release' their loved ones and accept their absence. Later, a second ceremony took place at MaMokoena's. Then the members congregated at the Catholic church for a meal of pap, boerewors and T-bone steak.

It had been difficult to pin Duma down with all the work that he is involved in. We had spoken a few times in between his appointments. He was either meeting Khulumani donors or taking them on township tours – 'So that unlike most of our government representatives, they should see for themselves what is happening', organising group counselling sessions or helping victims with applications for assistance. Even at the church in Zone 12, he excused himself at one point to make an announcement that some foreign government or organisation had donated wheelchairs, and people were asked to identify victims of violence who needed them so that they could apply. But despite such interruptions, we were eventually able to resume our talk about the TRC and other things.

'Who is the victim?' he had asked during one of our earlier meetings. 'The dead person or the survivor?' And, since he had raised the question, he had to give his own opinion, which was that, until the survivor achieves some psychological closure, he or she remains a victim of an act of injustice as long as it is not redressed. The victim of an unredressed injustice becomes a weight on the consciences of both the perpetrators and those who have the power of redress, but do not apply it.

Duma said that the one thing he would go on demanding, for the rest of his life, if it took that long, was his total exoneration from the murder of Councillor Jacob Khuzwayo Dlamini. He wanted a retrial, to establish objectively the innocence he had always vehemently averred.

Duma seemed to treat his life before 3 September 1984 as an insignificant phase. He said little about it, beyond the fact that he had wanted to be a teacher because employment without a profession was not very secure, and he made some general comments about the experiences of his contemporaries. But he did not have to be prodded to speak about his life after that fateful day.

The uprising in the Vaal Triangle of September 1984 began as a protest against rent increases proposed by the black local authority. On the morning of 3 September, twenty-six-year-old Duma Khumalo, 'an aimless student teacher, innocent of any politics and interested only in fun and girls', followed a crowd of Sharpeville residents to the house of Councillor Dlamini. They intended to frogmarch him to the township's administration offices to address their problems.

When Duma approached the councillor's house, he was firing a gun at the scattering crowd. Duma also ran for cover. In the mêlée, he gave first aid to someone who had been shot in the leg. By the time the notorious Riot Squad arrived on the scene, it was too late to contain the situation. In retaliation against the shooting, the mob had killed the councillor and torched his house and car.

On 5 September, two days after Dlamini's tragic death, Duma was picked up at his home by the security police. Machabane Theresa Ramashamola, the only female accused among the Sharpeville Six, was in one of a convoy of police cars. She said to him, 'Don't worry. We're coming back.'

'Wat sê jy, bitch?' a white security policeman snapped. 'What are you saying?'

Along with several others who had been picked up at random, Duma and Theresa were detained without trial under section 29 of the Terrorism Act.

Duma's interrogation was brief. He was asked, 'Wat weet jy?' [What do you know?] He answered, 'Niks.' [Nothing.] 'Jy gaan 'n baie lang tyd alleen bly,' was the promise. [You are going to be alone for a very long time.]

Duma knew that the security police could lock him up and forget about him, and he had a premonition of where he might end up if he were charged with the councillor's murder. Outraged by being picked on for nothing, he immediately tried to commit suicide by grinding and swallowing some glass, but although this made him bleed a little, it did him no serious harm.

Three days later, he was transferred from Vereeniging police station to Diepkloof Prison in Soweto, alias 'Sun City', and put in an isolation cell. Other 'political prisoners' from different factions, including Umkhonto we Sizwe and the Azanian People's Liberation Army (the armed wings of the African National Congress and the Pan-Africanist Congress respectively) and Inkatha, were being held in cells leading off the same corridor.

'At first it was quiet and I spent day and night wondering why I had been picked on,' Duma recalls. 'Was it Theresa who had taken the security police to my home? If so, why?' He tried to remember minute details of the events of 3 September, and could not find anything that would incriminate him.

The claustrophobic isolation cells were hot, and the detainees complained. The prison officials obliged by removing the shatter-proof glass peepholes from the doors to let in some air. Whether this was to allow the authorities to eavesdrop on the prisoners, nobody knew. The opportunity to shout across to other detainees through the door was a welcome relief. Voices started recognising one another and calling one another by name, although their owners had never seen one another before. There were heated political debates and arguments, from which Duma gradually began to understand the South African political arena.

He listened to all sides and wondered why, when the voices in here all agreed that the enemy was apartheid, they massacred one another on the outside.

Maybe belonging to a political organisation would have helped to get him out of this fix? Although the politicals nearly always wound up on the gallows, or on Robben Island for life or long stretches. He tried as hard as he could to resist thinking about conviction because, in the first place, he had done nothing wrong. The security police would come to their senses and release him. He would convince them, with nothing but the truth, that they had made a mistake.

The two months Duma spent at Sun City felt like two decades. In the running conversation among the detainees, he discovered that one could pay a visit outside to see if the world still existed by reporting ill, or better still, by claiming one had a tooth that needed to be extracted immediately. Some detainees lost several teeth this way.

Duma tried the same trick, and it worked perfectly the first time. The Jewish doctor he was taken to surprised him by assuring him that he would not die. The second time he decided to sacrifice a tooth, things went smoothly until he was returned to detention. Then the handcuffs couldn't be unlocked. He was taken to the prison workshop, where an oxyacetylene flame was used to cut them off. Of course, his wrists were fried in the process, and he screamed like hell.

Naturally, the detainees resorted to the only weapon they had to demand that they were charged or released: their own bodies. They went on a hunger strike. After several days, the prison officials brought in some irresistible delicacies, and the strike was soon forgotten.

At the end of two months, Duma was taken from his cell and transported to Krugersdorp's Oberholzer Court. There he learned for the first time that he had been held under section 29 for making petrol bombs, which he knew nothing about. Then he and some other detainees were released.

For eight of them, including Duma and Theresa, freedom was brief. They were immediately rearrested and formally charged with murder, subversion and public violence, without bail. Some other detainees, who were granted bail although they had confessed to assault, would turn up later as state witnesses.

So Duma embarked on the most profound emotional experience of his life.

On 23 September 1985, a little more than a year after they were first detained, the eight went on trial in the Pretoria High Court. Day after day, they listened helplessly as primed state witnesses recited damning evidence against them. There were many discrepancies in this evidence. For instance, one witness said that he had seen Duma pouring petrol into Dlamini's house through a window. Another said that he had seen Duma pushing Dlamini's car out of the yard before it was burned. Which of the two was right? The court seemed to believe they were both right somehow, and their *pro deo* defence did very little to expose the contradictions.

Even more distressing than the false evidence was the fact that the co-accused started turning against one another. Each now wished that the others would take the rap, as it became obvious that not just their freedom but their lives were at stake.

On 13 December, six of the original eight were found guilty on all charges and sentenced to death.[2] The judge found them guilty of murder by 'common purpose'. They could not believe it. They thought the state was only frightening them, just showing what might happen if people were careless with other people's lives.

After passing sentence, the judge remarked that there had been perjury in the evidence relating to accused number seven and eight, one of whom was Duma, and that there were doubts about the guilt of all the accused. When their lawyers sought to lodge an immediate application for a retrial, the judge said he did not have the power to overturn his own judgement, which he had already passed. The six were doomed.

Death row is like hell's or heaven's waiting room. There is a dignified air about the place and its inhabitants. Of course, there are loudmouths and jokers too, but everybody knows there is no anaesthetic for the painful emptiness that suddenly engulfs one. Duma says it seems as if the soul leaves the body the moment one is condemned and watches the body from a distance, waiting for eventual release.

After some time, you get used to the prison sounds and smells that punctuate the humdrum routine, as well as the sounds of motor cars and trains from outside, and the soul goes out there on the wings of the imagination. You make reluctant friends with the warders. Your people visit and cry, and you try to console them by telling them that you are going to heaven. The church sends a priest, who tells you to forgive them, for they know not what they do. Like Jesus. You know very well that this is different: the apartheid government and its judiciary know exactly what they are doing. But you don't want to lose a friend, when you already have so few and such a little time to live. You have resigned yourself to your bad luck and you almost look forward to the last day. The faces around you are no longer condemned prisoners, as they are called, but people, human beings. You are a community.

Yet there is no love in prison. The love you feel is buried deep inside your soul, and you hate it when it surfaces in your consciousness, because you know that you will never be able to express it if they really mean to hang you. In spite of that, you can't help thinking about your loved ones, and you can't tell them not to come and see you, because that is their right.

The Sharpeville Six, as they became known, spent more than two years on death row. Two of the six lodged an appeal against their sentence, which took two years to run its course, and then was turned down. Meanwhile, outrage was growing around the world. The families of the condemned prisoners sent deputations to the United Nations. There were protests involving the Anti-Apartheid Movement, Amnesty International, the South African Council of Churches and the World Council of Churches, all aimed at blocking the execution.

On 14 March 1988, they were informed that they would be executed four days later. In the coming days, the prisoners were weighed and their necks measured, in preparation for the hanging. Looking back, Theresa would remember this as the most horrifying moment of all. International protest reached a crescendo. On 17 March, just twenty-four hours before they were due to die, P.W. Botha finally succumbed to the pressure and granted the Sharpeville Six a stay of execution.

On 23 September, they were removed from death row. Strangely enough, Duma missed it. 'The clemency cells were worse than the death row cells. There was no singing, no noise at all.' The words of a death row warder kept ringing in his head: 'Jy's so maer, ons gaan jou vetmaak voordat jy hang.' [You're so thin, we're going to fatten you up before you hang.] Even then, Duma resolved to set the record straight if he ever got out of prison, and this would grow steadily into an obsession.

On 23 November, their death sentences were commuted to twenty-five-year prison terms. They refused. The deal was improved to eighteen years' imprisonment with reductions for good behaviour. Final offer. They signed with great reluctance, because this amounted to an admission of guilt on all the trumped-up charges that had put them in this life-and-death predicament.

Some three years later, on 10 July 1991, they were released as part of a politically negotiated deal.

But that was not the end of the story, at least not for Duma Khumalo. They had all been stigmatised with a gruesome murder they did not commit. Their chances of resuming normal, productive lives had been drastically compromised by their ordeal – spiritually, psychologically and materially. When the political fanfare surrounding their case was over, who would employ a former death row inmate? The only credible redress for Duma was nothing less than a retrial, which would give them a second chance to prove their innocence.

However, his five co-accused were so relieved at being saved from the noose that they simply wanted to walk away from the past, or to cash in on it by selling their stories to the media for a pittance. Duma was not impressed. He wanted his name cleared before he could resume his life as a free man.

He wrote a letter to the state president, F.W. de Klerk, requesting his intervention, to no avail. He wrote to the minister of justice, Kobie Coetzee. In 1995, after consulting Legal Aid, which referred him to lawyer Tony Richards, Duma decided on a protest action. He would deliver a written request for a retrial to the chief justice, care of the Sharpeville police station, and wait there until he received a reply.

The white policemen mocked him as he sat in the charge office, day in and day out, asking him why he did not go to Mandela, for whom he had nearly been hanged. Thanks to the support of Tony Richards, he was not thrown out of the police station. Some of the black policemen appeared to sympathise, advising him to eat well and exercise, so that he would be strong for his campaign.

Dr Fazel Randera of the TRC visited Duma during his protest and explained how the Truth Commission would be able to help him. The TRC had already been announced by then. But Duma could not wait for a process that would only start the following year.

He maintained the sit-in for sixteen days, without any reply to his request.

When his protest began to attract media attention, Duma was taken to the Vereeniging magistrates' court to discuss the matter with the chief magistrate. The magistrate embarked on an irrelevant explanation of why and under which laws Duma had been sentenced, and also ended up by asking why he did not go to Mandela.

This was the last straw. On the morning of 5 January 1996, Duma took an axe, went to the magistrates' court, and chopped Court B to splinters as an expression of 'disgust and contempt' for apartheid justice.

Violence begets violence, Duma says, when there is no relief from the anger that it stimulates in a victim. This is how he sees the incident in Court B. All the psychological, spiritual and physical violence he had been subjected to since 5 September 1984 exploded in an act of temporary madness. He is grateful that his anger was directed at inanimate objects rather than human beings.

He was promptly arrested and charged with malicious damage to property. Bail was set at R2 000, which he did not have, and so he was jailed. Tony Richards subsequently managed to have the bail lowered to R200, and it was paid by the Catholic Church. It was during the trial that Gill Eagle, who had been Duma's psychologist when he was first released, came to court and asked him to join Khulumani instead of fighting a lone battle. Duma joined.

The Truth and Reconciliation Commission was a beacon of hope for Duma, especially as it was going to be chaired by Archbishop Desmond Tutu. Not only did Tutu have first-hand knowledge of apartheid injustice, but in the first half of the eighties he had headed the South African Council of Churches, which had contributed immensely to the fight for the lives of the Sharpeville Six. Expectantly, Duma submitted his statement to the TRC. Maybe the truth would come out at last and he could resume his life with a clean slate.

He desperately needed a new start. His private life was not going very well. He carried two burdens of shame with him. He was regarded as a murderer who had callously deprived a family of its breadwinner, and he felt this keenly – 'especially when I see his destitute children.' He was also an adult who could not fend for himself, and depended on his wife for everything. After his release from prison, he had fathered a child, born, by an ironic coincidence, on 18 March, the same date on which he would have been hanged the previous year. It added to his unhappiness that he could not support his child. 'I started stealing items from the house to sell, so that I could give the semblance of contributing to the family livelihood by bringing some food.'

The ordeal of the Sharpeville Six was revisited in detail at the TRC hearing on 5 August 1996, which was held at the Vaal Technikon in Sebokeng. Even this event troubled Duma. His attendance might create the impression that he was seeking some kind of amnesty, when in fact he had never been guilty of anything. The people who had railroaded him onto death row were also not present to hear him insist on his innocence. And finally, his five co-accused had deserted him, so there was no one from his side to corroborate his evidence.

A documentary was being made about the TRC, in which former adversaries were brought face to face. Duma wanted to meet the prosecutor who had condemned him. This man, who had since become a judge, refused at first, but later changed his mind and met with Duma at the Union Buildings. Duma was surprised by the humility he had assumed, and also by how fast he had aged over the years. The judge claimed that he had gone into private practice after the Sharpeville Six case, and saved three lives from the gallows. He then confessed to Duma: 'In your case, I was pushed to ask for the death penalty.'

All in all, the TRC was a dismal and disillusioning experience for Duma. It had no powers to order a retrial, and could neither remove the stigma of murder nor help him to support his family. He was told in no uncertain terms by an official that the Commission was not a welfare organisation for the victims of apartheid.

Would some form of reparation ease his pain? Duma answers that he has come to realise, through his own experience and his work at Khulumani, that no amount of money can repair a wounded soul. No amount of money can bring a dead relative back to life or restore a lost limb. 'Only care, only we can grant one another reparation through care. Unfortunately, there are very few who know this or care enough. South Africans forget too easily, too quickly, except the surviving victims. I don't know about the perpetrators and their false witnesses.'

He thinks that the reparations of R800 million, announced in the budget address of the minister of finance, Trevor Manuel, at the beginning of 2001, should have been invested in long-term projects to provide employment for the victims of apartheid or their families. Otherwise, the money will just be a way for the judicial system to wash its hands.

Duma also thinks that reconciliation without justice is a strange, impractical notion. He says, 'There can be no absolute reconciliation between victim and perpetrator unless absolute justice is applied to repair the wrong that has been done to the victim. And justice can never be attained without getting to the bottom of the truth.' When a victim sees the perpetrator going about his life as if nothing ever happened, sometimes even mocking the victim, the pain is revived and deepens. 'The greatest flaw of the TRC was the lack of justice in its formula, and this left many open wounds. The truth it uncovered was only the tip of the iceberg.'

Perhaps truth becomes too valuable to take lightly when you have nearly lost your life on the basis of a lie? Perhaps helping others to speak out becomes even more important when you know what it is to be silenced?

Khulumani is very important to Duma. His work as an assistant project manager helps him to maintain his sanity, he says, because it sometimes reduces his own experience to a mere misfortune compared to that of others. People are walking around with bullets in their bodies, children were orphaned and maimed at Boipatong, bodies lie in unmarked graves. By helping people to cope with their daily problems, he feels useful to society, in spite of the mark of Cain which the legal system seems unwilling to help him remove.

Would it be correct to describe Khulumani as a grass-roots alternative to the TRC? It is more than that, Duma says. Khulumani has gone beyond being simply a mouthpiece for the victims of apartheid. It is a vehicle for providing ongoing counselling and support, through trained counsellors. In Khulumani, the survivors of family massacres even find foster relatives, who visit them and try to see to their welfare.

I ask Duma if there is any possibility that an incident like the one with the axe could have happened again, if Khulumani had not embraced him. He smiles and says he doesn't know. All he can say is that since joining Khulumani, he can see for himself how many people need him. He is doing what he can so that life might be slightly better for the weak.

Talking with him, I am reminded of the Nguni saying that when you have a thorn in your body, you use another thorn to remove it. But perhaps that is too literal. Duma says the anguish to which he was subjected by the prospect of capital punishment will always stay with him. 'I'm free, but I'm always haunted by people who died innocent. Their faces are with us more than those we see every day.'

One of the faces that stays with him is that of nineteen-year-old Andrew Zondo, whom he mentions often. One day he was there, and the next they took him away to hang him, young as he was. 'Who was the victim?' Duma asks. 'The dead man or those who survived him?'

'What do you think?' I respond.

'The survivors, the loved ones, those who go on living with the knowledge that their son was lynched.'

Duma and the victims he serves believe that truth is futile unless it is used to determine justice. If justice is not done to both the perpetrators and the victims, there will be no closure to the experience of apartheid. Duma says that violence prevails among the 'apartheid generation' because, while people were encouraged and trained to resort to violence as a means to an end 'when necessary', there has been no subsequent attempt under democracy to teach them otherwise.

However, most of the victims, the women, the children, the aged, were merely caught in the crossfire of a conflict they did not understand. Violence always has a ripple effect. It affects the perpetrator and the victim, their relatives, associates and communities, and eventually consumes the whole society.

He thinks the current government is infested with self-serving opportunists, who undermine the people's confidence in government at all levels. Often, these so-called leaders have no idea how much other people sacrificed so that South Africa could achieve democracy. He also thinks the government does not fully appreciate the invaluable, grass-roots work done by non-governmental organisations. Otherwise they would not be begging for funds from foreign governments or winding up their activities because of a lack of resources. Rather than being discounted, the contribution made by ordinary people to the liberation struggle should be the foundation of a patriotic commitment to bettering the lives of all South Africans. This history should be a compulsory subject at school, so that children grow up knowing that our democracy was achieved through bitter struggle.

Duma sees no difference between the application of justice by the old National Party government and by the current ANC one. Justice was difficult to come by then, and it is difficult to come by now. He blames this state of affairs on the fact that while there was a constitutional transformation, there was little if any transformation in the judicial system, as it remained under the control of the same corrupt officials.

Truth and justice. At the Catholic church in Zone 12, sixteen years after the events that have become the crux of Duma's life, we talked about the relationship between the two. He had a great deal to say on the subject. His major worry was that with one crucial witness, fact or account missing, the truth would always be incomplete. And no justice could be achieved on the basis of incomplete evidence, let alone deliberately distorted evidence, as happened in his case, where a chief witness confessed that the police had forced him to lie, and the judge later confessed that he had been instructed to give a certain verdict.

'In fact,' Duma said, 'I think justice is just a word, the concept itself is an illusion, something relative to who applies it to whom. For instance, the apartheid regime regarded hanging people as ultimate justice. The present government regards it as inhumane. See? Justice depends on who applies it, from the government of the day down to the police in charge of the case, because if they want a conviction, they get one. The police write you their own version of the statement and make you sign it. They write statements for the witnesses and rehearse them, so that they make no mistakes in court. And those in power endorse the process. That's what happened to us. I'm not telling you about anybody else.'

This is how justice failed Duma Khumalo, in his own words:

'On the day Dlamini was killed, the mob itself was on its way to demand or mete out its own version of justice relating to its grievances. Whether their collective intention was peaceful or otherwise can never be ascertained. Whether the violence was triggered by Dlamini's trying to repel the mob with his gun can also never be ascertained. Fact is, those people who marched on the councillor's house were ostensibly going to seek redress for the civic injustices that they perceived in their lives. They were out to seek justice from, or vent their frustrations on, a person who represented the Vaal Administration Board, which was the bane of their lives.

'As I told you, I was a young, apolitical student teacher with no personal gripes against Dlamini. I got involved by trying to help save Dlamini's car when the house was already burning. I was identified for helping casualties of the riot. Maybe if I hadn't helped, I would never have been noticed. That hurts. That is my truth.

'Then the security police, prejudiced against any anti-government sentiment, sought their own version of justice. An apartheid government collaborator had been killed, and justice had to be seen to be done. Someone had to pay. My co-accused and I were the unfortunate ones, and you know the rest of the story.

'In our case, there were several irreconcilable versions of the truth, and therefore of justice, depending on which side you stood.

'Dlamini's enemies must have thought that some form of justice, inhumane as it was, had been achieved through his death. I thought it was tragic and unfortunate. I had seen part of what happened, my co-accused had seen their part and so had the witnesses in the case, and none of us saw the same thing. Our statements were naturally different, while those of the rehearsed witnesses corroborated each other. The police themselves formulated what they thought was the truth on speculations arising from hearsay, and they paid or coerced informers to gather evidence.

'On the other hand, Dlamini's family, friends and supporters must have felt that justice was being done when the Sharpeville Six were put on trial. They must have believed each and every word of the fabricated evidence to be the truth, although not a single thread of evidence showed directly that any of us had killed Dlamini or torched his property.

'I had no doubt that I was innocent, but I could not help feeling that perhaps, just perhaps, one or more of the others had been directly responsible for Dlamini's death. It turned out later that my co-accused were nurturing the same suspicions about me and one another.

'When we were sentenced to death, many people must have believed that the truth had been uncovered. Why else had we been found guilty? And the six of us would have taken this stigma with us to our graves but for the outcry following the sentencing, which kept my hopes alive that the real truth would eventually be dug out from the rubble of lies, and absolve us – or me, at least.

'When our lives were spared at the last moment, I told myself that they had known all along we were innocent, but I was immediately disappointed when the sentences were commuted to jail terms. That meant that we were still guilty, but were being spared through the benevolence of the apartheid government. In fact, it was then I began to suspect we might become political bargaining chips.

'We were eventually pardoned for political reasons, not because the truth had prevailed. Dlamini's family probably felt cheated and betrayed, I thought, and would always point fingers at us. The Sharpeville community, and the world at large, would remain confused as long as the real murderers were continuing freely with their lives.

'That was why I started writing letters pleading for a retrial and resorted to the courthouse sit-in, which culminated in the axe debacle. I was seeking the truth. When I failed to find it, I sought release for my pent-up anger and frustration by physically attacking the supposed symbol of justice, the court. Perhaps I was even trying to make myself really culpable by performing a criminal act, once and for all ...

'I was beyond caring, because my right to tell my own side of the story had been violated, to the point where I nearly lost my life. I needed the restoration of my integrity, at least, before I could pick up the pieces of my life. Instead, the law wanted to suggest that I was mad by referring me to psychiatric counselling, which did not help in any way, except that I discovered Khulumani and the TRC. And even the TRC turned out to be just another farce. I was not seeking amnesty, which amounted to forgiveness for a crime, but complete absolution based on the revelation of the truth. The TRC was irrelevant to my case. My only hope was that the real culprits and the false witnesses might come forward and tell the truth, and so remove the stigma I carried.

'The chances of that happening are diminishing by the day. Dlamini's family can never reconcile with me. I can never reconcile with myself nor the police, the prosecutor nor the judge, until the truth of what happened is deciphered from all the different versions and made public. That is where the matter stands with me.'

Duma was becoming impatient to get back to the meeting. After sharing their meal with us, people were singing and dancing happily in the aisles of the church, while the invalids among them clapped their hands. Duma and I could not just sit outside talking while the people were singing and dancing. We joined in.

When it was time to leave, my friends were invited to return on 21 March for the Sharpeville Day commemoration.

What conclusions can we draw from the quest for redress undertaken by individuals like Duma Khumalo or groups like Khulumani? The victims of apartheid, of the violence and injustice perpetrated in its name, have their own versions of the truth, based on their experience. The perpetrators also have their own versions, based on their political and personal motivations. The paid or coerced collaborators have their distorted versions, laced with self-interest. The wider communities within which these acts took place have versions of their own. From this jigsaw puzzle, those who have the authority to arbitrate must piece together the truth. The public generally accepts the final pronouncements of the arbitrators. And that, unfortunately, is what the surviving victims must live with for the rest of their lives.

The truth has many voices, and it is often the loudest one, rather than the most deserving, that gets heard.

Notes

1. This text is based on an interview with Duma Khumalo, conducted on 23 February 2001 at the Catholic church in Zone 12, Sebokeng.
2. The four people convicted along with Duma and Theresa were Mojalefa Reginald Sefatsa, Reid Malebo Mokoena, Oupa Moses Diniso and Francis Don Mokhesi.

PART THREE

Outsider Assessments

7

THE TRC REPORT
What Kind of History? What Kind of Truth?

Deborah Posel

> Fundamental to all forms of justice is *official acknowledgement* of what happened.
>
> Justice Richard Goldstone[1]

The Truth and Reconciliation Commission's 'official acknowledgement of what happened' in South Africa from 1960 to 1994 has been a dramatic, wide-ranging process, spanning two and a half years of hearings, investigations and research, and issuing in the five-volume report presented to the state president on 29 October 1998. If the TRC's human rights and amnesty hearings represented the 'live', active, fluid, human face of its truth-finding process, the report is pre-eminently the site of the TRC's 'official' voice on the truth as found: formal, voluminous, weighty, considered, authoritative.

Spanning over 2 700 pages of text, this is a report relatively few are likely to read in anything like its entirety. It is long, unwieldy and often difficult to digest. Yet, even the bulky five volumes' worth is a highly edited distillation of the large archive assembled by the TRC which, I'm told, would overwhelm the average suburban house. Within parameters very firmly set by the enabling legislation, the TRC embarked on the 'daunting and formidable'[2] task of 'establishing as complete a picture as possible of the causes, nature and extent of the gross violations of human rights which were committed during the period from 1 March 1960 to the cut-off date [10 May 1994], including the antecedents, circumstances, factors and context of such violations, as well as the perspectives of the victims and the motives and perspectives of the persons responsible for the commission of the violations'.[3] Underscoring the vastness of this undertaking, Archbishop Tutu's Foreword to the report stresses that it offers '... a road map to those who wish to travel into our past. It is not and cannot be the whole story; but it provides a perspective on the truth about a past that is more extensive and more complex than any one commission could, in two and a half years, have hoped to capture.'[4] This comment gives rise to two sets of questions which have prompted this paper.

The first set of questions is animated by the epistemological and methodological conundrum of the TRC: how does an inherently selective writing of only part of the story about the past present itself with the authority and objectivity of truth required of an official state commission?[5] How are the concepts of 'truth' and 'objectivity' understood in this process? How are decisions made about what to cut out, what to leave in? What counts as sufficient evidence for producing definitive findings about what happened in the past?

The second set of questions concerns the version of South Africa's recent past that has emerged as a consequence of these choices. How has the story about the commission of gross human rights violations been written in the report? How 'extensive' and 'complex' is it as an historical text?

In addressing these questions, the paper begins with an exploration of the various facets of the TRC's mandate, and demonstrates three key tensions that inhere in it. The paper then examines the discourses of truth and method that are produced in the Commission's attempts to manage these tensions. And lastly, the paper traces the imprints of these discourses on what the report has written about the country's past.

In line with the genre of an official state commission, the report presents itself as the work of a team of 'observers' of the past, who assembled and collated a series of facts about gross human rights violations, to produce the objective, authorised version of the country's recent past. But a closer reading reveals a different process of knowledge production. The report contains a version of the past that has been actively crafted according to particular strategies of inclusion and exclusion, arising from the complexities of the TRC's mandate. Part epistemological and methodological, part moral, the effect of these discursive strategies is to produce a primarily descriptive rendition of the past, uneven in its discernment of detail and indifferent to the complexities of social causation. The TRC's 'truth' about the past is neither 'complex' nor particularly 'extensive' (despite its length). With little explanatory and analytical power, the report reads less as a history, more as a moral narrative about the fact of wrongdoing across the political spectrum, spawned by the overriding evil of the apartheid system. In so doing, the report goes a long way towards fulfilling one part of the Commission's mandate – but to the exclusion of others.

The Mandate

As many commentators – including the authors of the report – have stressed, the TRC's exercise in retrieving South Africa's recent past was shaped in absolutely fundamental ways by the mandate of its enabling legislation and the political moment within which it was conceived and enacted.[6] The mandate was multifaceted. The Commission was to be an excavation of truth about gross human rights violations, both in respect of individual cases presented to the Commission and more generally, by way of establishing 'systematic' local and national patterns of gross human rights violations. The truth-finding process was to be both descriptive (what happened) and explanatory (why it happened), the latter understood to involve establishing the 'antecedents' and 'causes' for gross human rights violations, as well as the 'motives and perspectives' of victims and perpetrators. Understanding why gross human rights violations had taken place was seen as crucial to the future of democracy in the country: 'It is only by accounting for the past that we can become accountable for the future.'[7]

That this was intended as a serious and ambitious pursuit was signalled by the considerable powers and resources placed at the disposal of the TRC. Its powers of subpoena, search and seizure were formidable, 'much stronger than those of other truth commissions'.[8] In theory, the Commission had unlimited access to archival materials otherwise wholly unavailable to scholars of the past. The Commission also had a budget and staff significantly larger than previous state commissions in this country, and well in excess of other truth commissions elsewhere in the world.[9] This included a sizeable Research Department.

The TRC 's mandate was also deeply moral: access to truth was to lay the foundation for a more humane, just social order, passing resolute moral judgement on the past but in ways which reconciled a previously divided society to a common future rooted in a 'respect for human rights'.[10] 'Reconciliation' itself had various dimensions, inspired by a cluster of meanings of the idea.[11] The TRC was to initiate processes of individual, interpersonal and collective 'healing', through the catharsis of finally exposing the truth about gross human rights violations previously kept hidden. Here, reconciliation was to be an affirmation of *ubuntu*, a 'recognition of the humanity of the other'. The idea of reconciliation was also explicitly tied to the project of nation-building, 'imagining' a new form of national community based on a 'collective memory', a 'shared' history. Exposure to truth was to lay the basis for a national consensus about the past and how to overcome its legacy in the future – 'some essential lessons for the future of the people of this country'.[12] Lastly, reconciliation was also understood as an act of compromise, born of the country's negotiated transition.

Itself the product of a political compromise, the TRC was seen as a crucial vehicle for attempting to stabilise and reproduce the politics of transitional justice.

Finally, all of this was to be undertaken 'as expeditiously as possible',[13] within a period of two years.

Ensuing Tensions for the Encounter with the Past

The TRC's mandate was not simply vast; it straddled at least three internal tensions, arising from the conflicting pressures that moulded the Commission's efforts to write the past.[14] Let us deal with each of these tensions in turn.

Achieving 'Objectivity' While Acknowledging Contending Subjectivities

The legitimacy and credibility of the TRC as an official, authoritative account of the recent past rested profoundly on a demonstrable objectivity and impartiality. With rival political parties angling to accuse the whole enterprise of bias, Commissioners had to elevate the TRC above the political realm into a domain uncontaminated by such differences and disputes.[15] The quasi-judicial character of the TRC as an official state commission was crucial, offering a range of signifiers for a sober, thoughtful and impartial set of proceedings. The TRC's report was presented in a similar vein, as 'a comprehensive report ... based on factual and objective information and evidence collected or received by [the Commission] or placed at its disposal'.[16] At the same time, however, the TRC began from the recognition of a deeply conflictual past, which produced competing perspectives, judgements and versions of what had happened and why – particularly in respect of the highly charged issues of violence and violation. As the report put it, 'the telling of the truth about past gross human rights violations, as viewed from different perspectives, facilitates the process of understanding our divided pasts'.[17]

The TRC, then, had to contain the tensions between two different notions of historical knowledge. On the one hand, the past was the site of contending constructions and perspectives, each 'truthful' to those who proposed it. On the other hand, the past was a procession of 'facts', visible from the elevated and perspicacious vantage point of the Commission. By 'collecting' and 'receiving' these data, the authors of the report were to write the past in a way that transcended conflicting perspectives; the official truth had to be one to which all South Africans would consent, as an authoritative, impartial account.

The 'healing' function of the TRC brought this tension to the fore in yet another way. If the TRC was to produce the 'official', authorised verdict on the past, it also had to legitimate the voices and perspectives of victims whose stories had not previously been told, allowing that their intense pain and suffering automatically gave a certain authenticity to their version of events. This was their 'truth', and the Commission had to acknowledge it. Even more than this, the TRC pledged to allocate a special place to these testimonies in the overall structure of its proceedings. Central to its 'healing' mission was a commitment to a 'victim-centred' process, which would allow the victims of gross human rights violations to tell their own stories, thereby restoring their dignity and humanity.

Competing Versions of 'Completeness'

At the outset, the TRC issued an open invitation to all South Africans to tell their stories of gross human rights violations, in the knowledge that in the three and a bit decades spanned by the commission, there were many thousands of previously untold stories to tell.[18] The enabling legislation required that the Commission accept statements from all South Africans who wished to make them, and committed the TRC to documenting these narratives in a 'report providing as comprehensive an account as possible of the activities and findings of the Commission ...'[19] In many communities, this prospect created high expectations: people saw the TRC as an opportunity to piece together a comprehensive and detailed account of turbulent and divisive episodes in their histories, to clarify exactly who had been responsible for past traumas, how and why these had been inflicted, and to dispel any lingering doubts about who had or had not been an informer[20] – a particularly sensitive issue for many communities. These are expectations which squared with, and indeed validated, the Commission's commitment to the catharsis of truth-telling, as the basis of reconciliation at an interpersonal and community level.

Yet, the TRC's thinking was simultaneously subject to a different logic about how much of the past it was necessary to expose. If the idea of individual, interpersonal and communal catharsis validated the impulse towards completeness, the version of reconciliation as a national break with a divisive past pulled in a different direction. This nation-building exercise – creating a 'shared' national history – did not require a comprehensive, detailed narration of individual and community histories. The goal was rather to produce enough truth to demonstrate and exemplify the inequities of the past. A sample of the truth rather than the whole would suffice to establish the desired consensus. From this perspective, the global truth about the past was, in a fundamental sense, 'already known'. As Commissioner Mary Burton put it,

> a commission of truth ... must gather in stories to reach that truth which is, in a way, already widely known and accepted. But we need to make it legitimate through that process. We need to tell and record and validate that truth. We need to acknowledge the wrongs, not only in terms of justice and hurt but also the terrible loss.[21]

Here, the historical exercise was primarily to narrate a moral truth about wrongdoing, conflict and injustice, and it was one which could be represented effectively by a relatively small number of carefully selected individual cases that exemplified collective 'truths'. Indeed, the danger to be avoided was exactly that of 'overly individualis[ing] the horrors of apartheid and provid[ing] merely a piecemeal picture of the past, at the expense of necessary attention to its systemic and collective evils'.[22]

The politics of the TRC created additional reasons for a deliberately attenuated, rather than a 'complete', version of the past. The Commission acknowledged from the start that it was poised on a knife-edge, mandated to expose truths in the interests of 'reconciliation' but in the knowledge that the exposure could provoke pain, anger and further violence just as readily as impulses to forgive and 'reconcile'. The new state itself was walking a political tightrope in respect of the conflict between the African National Congress and the Inkatha Freedom Party, which created a further difficulty for the TRC. Writing a chapter about a violent past which continued to engulf the present could have worsened the conflict still further. From the start, the IFP had registered its contempt for the TRC process and refused to participate, in the midst of renewed eruptions of violent conflict in KwaZulu-Natal. The TRC had to assert its moral authority through its powers of truth-telling, yet not overexpose the past in ways that might exacerbate the problems of the present.

The tension between writing the history of gross human rights violations as a series of essential exemplars, rather than as a comprehensive record, in turn implied competing versions of the very purpose of history and its relevance to the future. From the perspective of nation-building, the TRC has the status of an event, rather than an ongoing process of disclosure over many years. As Asmal et al. put it, 'the TRC's best chance to change the nation's paradigm of itself [is] through a short, sharp hammer blow of a new beginning ... The TRC ... must not become ensnared in the banalities of subpoena and cross-examination, nor in the narrow business of determining individual guilt or innocence. We already have the courts to do that. Nor must the TRC convert itself or some form of itself, into a permanent bureaucracy ... [this] would let boredom in upon magic.'[23] By contrast, the commitment to producing an increasingly comprehensive record of the past implies an acceptance that the TRC is a beginning rather than the end of an encounter with history, one which has no necessary deadline or schedule.

Ambiguities in the Object of Historical Inquiry

The tension between writing 'as complete' an account of the past 'as possible' and merely distilling some 'essential' exemplars was magnified by the ambiguities in the TRC's object of historical inquiry. The TRC's truth-telling mandate was partly descriptive (what had happened, when, who had done it), partly explanatory (why, with regard to structural, institutional causes as well as motives and perspectives of relevant historical actors). In respect of the first part, the TRC's object of inquiry was strictly limited to gross human rights violations, rather than human rights violations in their entirety. And a precise definition of gross human rights violations was provided, so as to exclude many of the routines of apartheid degradation and humiliation from the TRC's ambit (a feature that has attracted intense criticism from various commentators, notably Mahmood Mamdani). From this vantage point, the apartheid system itself was not the subject of the TRC's investigations; rather, it was the 'background',[24] the 'political landscape' on which the picture of gross human rights violations was to be painted. However, the TRC was also expected to account for why gross human rights violations had been perpetuated, placing individual actions in their broader structural and institutional context. This *did* require an engagement with the apartheid system, not merely as the 'backdrop' but as the source of gross human rights violations. The nature of apartheid was simultaneously mere background to the Commission's investigations and absolutely central to its findings.

How Did the TRC Manage these Tensions?

The nub of each of these tensions was epistemological and methodological, in some respects not unlike the routine challenges confronting practising historians: how to reconcile conflicting versions of the past; how to paint a national picture that takes sufficient account of regional or local specifics; how to adjudicate between different types of historical evidence (particularly the tensions between oral and written modes of recording the past). But they confronted the TRC in a particular form: how to construct knowledge about the past in a form that satisfied a range of competing criteria of adequacy and validity arising from the different facets of its mandate?

One of the striking and unusual features of the report is the extent to which its authors reflect explicitly on their (perceived) epistemological and methodological options. There cannot be many official state commissions that ponder the question of the possibility of objective knowledge,[25] explore the meaning of 'truth',[26] invoke historical sociologist Max Weber as a methodological role model,[27] and render their research process as a 'dialectical encounter' with disparate sets of data.[28] Yet, for all this, the dominant epistemological and methodological underpinnings of the report are conventional fare for the genre of the official state commission.

A Rainbow of Truths

The Commission was mandated to acknowledge the contestedness of history and yet deliver the authoritative, official verdict on the recent past. Unusually for a state commission, the report names the problem of truth at the outset:

> But what about truth – and whose truth? The complexity of this concept ... emerged in the debates that took place before and during the life of the Commission ...[29]

The solution presented in the report is to differentiate between 'four notions of truth: factual or forensic truth; personal or narrative truth; social or "dialogue" truth ... and healing and restorative truth'.[30] As spelt out in the report, 'factual or forensic truth' refers to the 'familiar legal or scientific notion of bringing to light factual, corroborated evidence, of obtaining accurate information through reliable (impartial, objective) procedures'.[31] This sort of truth, argues the report, pertains to both 'findings on an individual level' and the more general findings on the 'contexts, causes and patterns of violations'. This, we are told, is the 'social scientist's approach' of 'analys[ing], interpret[ing] and draw[ing] inferences from the information ... received'.[32] According to the report, this is the notion of truth directly implicated in the TRC's mandate to produce a 'comprehensive report ... based on factual and objective information'.[33]

Yet, for the sorts of reasons identified earlier, there were other aspects of the Commission's mandate which required an acknowledgement that the stuff of history is subjectively and inter-subjectively constructed. To take account of this, three additional types of truth are then suggested.[34] First, the process of personal storytelling is deemed to generate its own type of truth: 'personal and narrative truth.' The concept is not defined explicitly, but invokes such ideas as 'the validation of the individual subjective experiences of people who had previously been silenced or voiceless'; 'captur[ing] the widest possible record of people's perceptions, stories, myths and experiences'; and 'recover[ing] parts of the national memory that had hitherto been officially ignored'.[35]

Another type of truth posited is 'social truth', which is defined by Justice Albie Sachs as 'the truth of experience that is established through interaction, discussion and debate', and is regarded by the report as the type of truth that embodies 'the closest connection between the Commission's process and its goal'. Social truth is to be found in 'try[ing] to transcend the divisions of the past by listening carefully to the complex motives and perspectives of all those involved'. Establishing this type of truth, it was stressed, 'could not be divorced from the affirmation of the dignity of human beings. Thus, not only the actual outcome or findings of an investigation counted. The process whereby the truth was reached was itself important because it was through this process that the essential norms of social relations between people were reflected.[36]

Finally, the report specifies a fourth type of truth, originating in a rejection of 'the popular assumption that there are only two options to be considered when talking about truth – namely factual, objective information or subjective opinions. There is also "healing" truth, the kind of truth that places facts and what they mean within the context of human relationships – both amongst citizens and between the state and its citizens. This kind of truth was central to the Commission.' 'Healing' truth is necessary because it 'was not enough simply to determine what had happened. Truth as factual, objective information cannot be divorced from the way in which this information is acquired; nor can such information be separated from the purposes it is required to serve.[37]

This is a very wobbly, poorly constructed conceptual grid. The grounds for differentiating the four types of truth are poorly specified and remain rather opaque. For example, the marker of 'healing truth'(putting truth in the context of human relationships) seems largely to reiterate the criterion for social truth (reflecting the essential norms of social relations). And the notion of 'healing truth' is defined in a way that undermines the very possibility of factual or forensic truth, rather than as constituting an additional 'type' of truth alongside it. If '[t]ruth as factual, objective information cannot be divorced from the way in which this information is acquired ... [or] the purposes it is required to serve', then the earlier definition of factual or forensic truth does not make sense. More generally, the differentiation between various types and sites of evidence is elided with the case for qualitatively different types of truth.[38] Moreover, definitional problems aside, the typology of truths *restates* the original challenge of how to manage the tensions between competing versions of the past. If the 'forensic' version of events is at odds with the 'social' truth in any particular community, on what basis is the conflict to be adjudicated?

The report's foray into epistemology stops short of considering these questions of how one type of truth relates to or impacts upon another. This is no surprise, because the tacit logic of the exercise is to separate the four 'types' of truth into apparently distinct, unrelated sorts of undertakings. For herein lies an apparently neat resolution to the dilemma of truth-telling confronting the TRC. Different facets of the Commission's mandate seem each to be taken care of by means of a distinct type and standard of truth, each of which services a particular type of 'reconciliation'. Giving individual victims a voice in the hearings illustrates the TRC's commitment to personal truth; getting victims and perpetrators to speak to each other and hear each other's perspectives is an instance of social truth; creating a forum for national reconciliation enacts healing truth; and the report becomes an exercise in factual or forensic truth. Seemingly, then, each type of truth would have its place in the proceedings, thereby managing to reconcile subjective, inter-subjective, contextual and objective truths as though they were unrelated, separate sorts of pursuits.

On this basis, the report then proceeds to take a conventionally positivist stance on the source of its own authority as the official, objective version of the past. Presenting four distinct types of truth allows the Commission's written report to preserve its status as the official, impartial, disengaged verdict on the past: factual or forensic truth is distinguished as that type of truth which is *not* embedded in social relations or social norms, and which is *not* established through dialogue and interaction. So the judgements on the past written in the report are delivered as the deliberations of 'the onlooker, the outsider, the observer, the recorder, the evaluator, the scientist'.[39] If the impact of varying and competing subjectivities is felt in oral testimony (the realm of the hearings), the written text gives expression to an objectivity that is seemingly divested of subjective intrusions or contaminations. Findings on gross human rights violations are presented in quasi-judicial form, as impartial verdicts on the past. The apartheid 'context' within which gross human rights violations took place is written in a 'factual' mode, effacing any sense of historiographical debate or contestation (more on this later). So the contestedness of South Africa's recent past seemingly detracts little from the authority of the official commission.

There are a few moments in the report that reveal flashes of a more sophisticated position on truth. A brief footnote buried in a methodological appendix suggests that at least one of the authors of the report saw objectivity as 'knowledge that is inter-subjectively reliable, that is, knowledge ... which the involved actors can agree is held in common between them'[40] – in other words, that truth is a judgement taken by particular communities of truth-tellers (the TRC being one) according to shared norms and standards of evidence. And at another point, the reader is alerted to the Commission's heterogeneous and contested engagement with the past:

> While its overall aim is to be even-handed and as objective as possible, to view the Commission as homogeneous, as all of one piece, is a rather oversimplified approach. The Commission is made up of many people with different perspectives ... This is not to decry the efforts of the Commission to be objective. It is an honest admission that the perspective of the Commission and its members is a complex one.[41]

This version of the report treats it as a more contested, contextual and interpretative exercise than the detached findings of 'the onlooker, the outsider, the observer'. It begins to blur the earlier typology of distinct, unrelated truths, which treats subjectivity and objectivity as unrelated modes of knowing. But this position is marginal in the report as a whole, which resolutely reproduces the discourse of factual, forensic truth as its vantage point on the past.

Trying to Make a Little Go a Long Way

One of the other epistemological and methodological dilemmas deriving from the TRC's mandate was how to capture the vast and complex phenomenon of gross human rights violations for the period 1960 to 1994, accounting for what happened and why, but without succumbing to the sort of detail that was morally unnecessary, politically inexpedient and unduly time-consuming.[42]

Processes of selection, summary, truncation and exclusion were fundamental to the workings of the TRC. Overwhelmed by the vastness of its mandate, the TRC sought to transform it into a more manageable undertaking. Some of these choices were more ad hoc, reactive and contested than others. Nevertheless, in aggregate, these methodological judgements in turn had a profound effect in shaping the TRC's discourse on the past as written up in the report.

The TRC's starting point on this front was to treat local cases as instances of national patterns. Overwhelmed by the 21 298 statements taken in respect of nearly 38 000 gross human rights violations, the TRC hearings showcased a sample, crafted on the basis of a careful political balancing act, reflecting the diversity of the victims (representing different ages, races and genders), a regional and historical spread of cases, and a commitment to even-handedness (reflecting gross human rights violations across the political spectrum, from the right wing to the left).[43] The TRC report then distilled, selected and summarised even further: 'It was not possible to include every case brought to the Commission;

rather the stories that illustrate particular events, trends and phenomena have been used as windows on the experiences of many people.'[44] The idea of opening exemplary 'windows' on the past also governed the selection of ten 'event hearings', which 'aimed to provide detailed insights into particular incidents that were representative of broader patterns of abuse'.[45]

The strategy of creating 'window cases' is recast in the report under the rubric of Weberian social science. This Weberian flirtation begins by endorsing the view that to understand gross human rights violations requires inserting them into a context formed by 'the relevant web of social networks and contingent cultural meanings'. This position, in line with the Weberian idea of *verstehen,* overcomes the limitations of 'decontextualised ... human rights reporting' and purely quantitative analysis of trends in the commission of gross human rights violations.[46]

In response, the report calls for 'methodological pluralism', identifying a seeming coincidence between Max Weber's notion of sociological method and the mandate of the Commission:

> Like the Commission, ... Weber recommends that analysts identify general factors in the universe of examples by applying ideal types – 'controlled and unambiguous conceptions' – which illuminate particular phenomena of study. However, the general factors must be understood in terms of the particularities of individual cases. This definition of a set of 'ideal types' is then applied to a universe of narrative (or semi-structured) statements taken in interviews with deponents ... At the Commission, the data processing teams implemented these 'ideal types', using a controlled vocabulary and a coding frame. The teams coded deponents' statements in standard forms before capturing the information on the database.[47]

Supposedly following Weber, the report then calls for a two-pronged process of researching gross human rights violations in the past: a method of 'ethnography' is needed to produce an understanding of the 'relevant social networks and contingent cultural meanings' in terms of which to make sense of individual cases; a process of typification then allows for a quantitative analysis of general trends and patterns. And here, seemingly, is a neat and efficient match between a respectably scientific methodological pluralism and dual facets of the TRC's mandate: analysing the 'context, motives and perspectives' leading to gross human rights violations requires 'historical or ethnographic reflection', while exposing 'systematic patterns' in gross human rights violations 'implies a quantitative treatment'.[48]

Invoking Max Weber might lend an air of methodological rigour and authority to the proceedings, but the parallels are ultimately spurious, in ways that reveal much about the limits of the TRC's research process and its powers of historical explanation. What Weber had in mind was to *link* ethnographic interpretations of the subjective meanings of social actions with a causal analysis of the measurable patterns in social behaviour across groups or societies at large. This, for Weber, would enable an explanation of why particular patterns of subjective meanings ('perspectives', in the language of the TRC) emerged at particular times and with particular effects. As a scientist, his goal was to understand the broader impersonal, structural constraints on how people thought and acted. His notion of ideal types was therefore intended to make fuller sense of individual cases by linking them to more general causative patterns. The TRC, however, proceeds along a rather different path. A great deal of time and effort seem to have gone into developing methods of data capture and coding which would facilitate the production of quantified trends in gross human rights violations. Individual cases of gross human rights violations were coded according to their 'type', and patterns in their occurrence were then quantified.[49] This exercise in quantification then produces a series of national and regional surveys of gross human rights violations, periodised according to the types and prevalence of these violations and disaggregated by age, race and gender. But the quantification bears little or no relationship to the narration of individual cases, other than in providing the basis for a (descriptive) periodisation. In the report, the quantitative data are presented as a preface to the national and regional 'profiles' of gross human rights violations, which narrate what happened and produce the TRC's judgements about who was responsible for them. But there is no explanatory link between the two kinds of exercises. The impulse of Weberian methodology, of understanding *why* individuals act the way they do by inserting their actions into a broader causal context, is stillborn.

Oddly, the report deals with the issue of 'motives and causes' in a separate chapter, also unrelated to the narration of gross human rights violations and the allocation of responsibility for them. This chapter contains a general discussion setting out different possible ways of explaining motives, ranging from 'the primacy of the political motive', through the idea of 'individualistic psychological explanations' (spanning 'human nature', 'psychological abnormalities', 'authoritarianism') to the idea of 'social identities' (including de-individuation, masculinity), ending up with a reminder that 'ideology is a form of power in which meaning (signification) serves to sustain and reproduce relations of domination'. Well, so what? In general terms, the chapter considers all of these factors relevant; in concrete terms, little if any of this is demonstrated, because this chunk of introductory psychology and sociology remains disconnected from the rest of the report.

The report's pseudo-Weberian method is responsible, then, for the unwieldy structure of the five volumes. Its text on the past reads as a rather disconnected compilation of discrete chunks of information: quantitative surveys of national and regional patterns of gross human rights violations; a disembodied general discussion of different approaches to understanding the motives and perspectives of the victims and perpetrators; 'background' sketches of the apartheid past; and narratives of cases of gross human rights violations and the findings reached about them. What the report lacks is an attempt to integrate and synthesise these into a unified analysis.[50] Instead, severing 'motive' from 'cause', and disconnecting both from the narration of individual cases, the report deprives itself of one of the essential tools of historical analysis.

As a consequence, the report reads as an often bland, largely descriptive account of what happened, when and how. One of the striking features of these narratives is that they convey almost nothing of 'social networks and contingent cultural meanings'. These are relegated to what the report calls the 'richness' of local histories which reside in the TRC's archives, beyond the realm of the report itself. Despite the notional commitment to an 'ethnographic' project, it seems to have been marginalised by the energy and effort that went into the quantitative research exercise – a point underscored by Commissioner Wynand Malan in his Minority Position submitted to the Commission.[51]

The descriptive recounting of what, when and how things happened is subject to other strategies of inclusion and exclusion. In respect of the few cases selected for the report, highly edited, condensed accounts of events and their context have been given. They have been pieced together, drawing on combinations of individual testimony and statements made in amnesty and gross human rights violations hearings, other victim statements, primary research undertaken within the Commission, and the occasional piece of secondary historical research. It is never clear why some aspects of the broader picture are deemed relevant and not others; nor why some scholars and not others are cited. But this raises the bigger question: how much information was considered 'enough' and according to what criteria of sufficiency?

The report has written the past history of gross human rights violations in a form that passes decisive moral judgements in respect of responsibility for these violations. The tacit criterion for deciding how much history is 'enough' was 'enough, in the eyes of various Commissioners and/or authors of the report, to pass moral judgement'. The report is written in such a way that findings allocating responsibility for gross human rights violations are the conclusions of narratives about what happened; there is no evidence for the findings over and above the narrative as it is presented. So the narrative produces the findings; but this also means that the narrative has been shaped by what has been deemed necessary evidence for those findings. Underlying the report's claims for the authority of its findings, then, is a self-effacing, circular process in terms of which the past is recorded only insofar as it is necessary to produce moral judgement; and the only basis for these judgements is the version of the past as it is written in the report.

How much evidence is considered sufficient as the basis for producing findings about responsibility for gross human rights violations? When this question is raised early on in the report, the issue of 'justification' is regarded as crucial: 'The act in question must have been committed with the objective of countering or otherwise resisting the said struggle',[52] and should have been demonstrably the 'result of deliberate planning'.[53] The Commission also insists on tracking the chain of command: 'it must be said that those with the most power to abuse must carry the heaviest responsibility.'[54] Yet, as suggested earlier, the establishment of the motives, the 'justification', and degree of planning attached to *particular* acts of violence is one of the most conspicuous lacunae in the report. And the gap is biggest in respect of those most senior in the relevant structures of command. Admittedly, there were some large obstacles in the Commission's way. The search for relevant state archival documentation revealed the systematic destruction of official records by the apartheid state, especially during the 1990s. Also, the politics of compromise disabled a more robust, insistent effort to subpoena key decision-makers in the hierarchies of either the state or the liberation movements. But the report's silences on questions of intentionality also reflect priorities and gaps in the research process itself, with the emphasis on the quantitative data-coding exercise dwarfing the process of 'historical or ethnographic reflection'.

This does not inhibit the report from making wide-ranging moral indictments, across the political spectrum. The amount of information and degree of detail accompanying these findings vary enormously, with some regions subject to a far fuller account than others and some findings presented more cautiously and in more qualified ways than others (for example, KwaZulu-Natal). In some cases, only named individuals in the police are held responsible for gross human rights violations. But in many others, the net of responsibility is thrown far more widely, with 'the state' or the relevant ministers held responsible for gross human rights violations committed by their underlings. Applying the Commission's own criteria for evidence, these findings often read rather baldly and at times are altogether flimsy, particularly in respect of earlier periods. For example, in the report on the 1960 Sharpeville massacre, the police in Vereeniging are held responsible for having deliberately opened fire on the fleeing crowds of anti-pass protesters, but so too are the 'state and the minister of police' – although the preceding narrative makes no mention of any processes of 'deliberate planning' between the various perpetrators.[55] Reporting on the deaths in detention of Ahmed Timol, Suliman Salojee and others, the report finds the minister of justice 'directly responsible for the failure of magistrates to take account of evidence presented to them of the torture and assault of detainees by the police', but again with no mention of the organisational linkages between them.[56] With similar omissions, the 'former state' was held responsible for actions undertaken by the South African Defence Force's Military Intelligence in Ciskei, as a result of which fifteen people died.[57]

All in all, the unevenness with which findings are made and motivated is striking, particularly in relation to the supposed need to demonstrate the 'motivations' and 'deliberate planning' along a chain of command. While many readers of the report would be unsurprised by, and sympathetic to, a finding that the apartheid state should take responsibility for the actions of Military Intelligence (for example), from a forensic point of view such findings in respect of 'the state' at large raise crucial questions about how much members of the Cabinet and other civilian structures or bureaucracies knew about the actions of the military, how far particular individuals and bureaucracies within the state acted independently and without authorisation from superiors, and what sort of coordinated planning characterised the apartheid state.

If the Commission's findings in respect of 'the state' and many of its senior decision-makers read as summarised and incomplete, they point to the way in which much of the report should be read – as primarily a moral narrative about the fact of evil in South Africa's past, for which the prevalence and character of gross human rights violations are ultimately sufficient evidence. Given the constraints of the political compromise, the disinclination to antagonise or incriminate leading politicians, the emphasis on the 'healing' process, as well as the problems of archival access, the TRC chose to deal with the highest echelons of decision-making in the state largely by ignoring them, and passing judgement on the system of apartheid itself as a crime against humanity. The state is then responsible as the author of the system, but without the TRC having to demonstrate much about its institutional apparatus or modus operandi.

Grappling with Apartheid

As suggested earlier, the apartheid system was the 'background' to the Commission's inquiry (insofar as its mandate was limited to *gross* human rights violations rather than human rights violations more generally and therefore the apartheid system in its entirety), and yet it was also the crux of its investigation, as the source of these gross human rights violations. The TRC's powers of historical explanation rested heavily on its ability to come to grips with apartheid. The previous section has exposed some epistemological and methodological reasons why the TRC report is ultimately more of a descriptive than an explanatory exercise. This section examines how these epistemological and methodological positions are manifest substantively, in the TRC's limited and rather unimpressive engagement with the nature of apartheid.

In several places, the report announces the TRC's discomfort with the exclusion of human rights violations more generally from its scope (although the mind boggles at how the Commission would have been strained by an even more extensive mandate). Many Commissioners, as well as the authors of the report, emphasised repeatedly the need to understand apartheid itself as the systematic violation of human rights, and to place gross human rights violations at one end of a continuum, with the day-to-day laws and institutions of apartheid at the other. Spurred by this insistence on taking the broader context into account in describing and explaining gross human rights violations, the TRC diversified its hearings in ways which promised to shed greater light on the social, ideological and institutional character of apartheid South Africa. In addition to the amnesty and human rights hearings, there were ten event hearings (as mentioned previously), institutional hearings on the business sector, media, medical profession, legal profession and 'faith community', special hearings on youth, women and military conscription, and political party hearings to allow for fuller interrogation of the actions and attitudes of their leaders and members. The TRC's Research Department also recognised the need to throw its net wide enough to encompass large chunks of the apartheid system. In short, there were some promising signs that a serious exercise in historical analysis was on the cards.

But it was not to be. The report sheds remarkably little light on apartheid, and adds very little to what we already know. A narrative on apartheid is constructed in bits and pieces, through a combination of general 'background' accounts, as well as national and regional 'profiles' on gross human rights violations. But this narrative is primarily descriptive. It is also extremely brief, selective and at times historically inaccurate. To a reader familiar with South Africa's recent history, much of this text seems to have been written by people with relatively little historical expertise. Swathes of existing research do not find their way into the report, even though writers occasionally make reference to one or other secondary text.

One of the more conspicuous gaps concerns the apartheid state. Curiously, the Research Department's list of fourteen 'strategic research themes' did not include one which dealt directly with the state, other than by way of research into the 'development of the security establishment', the judiciary and legal system. It seems that the state was not theorised, nor adequately conceptualised. As a result, the effort to understand its character and inner workings was rather desultory. Hampered in their efforts to read previously secret military and police records, researchers apparently did not probe elsewhere for evidence of the distribution of power, techniques of decision-making and methods of internal discipline deployed within the apartheid state.

In the light of the previous methodological discussion, these gaps can be read as symptoms of what emerged as the dominant logic of the report's global encounter with the past. Notwithstanding the TRC's mandate to account for why gross human rights violations occurred as they did, with reference to the motives, perspectives and 'deliberate planning' of the perpetrators, the report offers little on this front. It emerges as primarily a story of moral wrongdoing, for the purposes of which the complexities of motives, perspectives and planning on the part of state actors are far less important than their consequences, namely the commission of increasingly gross human rights violations.

The imprints of the report's notion of factual or forensic truth are also powerfully felt in its encounter with apartheid. Apartheid is written in the factual, forensic mode, as though it were a succession of 'facts' assembled and collated by the Commission. The report defines factual truth as the business of the social scientist; but only the most positivistic social scientists would recognise their practice in the Commission's writing. Any non-positivist would see the practice of producing truth as an interpretative exercise rooted in various theoretical assumptions about the object of inquiry and normative assumptions about the value and purpose of the inquiry. In the case of writing the history and character of apartheid, there is by now a large body of literature straddling a series of debates born of conflicting theoretical and normative assumptions. With the exception of the chapter recounting the hearings on business and labour,[58] none of this surfaces in the report, which otherwise lacks any explicit engagement with the *historiography* of apartheid, and therefore with the contestedness of its history.

This is ironic in view of the TRC's limited capacity to generate its own primary research on apartheid and its reliance on existing scholarship. The TRC's ideas of research, the relationship between primary and secondary research, the authority of particular scholars or versions of apartheid, remain something of a muddle in the report. One version of the research process speaks of a 'dialectical encounter' of primary and secondary research (but sheds no light on what this might be). Another version allocates far more limited powers of discovery to the TRC's own Research Department, suggesting that selected secondary texts authorised much of the data assembled: 'by continually evaluating the Commission's primary data in the light of the material already written on the subject the Research Department was able to enhance the evidence presented to the Commission.'[59] But the authors of the report are also at pains to emphasise that the appropriation of research was atheoretical – 'information only'[60] – as though any explicit recognition of a theoretical position would have contaminated its 'forensic' objectivity.

Inarticulately and inexplicitly, the report does take a position on apartheid, even if this is effaced as though it were historical fact. If we look for an answer to the question of how and why apartheid emerged, how and why it took particular forms, how and why it survived for over four decades, all the report has to offer is 'racism'. Indeed, apartheid and racism are often treated as interchangeable.

> [W]e cannot hope properly to understand the history of the period under review unless we give apartheid and racism their rightful place as the defining features of that period.[61]

Racism, however, pre-dated apartheid:

> Racism came to South Africa in 1652; it has been part of the warp and woof of South African society since then ... 1948 merely saw the beginning of a refinement and intensifying of repression, injustice and exploitation.[62]

But what then is 'racism'? Why did it 'come' to South Africa? Why was it 'refined and intensified' after 1948? The text is not consistent in its rendition of racism in South Africa, and therefore in its tacit historiography of apartheid, lurching between the view that racism in South Africa was quintessentially colonial (reproducing Mamdani's view that there was 'nothing particularly new or unique' to South Africa's version of colonial governance)[63] and the idea that apartheid – and therefore its particular incarnation of racism – was 'qualitatively different'.[64] Either way, the report tends to treat racism as an answer, not a question. We read about how racism is reproduced, through processes of socialisation in the family, schooling and the media; we are presented with familiar litanies of racist laws which institutionalise racial discrimination and oppression in various forms.

But once again the 'what' and 'how' are uppermost; *why* racism has shaped the South African social order is another of the bigger silences in the TRC's encounter with the past. Racism simply exists; it is 'part of the warp and woof of South African society', the motor of its history. Overall, there is little sense of the interconnectedness of racism and other divides in the society.

This inability to grapple with the complexities of social causation is compounded by the TRC's having to tie its account of apartheid to the story of gross human rights violations. Having to focus a narration of the past around the clash between 'victims' and 'perpetrators' provides very blunt tools for the craft of history-writing, ill-equipped for more nuanced understandings of political violence, ideological positioning, the politics of complicity and collaboration, all of which would have moulded a deeper, fuller sense of the nature and dynamics of racism in South Africa.

Once again, there are glimpses of other avenues into the past. The report on the business hearings acknowledges something of the effects of class in the shaping of a racist social order. The report on the 'special hearings on women' recognises gender as a power relation; and a brief discussion of masculinity as a factor in South Africa's repertoire of violence signals that there is more to the country's history of violation than simply racism. But these discussions are underdeveloped, and read as footnotes to the report as a whole.

Taking Stock

The TRC remains, in several respects, a remarkable achievement. One of its important successes has been in closing many individual 'dossiers' on the past, revealing what happened to sons, fathers, brothers, sisters, mothers and daughters who had 'disappeared', tracing their killers, identifying the circumstances that led up to these ghastly deeds; also, vindicating individual allegations about torture perpetrated in the liberation movements and previously denied. And, in many instances, these disclosures have been accompanied by the sort of catharsis and individual or interpersonal reconciliation that the TRC strove to achieve. There were others for whom this process was less rewarding, people whose stories have not been fully heard, who feel frustrated by the haste which accompanied the TRC's hearings and the inattention to the complexity of local histories of political conflict and violence.[65] Clearly, the task of unravelling these individual and local truths remains unfinished. But if one effect of the TRC has been to animate popular interest in understanding the past, this must count as a success, despite the limits of its own rendition.

The TRC's main focus, however, was a more global one on the nation at large. In this respect, one of its greatest achievements was its role as an historical 'lie detector', which created the possibility of a moral 'consensus that atrocious things were done on all sides'.[66] Enough detail about the fact and prevalence of gross human rights violations has been exposed to debunk any lingering attempts either to sanitise apartheid or to romanticise the struggle against it. As Archbishop Tutu puts it in the Foreword to the report:

> We know that the State used its considerable resources to wage a war against some of its citizens. We know that torture and deception and murder and death squads came to be the order of the day. We know that the liberation movements were not paragons of virtue and were often responsible for egging people on to behave in ways that were uncontrollable.[67]

In Michael Ignatieff's view, this should be enough: 'All that a truth commission can achieve is to reduce the number of lies that can be circulated unchallenged in public discourse.'[68] Yet the TRC was a more ambitious undertaking, its mandate creating higher expectations of its powers of historical analysis. Emphasising the need to learn from past mistakes, the Commissioners echoed the views of those who drafted the enabling legislation: it was considered crucial to expose why gross human rights violations had been committed, embedding the descriptive account in an analysis of the broader structural causes, the planned exercise of abusive power, as well as the intentions and perspectives of perpetrators. This required that the TRC grapple with what social scientists call the 'problem of agency', one which is also germane to most modes of sociological and historical analysis. In the words of Philip Abrams,

> the problem of agency is the problem of finding a way of accounting for human experience which recognises simultaneously and in equal measure that history and society are made by constant and more or less purposeful individual action *and* that individual action, however purposeful, is made by history and society ... People make their own history – but only under definite circumstances and conditions: we act through a world of rules which our action creates, breaks and renews – we are creatures of rules, the rules are our creations: we make our own world – the world confronts us as an implacable and autonomous system of social facts.[69]

This paper has argued that it is exactly the 'problem of agency' that caused the

TRC report to stumble. Previous sections have shown that the problem asserted itself on three fronts: epistemologically, in respect of the contestedness of truth; methodologically, in respect of the search for the appropriate 'methodological pluralism'; and substantively, in the need to anchor the actions of individual victims and perpetrators of gross human rights violations in the apartheid system. Whether proactively or reactively, the authors of the TRC report made epistemological and methodological choices which disabled the link between subject and object, agent and structure; and these choices in turn produced a version of the recent past which is largely descriptive.

The limits of the 'history' written by the TRC in turn inhibit its 'cathartic' and 'healing' qualities. With its powers of explanation stunted, the TRC cannot produce a consensus about *why* the terrible deeds of the past were committed. The increasingly familiar refrain among white South Africans that apartheid was merely a 'mistake' for which no one was responsible, that somehow the system propelled itself impersonally, may be one of the more ironic, unintended consequences of the TRC's rendition of the past.

To the extent that the report does venture into historical explanation, its consequences may once again be deeply ironic. The report's only answer to the question of why the country was subjected to such a violent and abusive past is itself in need of explanation – the prevalence and intensity of racism. But in the absence of an explanation for racism itself, the report fails to suggest any plausible grounds for transcending the racism of the past. If racism was part of the warp and woof of South African society, how can it be undone? The fact that it is embedded in the social fabric is also a measure of its tenacity. If we do not understand the conditions under which racism was produced, reproduced and intensified in South Africa, taking account of its interconnections with other modes of power and inequality such as gender and class, how can we transcend it?

Whatever the limits of its report, the TRC has created significant opportunities for an engagement with the past, which have not yet been realised fully. Its large archive promises to be an important resource for academic and popular historians, provided it remains open and accessible. It seems that the TRC has stimulated an interest in and enthusiasm for truth-telling, in communities intent on unravelling the complexities of their past. And there is much more to be said about the machinations of leaders in the apartheid state and the homeland governments, and the liberation movements which opposed them.

In the final analysis, it is a strength rather than a weakness of the TRC that it has initiated a process of truth-telling without seeing it through to completion. If 'the past is an argument',[70] then it should not be limited to a single distillation under one official rubric. The responsibility falls to a range of different research communities and intellectuals to diversify the terms of debate and prevent its premature conclusion. The stakes are high: as Ignatieff puts it, 'national identity [should be] a site of conflict and argument, not a silent shrine for collective worship'.[71]

Notes

1. *Business Day*, 7 March 1996 (my emphasis).
2. Truth and Reconciliation Commission, *Truth and Reconciliation Commission of South Africa Report*, 5 vols (Cape Town, Juta & Co., 1998), vol. 1, ch. 6, para. 2.
3. *TRC Report*, vol. 1, ch. 4, para. 31 (a).
4. *TRC Report*, vol. 1, ch. 1, para. 5.
5. For all Tutu's apparent insight into the TRC's having presented a 'perspective on the truth' about the past, not for a moment does he renounce the surety or veracity of the Commission as the official version of what happened.
6. See, for example, *TRC Report*, vol. 1, ch. 1, paras 7, 15.
7. *TRC Report*, vol. 1, ch. 1, para. 28.
8. *TRC Report*, vol. 1, ch. 4, para. 26.
9. *Ibid.*, para. 30.
10. *TRC Report*, vol. 1, ch. 1, para. 28.
11. *TRC Report*, vol. 1, ch. 5, paras 10-28.
12. *TRC Report*, vol. 1, ch. 1, para. 19.
13. *TRC Report*, vol. 1, ch. 4, para. 82.
14. For example, *TRC Report*, vol. 1, ch. 6, para. 27; vol. 1, ch. 5, paras 3, 4.
15. *TRC Report*, vol. 1, ch. 1, paras 34, 60.
16. *TRC Report*, vol. 1, ch. 6, para. 1(e).
17. *TRC Report*, vol.1, ch. 4, para. 3.
18. *Ibid.*, para. 133.
19. *Ibid.*, para. 31 (d).
20. H. van der Merwe, 'Community Reconciliation in South Africa: Lessons from the TRC's Intervention in Two Communities', Centre for the Study of Violence and Reconciliation seminar paper (Johannesburg, March 1999).
21. A. Boraine and J. Levy (eds), *Healing the Nation?* (Cape Town, IDASA, 1995), pp. 122-3.
22. K. Asmal, L. Asmal and R. Roberts, *Reconciliation Through Truth: A Reckoning of Apartheid's Criminal Governance* (Cape Town, David Philip and Mayibuye Books, 1996) p. 19. R. Wilson makes a similar point: 'The symbolic impact

of truth commissions lies in how they codify the history of a period. Popular memory of an authoritarian past is often fluid, unfixed and fragmentary and it is impossible to investigate all the cases brought to a commission, so truth commissions fix upon particular cases and events in order to create "the global truth" of an abusive period' (R. Wilson, 'The Sizwe Will Not Go Away: The Truth and Reconciliation Commission, Human Rights and Nation-Building in South Africa', *African Studies*, 55:2 (1996), p. 17).
23. Asmal et al., *op. cit.*, p. 27.
24. *TRC Report*, vol. 1, ch. 4, para. 51.
25. *TRC Report*, vol. 1, ch. 6, Appendix 1, para. 10.
26. *TRC Report*, vol. 1, ch. 5, paras 29-45.
27. *TRC Report*, vol. 1, ch. 6, Appendix 1, paras 13-15.
28. *TRC Report*, vol. 1, ch. 11, Management and Operational Reports, Research Department, para. 9.
29. *TRC Report*, vol. 1, ch. 5, para. 29.
30. *Ibid.*
31. *Ibid.*, para. 30.
32. *Ibid.*, paras 32, 33.
33. *Ibid.*, para. 31.
34. Researchers working for the TRC have pointed out to me that this typology was produced fairly hastily and relatively late in the day, rather than as part of a well-planned, forward-looking research strategy and epistemological position. It was therefore in the TRC report, rather than in the early stages of the research process, that the effort was made to contain conflicting positions and strands of argument about 'truth' by way of this typology.
35. *TRC Report*, vol. 1, ch. 5, paras 36, 37.
36. *Ibid.*, paras 39-42.
37. *Ibid.*, paras 43, 44.
38. Reconstructed in these terms, the typology would read as follows: the evidence for personal truth is the intensity of personal beliefs and feelings; the evidence for social truth is the emergence of a consensus, which may or may not have to do with 'facts' about the case; the evidence for healing truth is its effects in promoting reconciliation; and the evidence for factual or forensic truth is the objective 'facts' of the case. Thanks to Mark Leon for his insights on this point.
39. *TRC Report*, vol. 5, ch. 7, para. 51.
40. *TRC Report*, vol. 1, ch. 6, footnote 14 on p. 161.
41. *TRC Report*, vol. 5, ch. 7, para. 52.
42. Although the lifespan of the Commission was extended by a few months,

there was little sympathy for the idea of a more substantial extension beyond the two years within which it was originally expected to complete its work.
43. *TRC Report*, vol. 1, ch. 6, para. 33.
44. *TRC Report*, vol. 1, ch. 5, para. 38.
45. *TRC Report*, vol. 1, ch. 6, para. 37.
46. *Ibid.*, Appendix 1, paras 10, 11.
47. *Ibid.*, Appendix 1, para. 13.
48. *Ibid.*, Appendix 1, para. 12.
49. As the report points out, this is neither a census of gross human rights violations, nor is it based on a representative sample. It is a compilation of only those gross human rights violations reported to the TRC.
50. The report lacks an index, which makes it almost impossible for its readers to cross-reference and connect different parts of the five volumes.
51. In his Minority Position, Commissioner Wynand Malan picks up on this point: 'A qualitative analysis of the data that has been collected, especially from victim statements and testimonies or through the amnesty process, would have made a very valuable contribution to a better understanding of our society and the underlying endemic risks of the conflicts of the past repeating themselves in different forms. Unfortunately, we have not been able to undertake such an analysis ... It is recommended that institutions of learning and research, the private sector and civil society promote research programmes aimed at qualitative analysis of the data' (*TRC Report*, vol. 5, Minority Position Submitted by Commissioner Wynand Malan, paras 86, 87). The report, however, makes a recommendation calling for further quantitative analysis of its data (vol. 5, ch. 8, para. 21).
52. *TRC Report*, vol. 1, ch. 4, para. 123(b).
53. *Ibid.*, para. 124(c).
54. *Ibid.*, para. 80.
55. *TRC Report*, vol. 3, ch. 6, para. 42.
56. *Ibid.*, para. 63.
57. *TRC Report*, vol. 3, ch. 2, para. 342.
58. This chapter sees the conflicting positions taken by business and labour as mirroring competing stances in the 'long-standing debate over the relationship between apartheid and capitalism' (vol. 4, ch. 2, para. 8).
59. *TRC Report*, vol. 1, ch. 6, para. 48.
60. An account of the workings of the Research Department acknowledges the contribution of 'specialist researchers', but insists that '[t]his work was received strictly as *information only*. The insights gained, views expressed and

information submitted were all assessed in the first instance by the Research Department and ultimately by the Commission, which takes full responsibility for all information and findings included in the report' (vol. 1, ch. 11, Management and Operational Reports, Research Department, paras 26, 27).

61. *TRC Report*, vol. 1, ch. 1, para. 63.
62. *Ibid.*, para. 65.
63. *TRC Report*, vol. 1, ch. 2, para. 62.
64. *TRC Report*, vol. 1, ch. 1, para. 23.
65. Hugo van der Merwe discusses these frustrations in relation to the communities of Duduza and Kathorus. See Van der Merwe, 'Community Reconciliation in South Africa'.
66. M. Ignatieff, untitled, in *Index on Censorship*, 5/96, www.oneworld.org/index_oc/issue596/ignatieff.
67. *TRC Report*, vol. 1, ch. 1, para. 70.
68. Ignatieff, *Index on Censorship*, 5/96.
69. P. Abrams, *Historical Sociology* (Ithaca, Cornell University Press, 1982), pp. xiii-xiv.
70. Ignatieff, *Index on Censorship*, 5/96.
71. *Ibid.*

8

THE TRUTH AND RECONCILIATION COMMISSION AND THE PURSUIT OF 'SOCIAL TRUTH'
The Case of Kathorus

Philip Bonner and Noor Nieftagodien

Introduction

The South African Truth and Reconciliation Commission (TRC) was born of political compromise. Its central features crystallised at a critical point in the negotiations at the Convention for a Democratic South Africa (CODESA), when a political deal was struck between the main parties. In terms of this deal, political amnesty could be granted for politically motivated human rights violations, provided that individual perpetrators confessed to their crimes and, as was later agreed, victims were given the right to tell their stories of suffering and struggle.[1] This central purpose animated and constrained the Commission throughout its proceedings. In time, other objectives were added and priorities were redefined, but these always took second place behind the main business of catharsis and expiation. The TRC's preoccupation with public hearings and amnesty applications made a major contribution to reconciliation, but at a cost. All too often, as this paper hopes to demonstrate, any deeper understanding or explanation of what happened was sacrificed at the altar of these other concerns. Parts of the data collected by the TRC could almost certainly contribute to that understanding if they were made available, but they would have to be supplemented by further analysis and research. The collective wisdom of the Commission, as distilled in its five-volume final report, certainly fails in this regard. This paper, through an analysis of the Commission's investigation of events on the East Rand from the late 1980s to the early 1990s, tries to explain this failure.

The TRC's Mandate and Procedure

The Commission engaged in two central sets of inquiries aimed at identifying the victims and the perpetrators of gross human rights violations between March 1960 and May 1994. As part of this exercise it was explicitly mandated to investigate 'the antecedents, circumstances, factors, [and] context' of such violations, as well as individual motives and accountability.[2] In pursuit of these objectives, the Commission set itself the task of uncovering different kinds of truths – factual or forensic truth; personal and narrative truth; social truth (and 'dialogue truth'); healing and restorative truth. These distinctions are discussed fully elsewhere in this volume and need not detain us here.[3]

On the surface, these various kinds of truth-finding were fully congruent. Establishing a social 'truth', for example, could readily be seen as indispensable to a proper understanding of cause and accountability. In both practical and methodological terms, however, they proved inconsistent with one another. The Commission recognised 'at the outset' that the human and time resources it had at its disposal made it impossible for it to 'carry out all the tasks required of it simultaneously'. It therefore devoted its attention initially to the restoration of the human and civil dignity of individual victims of past gross human rights violations. It did so by 'creating opportunities for victims "to relate their own accounts" '. This was accompanied by extensive statement-taking and research to establish the whereabouts of victims and the identity of those responsible for violations.[4]

The quest to identify perpetrators and victims was relatively straightforward when the perpetrator was an agent of the state working to sustain the apartheid order.[5] Much more problematic, as the Commission soon realised, was civil conflict between different segments of the black community, especially that between the Inkatha Freedom Party (IFP) and the African National Congress (ANC), where perpetrators and victims often blurred into each other, and it was not clear 'who was "innocent" (defending) and who was "guilty" (attacking)'.[6] The distinction became particularly difficult to draw in relation to the era of negotiations (1990-94), when political violence escalated to unprecedented heights and 14 000 South Africans were killed. Of the 9 043 statements on killing gathered by the Commission, 5 695 concerned this period.[7] The majority of these deaths were connected to internecine political conflict between the IFP and ANC (although, as the report emphasises, this was often orchestrated at one remove by the state). The East Rand, and more specifically the Kathorus area, witnessed 'more intensive violence between the ANC and the IFP in the early 1990s than any other part of the country',[8] and hence presented a particularly difficult set of human rights violations on which to adjudicate.

The uncovering of forensic and narrative truth dominated the Commission's agenda for the first eighteen months of its existence. Only from mid-1997 did its emphasis shift to trying to understand the individual and institutional perspectives that gave rise to the gross violations of human rights, including contexts, causes, and political and moral responsibility. At a national level, this involved 'public submissions by, and questioning of, political parties, and a range of institutional, sectoral and special hearings'.[9] Together these threw light on the structural violence of apartheid, and on the moral responsibility of sectors of civil society for apartheid and the gross human rights violations carried out under its authority. But they did little to help the Commission comprehend what remained its most intractable problem – the causes and patterns of violence during the final decade of minority rule. This required addressing a different level of motivation and causation, which it seemed unable or unwilling to contemplate. There are suggestions that the Johannesburg office, which was far more strapped for resources than any other office of the Commission, being required to report on four times the number of people than any other regional centre,[10] confronted this problem more directly when it tried, without complete success, to focus its strategy on statements rather than hearings.[11]

The task of finding adequate social explanations for human rights violations was hampered fundamentally by other terms of the Commission's mandate. These excluded from consideration any human rights violations that could not be termed political. Only violations that were politically motivated were 'gross' and hence worthy of the Commission's attention. A qualifying clause directing attention to politically motivated violations 'which emanated from the conflicts of the past' potentially offered some latitude for the Commission's inquiries. In practice, however, the Commission seems to have interpreted this to mean political conflicts 'in the past'.[12] Such an apparent limitation presented researchers and analysts working for the Commission with daunting obstacles when trying to analyse and describe the 'causes, nature and extent' of civil conflict between 1990 and 1994.[13] Much that fed into this conflict was not party political at all, but socio-political in character and rooted in another area the Commission was required to exclude from view – 'the more mundane but nonetheless traumatising dimensions of apartheid life that affected every single black South African'.[14] For the period 1990-93, researchers from the Johannesburg office, with whose work this paper is primarily concerned, tried to square this political circle by smuggling socio-political dynamics and conflicts back in under the rubric of the political. For them, struggles simply needed to have taken place within a wider context of political conflict to qualify as political. This practice, while in some senses laudable, was potentially misleading and distorting. Issues that were not party political at all were represented as such. This bias has the potential to vitiate the aim of creating a human rights culture in South Africa, since grave (but not 'gross') human rights violations, which are provoked by socio-political conflict and persist when the context of party political conflict is removed, are not confronted, interrogated or in any way resolved.

One key aspect of the Commission's mandate that comprehensively precluded adequate social explanation was the requirement to make clear-cut findings on victims and perpetrators. The format of much of the report reflects this orientation, being designed so that each section can conclude with a finding. At points, the sections and findings are arranged chronologically, as in the case of the Soweto uprising of 1976. More typically, they are structured around categories of violation (public order policing, detention and torture, deaths in detention, covert action, and so on). The rationale for this procedure is furnished in Volume 5 of the report, where it is noted that the Commission 'recognised early on that it would not be able to investigate all the cases before it'. Its solution to this undeniable dilemma was to focus on 'specific "window" cases – representative of a far larger number of violations of a similar type and involving the same perpetrator groupings'.[15] In the case of civil conflict (mainly between the IFP and the ANC and its allies), the Commission isolated a number of 'iconic' events demanding closer attention, among which the conflict in Phola Park is significant for this study.

Volume 5 identifies a further presumption that helped to narrow down the most illuminating 'window' cases:

> Having identified the former state and the IFP as undoubtedly responsible for the greatest number of violations, the Commission directed its resources towards the investigation of those bodies.[16]

Later, the same volume adds a little more substance to this proposition:

> As early as 1982, Inkatha began to foster the concept of paramilitary training, particularly among its youth movement ... a process by which violence became institutionalised in KwaZulu ... In the period after July 1990, IFP violence spread to other regions, particularly the Transvaal.[17]

The report backs up these claims with figures extracted from the TRC database, showing that the IFP was 'allegedly responsible' for over 4 500 killings nationwide, compared to 2 700 for the South African Police and 1 300 for the ANC (figures then rendered as a ratio between the IFP and the ANC of 3.5 to 1).[18]

These passages encapsulate in a particularly condensed and arresting fashion the core methodology employed by those directing the Commission. A sharp dichotomy is established between perpetrators and victims, and incidents are aggregated into categories on the basis of which findings are made. For some purposes, such a procedure can be defended. Even if human rights violations committed against victims aligned with the IFP were under-reported, which seems to have been the case at some points in the Transvaal, IFP perpetrators nonetheless greatly predominated. They are thus the main human rights violators from the mid-1980s onwards, and this stands as one of the most powerful findings of the Commission. The problem is that such global figures shed little light on patterns of causation and motivation, and herein lies the fatal flaw of the report. Incidents are grouped into categories and abstracted from their historical sequence and context. The relationships between different categories of 'incident' are thus rendered opaque. Where 'window' episodes are selected, only immediate and triggering factors are taken into account as 'causes'. The possibility of an alternative explanation of the apartheid years and the immediate aftermath vanishes from view. Motivation becomes truncated, accountability leaches away. Historical process is utterly obscured, and explanations are reduced to a single political realm.

A similar problem limits the historical usefulness of statements taken by the Commission's researchers. The format of the 'statement protocol' evolved through several different versions. Version 4 required an initial 'brief description of the violation of human rights'. Deponents were guided by an inventory of the points their statement was expected to cover: '... briefly describe what happened to you or the person you are telling us about, please tell us what happened? Who got hurt, killed or kidnapped? When did it happen? Who did it?' The space provided for this information ran to 1½ pages (40 lines) of the statement form, although additional pages were furnished if a longer statement was given. Deponents were then asked further questions according to the categories of violation into which their experience fell (killing, serious injury or severe ill-treatment; torture; abduction; disappearance). Submissions in respect of killings, for example, required deponents to provide the name of the victim and when they were killed (½ to 1 line for each of these pieces of information); how they were killed (3 lines); whether a post-mortem was held, and if so, what its outcome was (4 lines); the identity of the perpetrators (5 lines); how the deponent had identified them (¾ line); what organisation the perpetrator was thought to belong to or support (½ line); who did what, who was in charge, who gave orders, who was with them (4 lines); where and when they last saw the perpetrator (1¾ lines); who witnessed the act (3 lines); and additional information (5 lines). Deponents were also asked whether they would like to meet the perpetrators (¾ line). Further on, deponents could indicate what they thought the consequences of making the statement would be for themselves, and what their expectations of the Commission were with regard to 'symbolic acts which will help us remember the past, honour the dead, acknowledge the victims and their families, and further the cause of reconciliation'. Only two sections of the statement form gave deponents any opportunity to venture an explanation of the event. In a section that followed directly after the 'description of the violation', deponents were asked to describe the political context of the act: 'For example, there was a mass funeral in the community that day, a stay-away boycott march, mutiny in the camp, political rally etc.' The truncated nature of this exercise, to which no more than 9 lines were devoted, is suggested by the phrase 'that day'. Only in dealing with the specific category of violation (for example, killing), were deponents asked, 'Why was the person killed?' and a princely 2¾ lines were provided for the answer.[19]

Earlier versions of the statement form were both more constrained and more expansive. Many of the questions posed in later versions did not feature, but deponents were also asked: 'What were the circumstances that gave rise to/ happened before the act (e.g. what was the victim doing at the time)? Why do you think this happened to the victim? What do you think motivated the act?' There were 3 lines for the answers to each of these questions. In addition, deponents were asked to furnish biographical details on education, occupation and political affiliation, and 6 lines were set aside for this. In practice, only political affiliation was usually recorded.[20]

What seems evident from each version of the form is that deponents were encouraged to offer only the skimpiest data on motivation, and to focus on the immediate antecedents of the act. The very structure of the form and the direction in which it steered the statement-takers precluded a consideration of the wider context. Only tiny windows were opened up on the lives of the victims whose experiences were recorded. The rest remained blank. No sense of cause or motivation could possibly be apprehended from such a procedure.

This paper addresses what it sees as the missing dimension of the TRC's historical explanation. It deals with a limited but important area of the Commission's concern, namely Kathorus on the near East Rand. It hopes to show that only by adopting a longer-term historical perspective, and by probing social and economic as well as political processes, can we arrive at a sense of the causes and motivations of the violence that occurred in Kathorus, and hence allocate accountability. It proceeds from the belief that a broader, more complex perspective can only be gained by much fuller documentation of the lives and world-views of a cross-section of the individuals concerned, as they evolved, intersected and eventually collided. This exercise, the paper argues, requires more intensive and relatively localised studies, which were clearly beyond the TRC with its limited time and funding.

Financial and time constraints, which were there from the outset, were beyond the Commission's control. What is more troubling is that an understanding of what was required to probe cause and motivation seriously also lay beyond the Commissioners' ken. There are signs that they did not even perceive the dilemma they faced, and this massive failure of comprehension left a black hole at the heart of the Commission's investigations. One gets the impression that the writers of the report believed they had made a passable attempt at an adequate reconstruction, giving due weight to cause and motivation. At least some of the researchers seem to have felt that they had succeeded in providing an alternative history. How else could they have observed, in the letter they dispatched to Leah Mokoena, the widow of Sam Ntuli, that 'we trust that your statements will help to establish the truth about our past and assist in achieving the healing that you and our country need'.[21]

Causes

Serious violence first erupted in Kathorus – the East Rand township complex of Katlehong, Thokoza and Vosloorus – in the form of a bloody taxi war in late 1989 and early 1990. This was some months before the launch of the IFP as a national political party in July 1990, the event to which the Commission attributes the origin of the conflict. In late February and early March 1990, 50 people were killed and 350 injured in the taxi war, in a portent of the bloodletting that would soon become routine in the region.[22]

But the taxi war does not make much of a showing in the TRC report. It commands three paragraphs, and features as an additional category of incident in the latter part of the Transvaal regional report. It is admitted through the back door, as it were, because it could be vestigially categorised as 'political'. As the writers explain: 'While the conflict was initially an economic dispute over control of taxi routes, it quickly became politicised.' Economic conflict, they state, often 'became intertwined with other dynamics, particularly the political conflict between the ANC and IFP'.[23] From the report's own account, the taxi conflict in Katlehong was only secondarily political and was therefore disqualified from 'iconic status'. As a result, despite its chronological priority, it is relegated to near the end of the regional report, long after subsequent, more directly political incidents have been discussed. It is thus disconnected from what followed and permitted no longer-term impact on subsequent events. This profoundly compromises any proper understanding of the evolution of conflict in Kathorus.

The taxi war was important to understand for two reasons, neither of which is grasped in the report. First, it formed the bloody prelude to the endemic violence in the area over the following three or four years, and was perceived by most of the main antagonists as being intimately connected with what followed.[24] Second, it condensed most of the socio-economic grievances and antagonisms that underlay the violence throughout the period. At the root of the conflict were the declining material conditions of both migrants and urban dwellers in Kathorus and the rest of the Rand in the 1980s and early 1990s. Of the two groups, migrants were the hardest hit. It is with them that this discussion begins.

In the late 1970s and 1980s, stock theft became rampant in many rural communities in South Africa, as a result of the dislocation caused by land betterment and resettlement programmes initiated by the state.[25] The district of Nqutu in KwaZulu-Natal, from which many Kathorus migrants hailed, was particularly hard hit. According to migrants, 'whole kraals were emptied and closed', thereby 'destroying the social fabric of these communities whose major building block is livestock possession'.[26] Stock thieves in Nqutu and elsewhere commonly converted part of the proceeds of theft into taxis. Migrant workers, who had been denuded of cattle by thieves, often gave up all hope of retiring to a conventional rural life, and also invested for their future security in the purchase of a taxi rather than cattle. Taxis were a logical alternative or supplementary investment, since migrants' distance from their rural homes ensured that there was a constant demand for transport.

In the 1960s and 1970s, the granting of licences to Africans to run taxis was tightly controlled. The easing of high apartheid, and the loosening of some of its more senseless restrictions in the aftermath of the 1976 student uprising, helped unfreeze the issuing of taxi permits to some degree. An important moment in this process was the appearance on the market of the Kombi or minibus, which could carry twice as many passengers as a car. Aspiring migrant entrepreneurs moved quickly to exploit the opportunity this presented, and set up taxi services between the homelands and the towns. Now migrant workers could be ferried back and forth between their homes and their workplaces several times a year, without consuming too much of their income or jeopardising their jobs. The real take-off came in 1986-7, when a number of the central components of apartheid regulation, the most notable of which was influx control, were either relaxed or abandoned. Among the various restrictive regulations that were scrapped at this time were limitations on the licensing of taxis. As a result, over the space of eighteen months, the number of Kombi licences issued leapt from

7 093 to 34 378.²⁷ Taxis quickly became the principal means of capital accumulation open to black South Africans. Almost as quickly, taxi routes became saturated with new operators, and competition became acute.

Even before deregulation, a number of local taxi associations had been formed with the aim of protecting their routes. It was estimated that between 38 and 60 per cent of taxi operators at this time were pirates, operating without permits and encroaching on the preserves of those who were officially licensed.²⁸ In Germiston, the taxi operators who initially plied the long-distance routes to KwaZulu-Natal formed the Germiston and District Taxi Association to suppress pirate competition. Elsewhere on the Rand, competition between legal and illegal operators and between rival taxi associations had already led to conflict and even killing.²⁹ In Katlehong, these rivalries assumed their own distinctive form, with Zulu-speaking migrant operators on one side, and operators who were permanently resident in the township on the other. Moses Maseko, former president of the Congress of South African Students (COSAS), places this development within the equally unfriendly economic context in which Katlehong's permanent township residents found themselves:

> You remember around this time ... a lot of people were retrenched, out of work ... Some, I would say ordinary citizens of Germiston, or Katlehong, some had to buy taxis because they [saw] it as a mushroom industry.³⁰

Throughout the Katlehong and Thokoza area, tensions began to rise.

At some point in the next months, the rival Katlehong Taxi Organisation (KATO) was formed by operators based in the townships as opposed to the hostels. The township association exploited their more intimate connection and familiarity with the township community. As Maseko observes:

> You know that a number of young people who were not able to go to university, and all those things, there was no other option but to look at possible jobs around, and they were employed within the taxi industry to be drivers ... Because COSAS was a strong organisation, they met us, [and] said, 'No, we will reduce fees for students, give us one rand ...' They [were] marketing themselves and, obviously, once there are economic issues, there will be politics coming in at the end of the day ... If I remember well, there was a situation where the Student Congress, we hosted a number of events, [and] KATO supported us.³¹

The stage was now set for the most bloody conflict the taxi industry in South Africa had ever seen.

Its trigger was the 'stick-away' stay-away called by the Congress of South African Trade Unions (COSATU) in June 1989. To prevent migrants and others from going to work during the stay-away, students obstructed the passage of taxis. One taxi, owned by a member of the Germiston and District Taxi Association named Ngobese, drove down the soon-to-be infamous Khumalo Street in Thokoza, in an attempt to beat the blockade. At Mnisi section, it was intercepted and attacked by student activists, and twelve passengers, including a pregnant woman accompanying a small child, were burnt to death. Migrants in most of Kathorus reacted with collective outrage. Over the following weeks, efforts were made to broker a truce and a lasting peace.[32] These failed when a second, purely economic variable intervened in the form of a local authority initiative to reallocate ranks and routes.[33] This provoked a new round of bloodletting, lasting from 24 February to 11 March 1990. In one particularly savage episode on 27 February, six pupils and teachers were murdered in a Katlehong school. Hostel vigilantes went from house to house hunting for township suspects and even raided a local hospital in search of wounded 'komblese' (comrades).[34] While many of the hostel dwellers taking part in the massacres were presumably members of Inkatha and its trade union wing, the United Workers' Union of South Africa (UWUSA), many were not. Many were not even Zulu-speaking, although there is evidence that Xhosa-speaking workers at Khalanyoni hostel, at least, were reluctant to take part in these acts. There is no sign of Inkatha being involved in any way at this point.[35] The conflict was secondarily political, at best, having been precipitated by reluctance to observe a political stay-away. Its real sources were socio-economic and socio-political. This, in effect, disqualified it from close scrutiny in the TRC report. Yet the conflict constituted the crucial preamble to the violence of mid-1990, without which the latter cannot be fully explained.

In August and September 1990, a fresh wave of violence engulfed Kathorus. The leading protagonists were Zulu-speaking and IFP-aligned hostel dwellers on one side, and Xhosa-speaking and ANC-aligned hostel dwellers and squatter camp residents on the other. Described thus, the violence was political, and was prompted by rivalry between the two political parties following the release of Nelson Mandela from prison and the unbanning of the ANC in February 1990. This is how it is interpreted in the final report. Once again, however, the deeper causes are fundamentally socio-political. Once again, they cry out to be explored.

In the course of the 1980s, the hostels in Kathorus decayed rapidly. Cash-strapped and corrupt local councils failed to carry out repairs. Services were frequently cut off, and effective administrative control was allowed to lapse. As apartheid unravelled in the mid-1980s and influx control was dropped, thousands of unemployed work seekers swarmed to the Rand. Many found accommodation in the hostels. To begin with, hostel regulations were relaxed so that people without employment could obtain a permit and a bed, provided they paid their rent. Maviyo Sithole recalls that he was fortunate to move into Buyafuthi hostel when 'rules governing residence in hostels were relaxed due to high unemployed', and confirms that 'people could get accommodation as long as they paid'.[36] Later, most notably in the Vosloorus hostel complex, even the payment of rent was not stringently enforced. By November 1988, the Vosloorus council reported that the number of paying residents in council hostels had declined to 50 per cent of the beds available. The other 50 per cent were occupied illegally. In addition, the number of women and children living in the hostels had climbed to alarming levels.[37] A significant minority of the new migrants were Xhosa, and a new edge of ethnic rivalry began to make itself felt in the job and accommodation markets. Zulu migrants speak of firms on the Witwatersrand being 'packed' with Xhosas, adding, for good measure, that 'if you are a Zulu you won't get a job'.[38]

Another result of the shift from high to no or low apartheid in the late 1980s was the mushrooming of squatter camps all along the Reef. Kathorus boasted several, including Crossroads and Phola Park. The camps were occupied by the overflow population from the backyard shacks of Kathorus, into which incredible numbers of people had packed during the late 1960s and 1970s, when no additional municipal houses were built.[39] These longer-term township residents were joined in the second half of the 1980s by a huge influx of new arrivals from the countryside and small rural towns.[40] For reasons which still need to be explored, Xhosa migrants were more likely to gravitate towards the camps than their Zulu counterparts, who still preferred a somewhat debased hostel life. An indistinct and intermittent line of cultural preferences thus separated migrants such as the Zulu from the populations of both the townships and the camps.

Phola Park was emblematic of these processes of urbanisation and their incipient rifts. It was laid out in 1987, only a stone's throw away from Khalanyoni hostel. Despite initial promises from the Alberton town council, it was never provided with basic facilities and its inhabitants lived constantly under threat of removal. By 1990, it housed between 17 000 and 30 000 of the most marginalised inhabitants of the Rand.[41] Positioned directly opposite Khalanyoni hostel, Phola Park embodied – in a face-to-face way not found elsewhere – the challenges that squatter communities and lifestyles presented to migrant culture.

Early on, broken-down walls at Khalanyoni granted Phola Park women access to the hostel to get water. According to a former Khalanyoni hostel resident interviewed by Segal:

> When Phola Park started to build up, more women started popping in. They would come and get water ... I didn't like it at all because a lot of women would stay and there would be a lot of corruption. They'd come for water but relationships started ... Only young guys like such style ... The feeling of the hostel changed.[42]

At the end of 1989, the Alberton town council decided unilaterally to demolish Phola Park and remove its residents to the relatively distant Zonkesizwe squatter settlement. Phola Park residents resisted and Thokoza Youth Congress members lent their support in this struggle. Some Xhosa-speaking hostel dwellers moved onto the vacant lots.[43] The rest of the Khalanyoni hostel residents held entirely aloof. The involvement of Youth Congress supporters, with whom Zulu taxi owners had been locked in conflict only a few months before, may well have deepened divisions between hostel and camp dwellers. The hostel dwellers' indifference certainly could not have helped.

Throughout 1990, the council persisted in its efforts at forcible removal. In July, two residents were killed by police when they tried to stop bulldozers from destroying their homes.[44] These conflicts further inflamed antagonisms between township residents or squatters and the authorities, which Zulu hostel dwellers did not share. A combustible situation thus existed in Khalanyoni and Phola Park, grounded in the poverty and competition for scarce resources that characterised late apartheid. Similar, though slightly less volatile, situations existed in other parts of the Transvaal, where the same ingredients were present in different mixes and measures. With hindsight, it is readily apparent that a single flashpoint could ignite conflict and spread through this whole field of social forces. This is what happened in July and August 1990.

The episode that provided the spark was a confrontation between IFP and ANC supporters in the Vaal township of Sebokeng, which erupted on 22 July 1990, leaving twenty-four dead and many more wounded. This, in turn, had its roots in a national stay-away called by the Tripartite Alliance the previous month. The stay-away was in protest against the IFP's role in the violence in KwaZulu-Natal, where IFP warlords in league with the security forces had waged a violent campaign against the United Democratic Front (especially the Youth Congress) and COSATU.[45] The anti-IFP campaign opened in the Vaal region on 2 July with a rally, at which speakers urged those present to remove all IFP supporters from Vaal townships. In the days that followed, ANC youths allegedly acted on these exhortations.[46]

The three-day national stay-away was observed all over the Witwatersrand and inevitably estranged Zulu-speaking workers, either on party political grounds or because they were prevented from going to work. Afterwards, the IFP announced its intention of relaunching itself as a national political party, and embarked on a campaign of intensive recruitment, which involved political rallies in many centres.[47] The political temperature began to rise in hostels all over the Rand, and there are suggestions that even as early as this, Xhosa migrants began to vacate the Khalanyoni hostel to take up residence in Phola Park.[48]

On 22 July, the IFP held a 'peace rally' at Sebokeng stadium. According to reports received by COSATU lawyers, Cheadle Thompson and Haysom, this was planned with violence in mind. During meetings at the predominantly Zulu and IFP hostels of George Goch, Jeppe and Denver in Johannesburg, individuals described as IFP 'warlords' instructed those present to carry arms and attack 'comrades and their property' in Sebokeng's hostels. On the day of the rally, 1 500 armed men were allegedly bussed into Sebokeng. ANC supporters had gathered outside the stadium, and they hurled stones and petrol bombs at the buses. After the rally, IFP members marched through Sebokeng, attacking the hostels and causing extensive loss of life. A struggle for control of the hostels raged over the following weeks, which the IFP eventually lost.[49]

The violence in Sebokeng heightened tension and suspicion between Zulu-speaking hostel dwellers and others all over the Rand, producing the climate in which conflict would erupt successively at Kagiso, Khalanyoni, and Vosloorus hostels. It is a comment on the extremely politicised interpretation of this violence that no serious study of the Sebokeng hostels and their relationship to the neighbouring communities was available to the Commission, nor was one undertaken by its researchers to contextualise or explain this initial eruption. The only information that appears to have been available to the TRC's staff was that the Sebokeng hostels were ANC-dominated.[50] It seems possible, even likely, that some of the same dynamics we have identified in Kathorus were also present there. In the absence of detailed material on Sebokeng, let us return to Kathorus.

Tensions mounted in the hostels and squatter camps of Kathorus early in August 1990. Rumours raced around in anxious apprehension of future violence. On 4 August, a letter that allegedly emanated from Vosloorus hostel was shown around Crossroads, warning that the Zulus intended to kill Xhosa-speaking people.[51] The next day, fighting broke out at the opposite end of the Rand in Krugersdorp, when Zulu migrants refused entry to non-IFP residents of Kagiso hostel following an IFP rally. Ten died in this fracas.[52] In the east, the paranoia intensified. Both Zulu and Xhosa hostel dwellers held meetings from which the others were excluded. Each feared the worst. On 8 August, many Crossroads residents stayed away from work. Shortly afterwards, a number of Xhosa residents were assaulted in nearby Lindela hostel and evacuated to Crossroads camp.[53]

On Sunday 12 August, a fight broke out between a Zulu and a Xhosa resident of Khalanyoni hostel, allegedly over a woman. Two Xhosa residents of either the hostel or Phola Park were killed in the subsequent conflict. The following day, Phola Park took revenge by attacking certain hostel residents. At this point, Zulu hostel dwellers began to exert pressure on other hostel inmates to join their ranks. Fearing violence, many fled, abandoning their few possessions in their rooms. Most took refuge in the neighbouring Phola Park squatter camp.[54] Now multiple flashpoints of violence ignited. Phola Park squatters attacked Zulu residents in Katlehong's Crossroads camp, forcing them to flee. They also congregated at the Xhosa-dominated Khuthatha hostel in Katlehong, where they planned an assault on the Zulu-speaking residents of the relatively isolated Lindela hostel. According to the testimonies of residents from both sides, many Zulus died on that night.[55] Police dockets provide some limited corroboration where they record taking a number of corpses away from Lindela hostel.[56] On 15 and 16 August, Vosloorus and KwaThema hostels, situated further east on the Rand, were cleansed of non-Zulu inmates.[57] On 15 August, Crossroads was attacked and razed by Zulu hostel dwellers. Its non-Zulu residents were expelled and relocated to Holomisa Park.[58]

Finally, Phola Park residents and Khalanyoni refugees attacked the Zulu redoubt of Khalanyoni, evicting its inhabitants and then dismantling it brick by brick. This last development, which was only fully accomplished late in 1990, must have seemed to Zulu hostel dwellers like a vindication of their worst fears. Many shared the belief that township residents, and more particularly the 'comrades', wished to obliterate the hostels and the migrant culture they nurtured. When squatters cannibalised Khalanyoni hostel to refurbish their shacks in Phola Park, every paranoid suspicion was confirmed.[59]

During the two-day orgy of violence around Phola Park and Thokoza, 203 people lost their lives.[60] Until this point, the violence was only secondarily party political; primarily, it represented the working out of several intersecting logics of competition, set in motion by both the construction and the partial dismantling of the apartheid system. A clearly party political component only began to intrude now. It is thus an appropriate moment to take stock of the TRC's account of the first phase of what was to become an increasingly internecine civil war. Once again, we need to distinguish between the collective view of the Commission (Volume 2) and the Transvaal regional report (Volume 3).

What is perhaps most striking about the collective view is its failure to comprehend, in any meaningful way, the dynamics that were *not* party political. The sociological contextualisation in Volume 2 is confined to the observation that:

> Many hostels in the Transvaal were inhabited largely by migrant Zulus from rural KwaZulu who had sought employment in the mines and industries in the Transvaal. Township residents viewed them as outsiders. The hostel residents used their common ethnic identity as a means of uniting in a hostile urban environment.[61]

The actual eruption of violence is understood almost exclusively in party political terms, being explained by 'tensions [which] came to a head shortly after the IFP launched a recruitment drive [in August 1990]'.[62]

The Transvaal regional report presented in Volume 3 is more sensitive historically and sociologically, but seems unable to pursue its intuition. It recognises the existence of 'a variety of other divisions, including generational, economic, territorial and personal, that impacted on the form that violence took and motivated people's participation in it',[63] but it fails to explore them. It situates the initial impulse towards conflict on the Rand somewhat earlier in the 'contest for power set in motion by the unbanning of organisations' early in 1990, but the explanation remains party political.[64] It recognises that the precipitating act of violence, which took place on 22 July 1990 at Sebokeng, was itself influenced by the nationwide anti-IFP stay-away at the beginning of the same month (something the collective view wholly ignores), but is unable to set it against the backdrop of hostel-township relationships in the area.[65]

One somewhat self-deprecating passage in the Transvaal report hints at the mandate and resource constraints cramping the research agenda, and may even explain some of the myopia of the report itself.

> In presenting these stories, background details have been used to situate the cases in their proper context. Hence, researchers and writers in the Commission have made use of secondary source material. The reports and publications of research institutes and monitoring bodies, both at home and abroad, have been extensively used.[66]

This highlights a problem the writers themselves might not have comprehended fully, namely, that the secondary reports and publications they refer to were both patchy and skewed. Close monitoring of events on the East Rand only began in August 1990, when a powerful party political component had already inserted itself in the conflict. Reporting by the Independent Board of Inquiry (IBI), for example, only starts in earnest at this point. As a result, most researchers are largely ignorant of earlier events. Thus, the taxi war is either ignored or misunderstood, while the attack on Lindela hostel and related events are totally absent from the reports of NGO monitors and scholarly social science researchers.

A generic statement by Nico de Goede, commander of the police unrest unit in Kathorus, which was attached to many murder dockets in this period and was accessible to the Commission's researchers, could have helped to plug at least some factual gaps. This records gatherings near Lindela hostel on 14 August and corpses being removed from the same site on that day and the next. De Goede's statement nevertheless has one key limitation, which it shares with the Commission, presumably because of their common preoccupation with forensic truth: it makes no effort whatsoever to establish motive or grasp broader context, merely attributing the violence to unspecified antagonisms between ethnic groups.[67] Since the Commission's researchers had no other data to highlight the importance of the Lindela hostel attack, it is not surprising that they passed over this episode in silence. Dozens of others, after all, crowded in immediately thereafter. The only means of remedying this deficiency would have been the extensive interviewing of participants in or bystanders to these events. But seeing that the victims of the Lindela hostel slaughter were migrant Zulus, whose political party, the IFP, refused to cooperate with the Commission, a major source of information was automatically cut off. To have interrogated onlookers, given the constraints the Commission operated under, would have seemed grossly indulgent. The upshot was that the dynamics of conflict could never be grasped fully.

In the absence of a more compelling explanation, the politicisation that occurred in late 1990 and especially in 1991 is therefore mistakenly read back into previous events. Squeezed between the mandate of the Commission, which required it to confine itself to gross human rights violations, and the severely limited scope of most of the available pre-existing research, the Commission's researchers and report were thus condemned to present a patchy and tendentious account, which avoids analysis and resorts largely to description, and from which process and explanation are almost equally absent.

Pauses

Once the violence that swept South Africa in 1990-94 was under way, it was pictured by the TRC as becoming self-generating and acquiring 'a momentum of its own'. A 'spiral of violence' took hold, 'fuelled by local dynamics in which proactive revenge attacks were carried out'. The gross human rights violations of this period assume an increasingly 'anonymous' character. Violence becomes 'random', indiscriminate and motiveless, except at the most brutal level.[68] Perpetrators are both faceless and increasingly dehumanised, driven by unconstrained visceral passions. Any vestigial logic or rationality disappears. The violence is self-explanatory. The Commissioners are conveniently absolved from any further task of explanation.

Once again, the Johannesburg regional report differs slightly from the collective opinion expressed in Volume 2. It shares the view that the violence became more pervasive and internecine as it continued, and developed a momentum of its own.[69] However, in this regional portrayal, the violence is neither as seamless nor as self-perpetuating as the other volume suggests. In particular, the report identifies different patterns and processes as operating in different places and at different times. As it explains:

> Initially, the primary locus of conflict occurred between squatter and hostel communities with conflict spreading to formal townships only later. The conflict led to a process of territorial polarisation with squatter camps and hostels becoming identified with either the ANC or IFP ... The process of political polarisation ... increasingly overlapped with ethnic identity ...[70]

With reference to Kathorus, the report also locates two secondary triggers of violence: the massacre of IFP supporters outside Thokoza stadium on 3 September 1991; and the ethnic cleansing that gripped Phenduka section in Thokoza and several residential areas bordering on the hostels in Katlehong in May 1993.[71] But even here, the understanding conveyed of the changing dynamics of different phases of conflict is deficient. One is left to infer from a *resumption* of violence that it had previously subsided. A sense of *pauses* or slowing down in the violence is otherwise absent and left entirely unexplained. As a result, the idea of new motives or causes supervening can never be contemplated. In a way, this deficiency flows logically from the Commission's overriding objectives and modus operandi. What could be more irrelevant than probing why violence declined?

The rest of this section deploys and augments the chronological framework presented in the Johannesburg regional report. It attempts to move beyond a description of the evolution of the conflict, as presented by the report, and to suggest at least elements of an explanation. It highlights extended pauses and changing tempos in the violence, and explores the extent to which new forces and new factors were responsible for reigniting conflict. In short, it tries to insert faces and motives.

As we have seen, the initial phases of the violence in Kathorus in July and August 1990 were, at most, secondarily party political. The IFP only gradually assumed some kind of orchestrating role. The ANC were barely involved. From mid-August, the pattern changed as the IFP and sections of the state security forces saw in the conflict a new field of political opportunity and launched a multi-pronged offensive against their political and social adversaries. Henceforth, key episodes in the violence bear all the hallmarks of party political direction. On 16 August, the first of a sustained sequence of train attacks occurred, culminating in the ghastly Jeppe station massacre on 13 September 1990, in which 37 commuters died and 270 were injured. All the available evidence, including the IFP's own admission, indicates that hostel dwellers affiliated to the IFP were centrally involved in these campaigns, along with undercover members of the security forces.[72] On 4 September, IFP members attacked inmates who were not Zulu-speakers at Sebokeng hostel. A week later, Zulu hostel dwellers attacked the houses of neighbouring Katlehong and Thokoza residents.[73] On 11 to 13 September, IFP members from Khalanyoni hostel attacked Phola Park squatter camp, burning 600 shacks and killing 80 residents.[74] Ample evidence attests to the active support lent by police in respect of arms, transport and active combatants. White men dressed in balaclavas, with their faces somewhat absurdly covered in black boot polish, fired gunshots and grenades into shacks and torched others with flares, shouting, 'Kom Zulu, kom.' Police Casspirs escorted the attackers and stood by throughout. At least one white combatant was killed, his body later being removed along with others by police Hippos and Casspirs.[75]

In late September, Phola Park residents retaliated by tearing down Khalanyoni hostel brick by brick. Zulu-speaking residents relocated to Zonkesizwe squatter camp. On 25 September, a curfew was imposed on Reef townships, and this had the immediate effect of stemming the violence.[76] Tensions mounted during the course of October between Zulu-speaking and Xhosa-speaking residents of Zonkesizwe. In mid-November, they flared into open conflict. According to the police, the cause was a boycott of rent and service payments in Kathorus, which led to services being cut even for those Zulu-speaking residents who had continued to pay. This was followed a week later by an attack on Holomisa Park squatter camp, which had been established to house mainly Xhosa refugees from Crossroads. Many of the people who fled Zonkesizwe settled at least temporarily in Phola Park. By 18 November, 3 000 Xhosa had moved from

Zonkesizwe to Phola Park, leaving it ruled by the Zulu.[77] Early in December, battles between IFP hostel dwellers and township residents racked Thokoza. Again these arose, in the police view, from the rent and service boycott. According to residents, IFP members visited houses with a list of 'wanted' people, which suggests clear collusion with the council and police.[78] It was in this period that self-defence units (SDUs) aligned with the ANC were formed in most East Rand townships.[79] Finally, in April 1991, Xhosa residents of Holomisa Park expelled all Zulu-speaking residents of the Mandela View camp, perpetuating the cycle of ethnic cleansing.[80]

A central component of these conflicts was clearly a struggle over apartheid space. Similar disputes and ethnic cleansings had been a feature of squatter politics as far back as the 1940s. Only the contending ethnic categories had changed. Such socio-political contestation was infused with and realigned by party political sympathies and interventions, notably political mobilisation by the IFP, 'third force' or police manipulation, and the revolutionary politics of boycott. Train violence, which would punctuate the following three and a half years, was another combustible cocktail of political and socio-political ingredients. The brutal, seemingly professional execution of many railway attacks and their sudden onset suggest that this was a cynical and orchestrated campaign of terror designed to demoralise and dislocate the Tripartite Alliance. The TRC marshalled convincing evidence for its finding that this was indeed the case.[81]

At the same time, many attacks appear to have been initiated by Zulu hostel dwellers themselves, in the context of a struggle for hegemony over the major means of workers' transport. Migrants often had to use the trains to get to work, and this brought them into conflict with supporters of the Tripartite Alliance. Tugged by rival fields of political force, workers of particular political persuasions gravitated to politically aligned railway carriages. Woe betide those who got into the wrong carriage. They ran the horrifying risk of being thrown alive or half-dead from a fast-moving train. Other train attacks took place in carriages where activists were directing 'political singing and sloganeering', which was evidently why they were targeted.[82] Later on, this struggle for political and social control over transport assumed its starkest form when Tripartite Alliance activists so thoroughly sabotaged the railway line between Germiston and Kwesine hostel in Katlehong that it was not repaired until 1994.[83]

From mid-December 1990 to January 1991, there was a downturn in violence. In the intriguing parlance of South African invented traditions, such lulls were shortly to be dubbed 'traditional'. The reason generally proffered was that factories closed down over this period and migrant workers returned home. Intermittent train attacks aside – 231 people were killed and 434 injured in train attacks between January and early September 1991[84] – violence only resumed on any scale in March and April of 1991. The character and distribution of this violence were different, although the objectives appeared more or less the same. Alexandra, for example, which until January had been an ANC stronghold, now became a battlefield, and by the end of the conflict two hostels and several nearby streets had been seized by Zulu-speaking migrants and subjected to IFP control. Apparently, similar contests occurred in Soweto's Meadowlands and Nancefield areas and in the neighbouring squatter camp of Power Park, as well as in Daveyton's squatter camps, by the end of which the ANC began to articulate more vociferously the demand for the wholesale dismantling of hostels. In all but the Nancefield incidents, the IFP appears to have been the main instigator of conflict.[85] In Kathorus, the violence dwindled to insignificant proportions in the first half of 1991, a pattern that was soon replicated over much of the Rand. June, July and August were quiet, at least by the standards of the time. It appeared that once the process of ethnic cleansing and territorial demarcation had reached a certain point, a stand-off had occurred. In an effort to consolidate a de facto truce, a National Peace Accord was signed between the contending parties on 14 September.

It came six days too late. On 8 September, gunmen armed with AK47s ambushed members of the Thokoza Hostel Dwellers Association, who were marching down the now notorious Khumalo Street in Thokoza towards the township's stadium, which lay at the thoroughfare's southern end. Sixteen were killed and thirteen injured.[86] On 29 September, Sam Ntuli, secretary of the Civic Associations of the Southern Transvaal (CAST), was intercepted by three men while driving along Khumalo Street and gunned down.[87] Just over a week later, at the end of Ntuli's funeral, which attracted one of the largest crowds of mourners ever seen in Kathorus, over twenty people were shot and hacked to death in two separate incidents.[88] The violence had reignited. From October to December 1991, violence swept across the Reef, with train attacks, drive-by shootings, and attacks on shebeens and parties being conspicuous features of this phase.

The trigger for the resumption of violence is unambiguous and is downplayed in the broader literature. As the Sithole Committee of the Goldstone Commission of Inquiry found, and the regional report of the TRC makes clear, conflict was precipitated by the Phola Park SDU, which launched a premeditated attack on Thokoza hostel residents on their way to a peace rally in Thokoza stadium. So carefully planned was the massacre that four separate units of the SDU were stationed at the corners of the stadium to carry out the deed. No clear motive has ever been ascertained, other than the general climate of political rivalry and conflict at the time. One particularly disturbing aspect of the episode, which emerged in the Sithole Committee's inquiry (and then in subsequent amnesty hearings of the TRC), was that two key SDU members involved in planning and executing the attack, Mucgugi Ceba and Motani, were also active police informers. There is thus a real possibility that members of the police knew of the attack in advance and did nothing to avert it. The Goldstone Commission nevertheless assigned sole responsibility for the deed to the Phola Park SDU, finding that it 'had little or nothing to do with defence and much more to do with blatant aggression [as well as being] a guise for criminal activity'.[89] This finding, and the broader contours of violence in the intervening period leading up to the presentation of its report, left the Goldstone Commission pondering an awkward question. 'Unlike the so-called Boipatong massacre,' the Commission observed,

> these incidents have all but disappeared from the agenda, and very little progress has been made in their investigation. This must leave innocent victims wondering whether there are different laws and different processes for groups attached to different political parties.[90]

The murder of Sam Ntuli ensured that the violence would rage on. The Sithole Committee was unable to identify the culprits, but later amnesty applications to the TRC by members of Thokoza's Khumalo gang identified gang members and senior figures in the local IFP as being involved in the crime.[91] IFP leaders had ample reason for wanting to get rid of Ntuli, as he was probably the most influential ANC-aligned leader in the region. Indeed, prior attempts had been made on his life, a point that is not adequately emphasised by the Sithole Committee and diminishes the force of its conclusions.

The reasons that gang members offered for why they took part in the murder were party political, at best, and cast a rare shaft of light on the murky, semi-criminal underworld of Thokoza politics, which would play an important role in the evolution of the conflict in the area. According to these accounts, Mbhekiseni Khumalo, already a self-appointed bishop of the Light of God Church of Zion, joined with members of the ANC Youth League early in 1991 to combat local criminals, in particular a gangster named Mugabe. It is unclear how far Khumalo was driven by self-interest at this point, but it soon became his dominating impulse. Over the following months, he acquired businesses and taxis, put known criminals on his payroll, and after being dumped by the local Youth League, began to associate publicly with the IFP. In mid-1991, the Khumalo gang and Youth Leaguers were embroiled in a bitter fight, as Khumalo tried to disarm and eliminate them. The Youth Leaguers retaliated by attacking his house. Khumalo now used his armed gang to eliminate those whom he perceived as a threat to his interests. His IFP connection was almost certainly incidental to his pursuit of mercenary goals. It was these that brought Sam Ntuli into his sights. According to gang members, Ntuli was top of his list because of his leading role in organising stay-aways, consumer boycotts and campaigns for affordable rents, all of which impinged in one way or another on Khumalo's business interests. From mid-1991, the Khumalo gang along with local IFP leaders planned to assassinate Ntuli. In September, they carried out their plan.[92]

The party political dimension of Ntuli's murder is thus as ambiguous as it was in the SDU's massacre of marchers at Thokoza stadium. Nevertheless, between them they precipitated a renewed bloodbath in Kathorus. Following Ntuli's funeral, ANC-aligned groups from Holomisa Park and Mandela View attacked KAPTA taxis, and taxi drivers connected with the IFP attacked mourners, allegedly objecting to the Ntuli funeral stay-away.[93] Conflict rumbled on through October and November 1991, although not as ferociously as in the same period a year earlier. In December and January, there was the 'traditional' lull. In February 1992, violence picked up, with shootings from a minibus in Katlehong that left six dead, a reprisal from Phola Park in which four were killed, hand-grenade attacks on Katlehong trains, and shootings outside Kwesine and Mazibuko hostels in Katlehong. The Easter weekend (3-6 April) saw another series of attacks from Phola Park on the IFP-aligned Crossroads and Zonkesizwe squatter camps, which left twenty-three dead and twenty-two injured. In early June, a series of taxi and train attacks rocked Soweto.[94] In the context of the time, these were relatively desultory. However, a new and decisive change of pattern was imminent. The inspiration was the attacks launched by IFP-aligned KwaMadala hostel dwellers and the third force on the residents of the Joe Slovo squatter camp at Boipatong on 17 June.

The Boipatong massacre, despite all intuitions, assumptions and explanations to the contrary, was not the trigger of a new wave of violence. Ordinary people in South Africa and around the world recoiled in horror at the death toll of forty-five and the evidence of police complicity. Even so, few direct reprisals occurred. The CODESA negotiations were derailed, but this atrocity, along with its counter-provocation at Bisho in September, brought both principal parties to their senses, and a new round of negotiations began. The shift in negotiating position on the part of the government was particularly marked. Facing deadlock, and conscious of the discredit into which the National Party and its destabilising agenda were once again falling, a reformist faction of the Cabinet, led by Pik Botha and Roelf Meyer, pressed for a loosening of the party's alignment with the IFP and a closer accommodation with the ANC. This found formal recognition in the Record of Understanding in September 1992. Once this had been reached, President de Klerk made his first serious effort to rein in the security forces. In particular, the Goldstone Commission was given wider scope for its investigations, and a raid on a Military Intelligence front company on 11 November 1992 yielded hundreds of incriminating documents on state complicity in the violence, as a result of which twenty-three senior army officers were pensioned off. The effects of these events on hit-squad actions and on violence more generally were pronounced. From the end of the year, hit-squad atrocities, train attacks, and the numbers killed in massacres on the Reef tailed off dramatically, as official state sponsorship was withdrawn. The main exception to this pattern was KwaZulu-Natal, where an increasingly politically isolated IFP continued its former ways.[95]

The shift in state involvement in the violence did not signal its end so much as change its character. July and August 1992 were as tranquil as the same period the year before, Boipatong notwithstanding.[96] According to the IBI's monthly reports, tensions began simmering again in Thokoza, Vosloorus and Sebokeng in September 1992, but few deaths or open clashes occurred. In October, IBI reports record a low-intensity war taking hold in Thokoza. Much of the violence is described as 'retaliatory', because 'the SAP in the area seem to be unconcerned'.[97] For the first time, the reports begin to portray the violence as becoming endemic and 'feeding off itself'. By this stage, criminal acts, carried out under the auspices of allegedly politically motivated SDUs and self-protection units (SPUs), were becoming an increasingly important component of the violence. At the end of 1990, SDUs had been formed in various townships to protect communities against attack from hostel dwellers and the security forces. Money was collected to arm these units.[98] Initially, the SDUs played a valued role. However, they gradually became a law unto themselves, a problem that was recognised by leaders of both the ANC and Umkhonto we Sizwe. Part of the problem was that the SDUs had become detached from the township's political organisations. According to Sochs Khanyile, a leading activist in Thokoza from the mid-1980s,

> at that stage organisation was more on fighting those who were fighting us than political issues. If you have such an organisation what tends to happen is that people who lead it are people who can be able to form strategies of defence ... it was then we begin to see not political persons but commanders. They were the ones who were going to run the area because it's a situation of war.[99]

Khanyile himself gave way to the commanders. The militarisation of the main organisation involved in the conflict had profound consequences. Although some SDUs remained loyal to the political cause for which they had been created, many became susceptible to criminalisation. When the ANC Youth League tried to impose some 'political discipline' on deviant SDUs, its members were attacked.

The changing nature of the conflict is captured in the assassination of Prince Mhambi and four other members of the Phola Park residents' committee on 8 October. It soon transpired that Mhambi and his fellows were the victims of a coup staged by increasingly criminalised Phola Park SDU members, anxious to get their hands on new resources being funnelled into the area by philanthropic groups on the outside (although an explicit motive was never acknowledged in the subsequent trial).[100] In the Vaal Triangle, a reign of terror by rampaging youths and ill-disciplined members of the SDUs also began to claim attention. Between May and October, it is thought that 186 individuals lost their lives and 486 were robbed, as the violence increasingly took on the character of a delinquent criminal binge.[101]

Shortly before the formation of SDUs in Kathorus, armed reinforcements had been brought in from KwaZulu-Natal, many of them stock thieves and hit men, to form the IFP-aligned SPUs.[102] Genuine workers were forced to participate in their attacks on the townships, or to leave the hostels or even the Rand. Criminalised IFP-aligned gangs such as that led by Mbhekiseni Khumalo were also given a free hand to pursue their own mercenary interests under a political flag. In December 1992 and January 1993, they embarked on a spree of killings of this kind. Amnesty hearings would subsequently reveal that the attack on the Ngema tavern later that year was motivated by the desire to eliminate business competition.[103]

This undercurrent of criminality, which was only partly curbed by the ANC, may well have been responsible for the largest part of the violence in late 1992 and early 1993. This is registered in the TRC's Transvaal regional report, but as a distinct category of violence and disconnected from any broader process, and so little light is shed on the evolving patterns of conflict.[104] Party political violence continued to drop through the first quarter of 1993. Even the assassination of Chris Hani on 11 April only provoked a brief backlash (260 dead). IBI reports noted that incidents of political violence were at their lowest in the first quarter of 1993 than they had been since 1989.[105]

It was only in May 1993 that a decisive new round of violence began, and it would persist unabated until the end of the year. In this period, large sections of Kathorus were razed, hundreds of people died, and bodies were left to rot for days on the ground. The trigger was a march organised by Phola Park residents along Khumalo Street to the hostels at one end. Local ANC structures had not been consulted about the march and few leaders attended. When marshals called on the marchers to stop one hundred metres from the hostel, armed Phola Park residents surged forward. Hostel residents immediately fired at the marchers and there were many casualties. Kathorus now erupted in flames.[106]

Information on this final phase of the violence is very sketchy, and we must rely on a few fragmentary participant accounts and the often rich data contained in IBI reports. Nevertheless, it does appear that a somewhat different mix of causes and motives stirred up the violence. From January 1993, new efforts at ethnic mobilisation and ethnic cleansing occurred in the township areas bordering Thokoza (notably Phenduka section) and around the Katlehong hostels. Residents of these areas were forced to attend meetings, pay protection money and participate in SDUs, or to flee. Relatively few deaths occurred.[107] Why these things happened at this time, we do not know. In April 1993, several mourners marching to Chris Hani's funeral were shot outside Kathorus hostels, but these were apparently disconnected episodes. Then in May, the Khumalo Street march took place. Like the TRC, we do not know what prompted this event, but the immediate aftermath suggests that at least some of the Kathorus SDUs had decided to mount an offensive against the strongholds of the IFP. In July, a sequence of attacks was launched against IFP-supporting hostel dwellers in Mshayazafe hostel on 5 July, against IFP mourners from Buyafuthi hostel in Katlehong shortly thereafter, and against IFP commuters at a Wadeville taxi rank on 18 July, all of which were reported in a sketchy way and without real motives being offered.[108] At some point during this period, the Kwesine railway line was also sabotaged by SDUs, bottling up IFP hostel dwellers for extended periods. Hostel dwellers retaliated by driving out all non-IFP residents from the houses adjoining the hostel. Between 3 July and the end of August 1993, 544 bodies were found on the East Rand.[109]

This final phase of the violence overlapped with and was overtaken by another set of motives and triggers. Yet again, these centred on taxi routes and on rivalry between taxi associations based in the hostels on the one hand and the townships on the other. In a series of drive-by shootings targeting commuters waiting at taxi ranks, forty-eight people died and forty-five were injured. Rival taxi owners, mainly those aligned with the IFP, played a central role in these attacks. The police claimed that the attacks were prompted by two factors: the circumvention of the Khumalo Street (hostel) route by township taxi owners and commuters, following the eruption of violence in July; and the state of siege that hostel dwellers found themselves in after the Kwesine railway line was sabotaged.[110] This phase of the violence is discussed in the Transvaal report of the TRC, but again abstracted from its context in a separate category of 'taxi violence' and in more or less the same breath as the taxi war that started the conflict in 1989.[111] In a curious way, though in radically transformed circumstances, the vicious war had come full circle. It would only finally stop spinning after the first democratic elections in South Africa in April 1994.

Conclusion

The tasks set for the TRC were well beyond its capacities to carry out. The multiple mandates with which it was charged and the limited resources it had at its disposal forced it to rank in order of priority the different types of investigation it could undertake. The political imperatives of the time impelled it to place the pursuit of forensic truth and restorative truth at the top of its list. This left little time and capacity to probe the larger issues of context and motivation. Perhaps it was unavoidable that the report would fail to present an adequate alternative history or set of social truths. However, the constraints and pressures that shaped the Commission's agenda were only partly responsible for the report's explanatory vacuity. The Commissioners and research teams must also bear some of the responsibility for its failure to uncover social truth. Such an exercise, this paper argues, would have required much more finely grained local studies, drawing on larger slices of life history, than the snapshot victim statements that furnished much of the raw material of the report. We have deployed such material here – albeit unevenly – in an effort to explain the evolving conflict in Kathorus between 1990 and 1994. There are hints in the report that the researchers gathered data which do not feature in their account, but which might well contribute to a better explanation of the events described. Sadly, the Commission refuses to give researchers access to these data. At our last request, its officials would not even tell us what kinds of information they had on their database or which section 29 hearings took place on the East Rand.[112]

Notes

1. Truth and Reconciliation Commission, *Truth and Reconciliation Commission of South Africa Report*, 5 vols (Cape Town, Juta & Co., 1998), vol. 1, ch. 4, para. 21.
2. *TRC Report*, vol. 1, ch. 4, para. 4(a) and paras 83, 85.
3. *TRC Report*, vol. 1, ch. 5, paras 29-45.

4. *TRC Report*, vol. 1, ch. 4, para. 34.
5. *Ibid.*, paras 102, 103.
6. *Ibid.*, paras 72, 77, 89-90, 105-6. The quote is in para. 143.
7. *TRC Report*, vol. 2, ch. 7, para. 7.
8. *TRC Report*, vol. 1, ch. 12, para. 44(n); vol. 2, ch. 7, paras 8-28.
9. *TRC Report*, vol. 1, ch. 4, para. 35.
10. *TRC Report*, vol. 1, ch. 12, paras 3-4.
11. *Ibid.*, para. 37.
12. *TRC Report*, vol. 1, ch. 4, paras 121-4.
13. *Ibid.*, para. 32. See also vol. 1, ch. 5, para. 33.
14. *TRC Report*, vol. 1, ch. 5, para. 107.
15. *TRC Report*, vol. 5, ch. 6, para. 58.
16. *Ibid.*, para. 73.
17. *Ibid.*, para. 115.
18. *Ibid.*, para. 118.
19. University of the Witwatersrand (UW), Independent Board of Inquiry (IBI) documents (not yet inventoried); for an example, see the Version 4 declaration of Sephoa Sarah Shokwa, 4 December 1996.
20. IBI documents; for example, Human Rights Violations statement draft, 10 May 1996. Statement, Leah M. Mokoena, 20 May 1996.
21. IBI documents, P. Kelly, Regional Manager, to L. Mokoena, 17 July 1991.
22. M.M. Khoza, 'Routes, Ranks and Rebels: Feuding in the Taxi Revolution', *Journal of Southern African Studies*, 18:1 (March 1991), p. 245.
23. *TRC Report*, vol. 3, ch. 6, paras 666, 665.
24. P.L. Bonner and V. Ndima, 'The Roots of the Violence on the East Rand', African Studies Seminar, paper presented on 18 October (University of the Witwatersrand, 1999).
25. A. Sitas, 'African Worker Responses on the East Rand to Changes in the Metal Industry, 1960-1980', Ph.D. thesis (University of the Witwatersrand, 1983), p. 261; and J.B. Peires, 'Traditional Leaders in Purgatory in Local Government in Tsolo, Qunu and Port St Johns, 1990-2000', *African Studies*, 59:1 (July 2000), pp. 98-104.
26. Interviews: S. Manyathi, Zonkesizwe, Kathorus, 25 August 1996; M. Sithole, Buyafuthi hostel, Katlehong, 4 August 1996; N. Ndima, Buyafuthi hostel, Katlehong, 4 August 1996.
27. Khoza, *op. cit.*, p. 245.
28. C. McCaul, *No Easy Ride: The Rise and Future of the Black Taxi Industry* (Johannesburg, South African Institute of Race Relations, 1990), p. 14.
29. Khoza, *op. cit.*, p. 245.

30. Interview, M. Maseko, Katlehong, 18 March 1990.
31. Interview, M. Maseko, Katlehong, 18 March 1990.
32. Interviews: K. Ngobese and W. Magubane, Kwesine hostel, Katlehong, 3 August 1996; P. Buthelezi, Nqutu, 25 November 1995; M. Sithole, Buyafuthi hostel, Katlehong, 4 August 1996.
33. Khoza, *op. cit.*, pp. 245-7.
34. *Ibid.*
35. Interviews: Phola Park, October 2000 to March 2001.
36. P.L. Bonner and N. Nieftagodien, *Kathorus: A History* (Johannesburg, Maskew Miller Longman, 2001), pp. 121, 124; Interview, M. Sithole, Buyafuthi hostel, Katlehong, 4 August 1996.
37. Vosloorus Archives (VA), B2/19, Agenda, 30 November 1989.
38. Interview, P. Mlambo, Katlehong, August 1996.
39. G. Ruiters, 'South African Liberation Politics: A Case Study of Collective Action and Leadership in Kathorus, 1980-1989', MA thesis (University of the Witwatersrand, 1995), pp. 33, 39, 41-2; H. Mashabela, *Townships in the PWV* (Johannesburg, South African Institute of Race Relations, 1989), pp. 94-5.
40. UW, Historical and Literary Papers, Papers of the Community Research and Information Network, Report by Julian Baskin, 2 July 1991.
41. Lawyers for Human Rights, 'Phola Park, 10-13 September 1990 as witnessed by the residents', Johannesburg, 1991, p. 3.
42. L. Segal, 'The Human Face of Violence: Hostel Dwellers Speak', *Journal of Southern African Studies*, 18:1 (March 1992), p. 211.
43. H. Sapire, 'Politics and Protest in Shack Settlements of the Pretoria-Witwatersrand-Vereeniging Region, South Africa, 1980-1990', *Journal of Southern African Studies*, 18:3 (September 1992), pp. 693-4.
44. Lawyers for Human Rights, 'Phola Park', p. 5.
45. J. Baskin, *Striking Back: A History of Cosatu* (Johannesburg, Ravan Press, 1991), pp. 327-42.
46. *TRC Report*, vol. 3, ch. 6, para. 549.
47. *Ibid.*, para. 540.
48. Sapire, *op. cit.*, pp. 687, 695.
49. Independent Board of Inquiry into Informal Repression (IBIIR) submission to the TRC on the Reef Violence, 12 December 1996, pp. 6-7.
50. *Ibid.*, p. 6.
51. UW, Historical and Literary Papers, IBI holdings, File 'Phola Park', Statement of V. Ngqwemla, 1283 Crossroads, Katlehong (no date).
52. UW, Historical and Literary Papers, IBI holdings, IBIIR monthly reports,

August 1990.
53. UW, Historical and Literary Papers, IBI holdings, File 'Phola Park', Statement by V. Ngqwemla, 1283 Crossroads, Katlehong (no date).
54. UW, Historical and Literary Papers, IBI holdings, IBIIR monthly reports, August 1990, p. 5.
55. Interviews: N. Ndima, Buyafuthi hostel, Katlehong, 4 August 1996; N. Mbo, Phola Park, 1998.
56. IBIIR dockets; see, for example, Ref JB/01980, Ms F.E. Chauke. Generic statement by N.C. de Goede, Unrest Unit, Thokoza, Katlehong, Vosloorus, 16 November 1990.
57. IBIIR monthly reports, August 1990, pp. 13, 21-2, 25.
58. *Ibid.*, p. 9.
59. IBIIR submission to the TRC on the Reef Violence, 12 December 1996, p. 9.
60. IBIIR monthly reports, August 1990, p. 3.
61. *TRC Report*, vol. 2, ch. 7, para. 203.
62. *Ibid.*, para. 87.
63. *TRC Report*, vol. 3, ch. 6, para. 531.
64. *Ibid.*, para. 528.
65. *Ibid.*, para. 549.
66. *TRC Report*, vol. 3, ch. 1, para. 3.
67. IBI documents; see the generic statement by N.C. de Goede, 16 November 1990, in docket Ms F.E. Chauke, Ref JB/01980.
68. *TRC Report*, vol. 2, ch. 7, paras 1, 460, 503; vol. 3, ch. 6, paras 523, 534, 537.
69. *TRC Report*, vol. 3, ch. 6, paras 523, 534, 537.
70. *Ibid.*, para. 542.
71. *Ibid.*, paras 619, 622-4, 633.
72. IBIIR monthly reports, August 1990, p. 13.
73. IBIIR monthly reports, September 1990.
74. *Ibid.*
75. Lawyers for Human Rights, 'Phola Park', pp. 1-38.
76. IBIIR monthly reports, September 1990, November 1990.
77. IBIIR monthly reports, November 1990, December 1990, January 1991.
78. *Ibid.*
79. *TRC Report*, vol. 2, ch. 7, para. 450.
80. IBIIR monthly reports, April 1991, pp. 17-18.
81. *TRC Report*, vol. 2, ch. 7, paras 80, 130-36; vol. 3, ch. 6, paras 648-52, 660-68.

82. *TRC Report*, vol. 3, ch. 6, para. 647; IBIIR monthly reports, April 1991, p. 19.
83. UW, Historical and Literary Papers, Police Reports and Memoranda 96 2691/E47, Investigations into the existence of a third force as a result of massacres on the East Rand, attacks on policemen and train violence (no date; 1993).
84. IBIIR monthly reports, February 1991, p. 6; March 1991, pp. 1, 21; April 1991, p. 19.
85. IBIIR monthly reports, March 1991, p. 13; April 1991, pp. 12, 16; May 1991, pp. 15-19, 29-30; September 1991, p. 26; October 1991, p. 26.
86. IBIIR monthly reports, January-May 1991; June 1991, p. 11; July 1991, p. 2; August 1991; September 1991, pp. 16-19, 29.
87. IBIIR monthly reports, September 1991, p. 14; October 1991, pp. 22-6; Report of the Committee of Inquiry into the phenomenon and causes of violence in the Thokoza area under the chairmanship of Mr M.N.S. Sithole (Sithole Committee Report), 3 June 1992, pp. 7-14.
88. Sithole Committee Report, pp. 14-27.
89. Sithole Committee Report, pp. 7-15, especially pp. 14, 59. For the Motani reference see IBIIR monthly reports, March 1993, pp. 30-31.
90. Sithole Committee Report, p. 33.
91. *Ibid.*, p. 17.
92. IBIIR monthly reports, February 1991, p. 6.
93. Sithole Committee Report, pp. 18-24.
94. IBIIR monthly reports, November 1991, pp. 8-11; December 1991/January 1992, pp. 12-13; February 1992, pp. 13, 15-17; March 1992, pp. 20-21; April 1992.
95. R. Taylor and M. Shaw, 'The Dying Days of Apartheid', in D.R. Howarth and A.J. Norval (eds), *South Africa in Transition: New Theoretical Perspectives* (London, Macmillan, 1998), pp. 18-24.
96. IBIIR monthly reports, July 1992, August 1992.
97. IBIIR monthly reports, October 1992.
98. Interview, S. Khanyile, Thokoza, 23 February 1999.
99. *Ibid.*
100. IBIIR monthly reports.
101. IBIIR monthly reports, May-October 1992.
102. Bonner and Ndima, *op. cit.*, pp. 22-3.
103. IBIIR monthly reports. For the amnesty hearing see www.truth.org.za/amntrans/1999/99090609JHB/990906jh.
104. *TRC Report*, vol. 3, ch. 6, paras. 678-98.
105. IBIIR monthly reports, April 1993, p. 1.

106. IBIIR monthly reports, May 1993, pp. 32-4.
107. IBIIR monthly reports, January, February 1993.
108. IBIIR monthly reports, July 1993, pp. 19-22.
109. IBIIR monthly reports, August 1993.
110. UW, Historical and Literary Papers, Police Reports and Memoranda 96 2691/E47, 'Investigations into the existence of a third force'.
111. *TRC Report*, vol. 3, ch. 6, paras 665-9.
112. Judge Denzil Potgieter (TRC Legal Department) to Noor Nieftagodien (History Workshop), 4 June 2001.

9

NATIONAL NARRATIVE VERSUS LOCAL TRUTHS
The Truth and Reconciliation Commission's Engagement with Duduza

Hugo van der Merwe

Introduction

One of the central goals of the Truth and Reconciliation Commission (TRC) was to 'uncover the truth' about South Africa's human rights abuses. This paper explores different understandings of the nature of this truth, by examining the tensions between the views of the TRC and those of a range of community stakeholders in Duduza, a township near Johannesburg.[1]

A central component of the TRC's reconciliation agenda was to develop and promote a common understanding of the history of the apartheid conflict. Through collecting individual stories and convening a hearing on human rights violations in Duduza, the TRC reflected to the community certain images of its own history. While Duduza residents were extremely interested in revealing and recording the truth about the past, they found the TRC process problematic in many ways. They felt that the type of information considered relevant and the space for complexity in the narratives were too constrained. Community reconciliation and local history, as perceived by the residents, required a much more involved, long-term engagement with the dynamics of local conflict.

The TRC's Engagement with Local History

While the TRC's mandate covered a range of responsibilities, section 3(1) of the enabling legislation spelled out its specific objectives:

> The objectives of the Commission shall be to promote national unity and reconciliation in a spirit of understanding which transcends the conflicts and divisions of the past by –

(a) *establishing as complete a picture as possible of the causes, nature and extent of the gross violations of human rights which were committed ... by conducting investigations and holding hearings;*
(b) facilitating the granting of amnesty to persons who make full disclosure of all the relevant facts relating to acts associated with a political objective and comply with the requirements of this Act;
(c) establishing and making known the fate or whereabouts of victims and by *restoring the human and civil dignity of such victims by granting them an opportunity to relate their own accounts of the violations of which they are the victims, and by recommending reparation measures in respect of them;*
(d) compiling a report providing as comprehensive an account as possible of the activities and findings of the Commission ... and which contains recommendations of measures to prevent the future violations of human rights.[2]

The Act did not specify exactly how the TRC should go about 'establishing as complete a picture as possible of the causes, nature and extent of the gross violations of human rights', nor how it should grant victims 'an opportunity to relate their own accounts of the violations'.[3] It was also not clear how these objectives could be achieved in a way that would 'promote national unity and reconciliation in a spirit of understanding which transcends the conflicts and divisions of the past'.[4]

The TRC operationalised these specific objectives in relation to particular communities by collecting statements from local victims and then holding a community hearing on gross human rights violations. These community hearings became the dominant focus of the first one and a half years of the TRC's operation, shaping the public image of its work and setting the scene for its subsequent amnesty hearings, investigations and published findings. Between April 1996 and May 1997, eighty such community hearings were held. These were public meetings lasting between one and three days, during which ten to twelve victims told their stories to a panel of Commissioners and a hall full of community members and local and international leaders.

These hearings served a number of functions for the Commission. First, they focused on victims, giving them an opportunity to speak out, to be listened to by representatives of government, to express their feelings in public, and to explain what they wanted with regard to truth, reparation and healing.

Second, the local community had the opportunity to find out directly from the victims what had happened, to clear up suspicions about who was involved in which abuses, and to break the culture of silence and mistrust among community members. It was hoped that this process would promote understanding among different groupings in local communities, and among political parties and different races.

Third, the community hearings provided a powerful media image that could be conveyed to the country as a whole. Night after night, for several months, national television presented South Africans with the stories of atrocity and suffering related by victims at the hearings. The goal of this national message was to allow the whole country to confront its past, and to make it impossible for people to deny the suffering that had been caused by the conflict.

Using Duduza as a case study, this paper demonstrates how the tension between these different levels of intervention – personal, community and national – ultimately undermined the TRC's ability to make an effective impact on the personal and community levels. The TRC probably impacted most effectively at the national level, largely through the extensive media coverage of its victim and amnesty hearings. While the nature and extent of this impact may be debated, the profile it received and the level of public interest give some indication of its significance.[5]

Duduza

Background to the Conflict

Duduza is a black township that forms part of the Greater Nigel area on the East Rand. Nigel itself is an historically white town, with neighbouring African, Indian and coloured townships. The total population of the town and townships is between 150 000 and 200 000, and over half these people live in Duduza.

Duduza has experienced a great deal of political conflict over the last thirty years. There was some violence here in the wake of the 1976 Soweto uprising, in which a number of youths were shot and killed by the police. After a period of relative political calm, the community mobilised again in the early 1980s under the leadership of the Duduza Civic Association, a locally based political structure aligned with the African National Congress (ANC). In 1985, violence erupted after police fired on a march organised to protest against the bucket sewage system used by the Duduza Town Council. Over the following two years, there was ongoing violence between members of the community, the police and the council. Black policemen and councillors living in the township were chased out and the area was made 'ungovernable', meaning that state structures were effectively expelled. Youth leaders emerged during this period and took a harder line.

The police response to protest action also became more drastic and brutal. In one incident, the police attacked the house of a Duduza Civic Association leader, killing his two daughters. In a revenge attack by youths, a white woman from a nearby farm was ambushed and killed. The police made extensive use of detention and torture, and of assassination in some cases, to suppress political protest in the area. They also infiltrated local political structures, and in 1985 orchestrated the 'zero hand grenade' incident, in which a number of Duduza activists were killed.[6] The murder of alleged police informer, Maki Skhosana, was linked to this incident. Rumours spread through the community that she had had a relationship with a police operative and had informed on the victims. She was beaten and stoned to death by members of the community, and her body set alight and mutilated. A number of people were subsequently convicted and imprisoned for the murder.

Tension also arose around the presence of Inkatha Freedom Party (IFP) supporters in Duduza hostels. In 1991, violence erupted when IFP supporters, who had been chased out of hostels in the neighbouring townships by ANC members, fled to the Duduza hostels. The conflict that emerged was both among hostel dwellers, and between the hostel and community residents. Eventually, residents burned down and demolished the hostels. Some of the hostel dwellers were absorbed into the community, while others fled to other townships.

After the democratic transition of 1994, political tensions in Duduza continued in other forms. One source of conflict was the local government election for the Greater Nigel Council in 1995. There were allegations of intimidation around the nomination and election of candidates to represent the ANC on the council. The ANC candidates who finally represented Duduza, which had been allocated six of the ten council seats, won by a wide margin against National Party (NP) and independent candidates. The three seats in the white neighbourhood of Nigel, an area previously held by the Conservative Party and contested in 1995 by the Freedom Front, were won by the NP, while the ANC narrowly won the seat in the coloured and Indian area against NP opposition. The ANC thus held 70 per cent of the seats in the Greater Nigel Council, which meant they could make budgetary decisions without having to reach consensus with the NP.

These are the broader, visible dynamics of the conflict. But while there were certain clear battle lines between some groups, many internal divisions also arose as the conflict metastasised. The cohesion of the community was destroyed as suspicions, allegations of complicity, retribution and competition for leadership led to violent internal struggles and suppression of internal dissent.

By infiltrating activist groups and planting rumours, the state security forces created and fostered suspicion among residents. In the face of state repression, these organisations were also forced to operate secretively, thus undermining their democratic ideals. Internal conflicts were not always managed constructively, and coercive power struggles developed between different factions. One victim commented on the state of community relations: 'The whole community needs reconciliation. The police had infiltrated the comrades and informers were used. We don't trust anybody any more. All victims are suspicious.'[7]

The TRC's Involvement in Duduza

The TRC held a one-day human rights violations hearing in Duduza on 2 February 1997. The hearing combined cases from Duduza and the neighbouring communities of Ratanda, KwaThema and Tsakane. Rather than being a community hearing, in the strict sense, this was a regional hearing that tried to cover the Far East Rand. In preparation for the event, the TRC met with various individuals and parties, including the Town Council, the Civic Association, trade unions and churches.

TRC statement-takers came to the area and collected statements from the public on a specified day. Additional statements were collected by the Khulumani Support Group. This group, which counsels and supports the victims of apartheid, was not included in the Commission's consultative workshops with the community.

The TRC also contacted a range of people in the communities to encourage their participation in its activities. The main conduit between the TRC and the communities was the local political leadership of the ANC and NP. However, these leaders were not effective in mobilising community involvement in the process. They seemed to have no effective way of channelling information on the TRC to their supporters. Some victims felt that this was a deliberate attempt to suppress certain stories that might have implicated these leaders and their colleagues. Few of the victims interviewed in Duduza had received any information about the TRC through the political structures or the Commission itself.[8] Most had relied on their own networks or on Khulumani for this information.

While the TRC also liaised with religious leaders, this interaction was confined mainly to using church structures to provide publicity about statement-taking and the public hearing. Church leaders felt that they had not been included sufficiently in the broader process; for example, they were excluded from the planning activities, which were steered by local political leaders.[9] One church leader commented: 'The TRC used the church structures to access the community. We were, however, not requested to join any committees. They mainly liaised with the ANC on things like the venue and so on.'[10]

The hearing was well attended: the hall was full and loudspeakers had to be set up outside. Most of those present were local Duduza residents, while a few people came from Ratanda, KwaThema and Tsakane. Only one white person from Nigel, a National Party councillor, seems to have attended.

Of the nine cases heard on the day, three concerned residents of Duduza and six concerned the neighbouring communities. The witnesses from Duduza who told their stories were some of the surviving victims of the 'zero hand grenade' incident; the sister of Maki Skhosana; and someone who was both tortured by the police and accused of being a police spy. Whereas the three Duduza cases were all related to the period of intense repression and resistance in the 1980s, the remaining six covered a range of incidents, spanning the past thirty years and involving various political organisations.

Together, the nine cases presented a very diverse array of experiences of victimisation. Most implicated the state security forces, but some related to violence between the IFP and ANC. Others involved incidents of taxi violence, where the perpetrators were unknown, and one case involved a person who had disappeared in the 1960s, apparently when he had gone to join the liberation movement in exile. The hearing thus incorporated a number of different communities, each with quite different conflict dynamics and types of victimisation. There was no obvious underlying cohesion to the various stories told. Trying to construct such a unifying narrative or to engage victims about the meaning of their experience would be complicated. If one included the hundreds of other victims who made statements but did not appear at the hearing, the task would be even more daunting.

Competing Narratives

In the process of collecting stories, doing investigations and conducting public hearings, various aspects of the TRC process became contested. Four key areas of contestation that illustrate the underlying tensions are discussed below: the social contextualisation of victimisation; the definition of a relevant abuse; the nature and identity of the perpetrator; and the choice of key victimisation incidents.

Social Contextualisation

Victims' stories about their suffering contain various levels of social contextualisation, ranging from the intensely personal to the more abstract. Here I will identify four contextual levels: personal, community, national and systemic. While one account of victimisation can cover all four levels, the stories of victims more often focus on one or two.

For many victims, their personal trauma, the effects of the victimisation on the lives of themselves and their families, is a key part of the story. Relating this part of their story is important because they want their suffering to be understood and acknowledged. They speak of pain, humiliation, fear, anger, and a struggle for survival and psychological healing. Some victims give insulated accounts of their experience, focusing on the social, economic and psychological repercussions on their own lives. Rather than looking for social explanations for their suffering, they speak as if the experience was arbitrary and without meaning. Personal suffering seems to have isolated them from their society and left them in a self-referential world.

A second layer of many victims' stories is the community context within which the victimisation occurred. Many stories fit into a local history, and feature other local actors and events that are specific to that community. The conflicts of the past took a particular shape at the local level, with communities often internally divided between activists and collaborators, or between rival groups of activists. For many victims, a central aim of their story is to make sense of the dynamics of an evolving local conflict and to contextualise themselves within it. Furthermore, the legacy of past conflict is often still embedded in the local milieu. People still mistrust and resent one another, and remain suspicious about who did what to whom. Uncovering the truth about the past is seen as a way of resolving these ongoing tensions.

A third layer refers to national political struggles. Victims draw a connection between their experience of victimisation and key national events or dynamics. They often demonstrate a deep political awareness, which allows them to describe their own suffering in relation to a particular phase or campaign in the broader liberation struggle, or in relation to particular political organisations and repressive state strategies. Some victims, especially those who were activists or leaders, place their stories mainly in this national context. They see their opponents not as independent actors but as agents of the apartheid system.

A fourth layer of meaning concerns the apartheid system itself and the severely repressive strategies required to maintain it. This systemic context is closely tied to national political dynamics, but implies a further level of abstraction. Here the victims understand their own experience in relation to the root causes of the conflict, whether racism, capitalism, colonialism or some other form of systematic oppression. Instead of regarding the conflict as being simply between the security forces and the community, or between rival political parties, these stories address broader social divisions.

This may seem like an obvious backdrop for stories of victimisation, but the victims themselves are not always aware of it. Take the case where black victims were abused by fellow blacks. Some victims interpreted this in the broader context of apartheid, drawing a link, for instance, between the maintenance of white privilege and the homeland system. But others saw their victimisation as solely a reflection of internal community divisions.

To uncover the truth about a particular human rights abuse, one needs to place it within its context, ideally drawing on all four levels of explanation. However, the reality is that different people prioritise different levels of social analysis. Victims do not all make sense of their experiences in the same way, and neither do those who intervene in conflict situations, such as researchers, peacemakers or politicians. At best, the contextualisations of outsiders fail to encompass the full range of explanations. At worst, they impose an interpretation, and undermine the attempts of victims and communities to rebuild a sense of meaning.

The TRC's formula for uncovering the truth and making sense of a victim's experience was to contextualise the abuse within the national political conflict. The attempt to engage victims with the national narrative arose from an understanding of reconciliation as essentially 'national reconciliation' between race groups and political parties. For many victims this made perfect sense. They felt validated by having the Commission acknowledge their contribution to the struggle for liberation, and were better able to come to terms with the consequences of suffering by having it associated with noble political goals.

But for victims who prioritised other levels of meaning, the focus on the national struggle was sometimes experienced as a hidden agenda. Some victims, who were intent on clarifying local patterns of abuse, and exposing local perpetrators and collaborators, saw the TRC's emphasis on the bigger picture as suspicious. They thought the Commission was trying to keep secrets. Whereas some saw a conspiracy between local ANC leaders and the TRC (which was generally regarded as an ANC body), others simply saw a lack of concern about local needs. Two comments by victims illustrate the seriousness of these misgivings:

> The community is dissatisfied with the TRC hearing because certain facts remain hidden. There is an ANC conspiracy to cover up, especially the hand grenade incident. One person who gave a statement contradicts evidence given at the TRC hearing.[11]

> The Commissioner who met with the ANC arranged a special deal to hide the truth. Many local ANC leaders were implicated by victim statements. They were afraid of what might come out.[12]

Rather than seeing the TRC as a victim-centred process, many victims thought they were being used to present a politically skewed national narrative of the past.

Defining Relevant Abuses

There was general dissatisfaction among community members that the TRC did not address a broad enough range of abuses. The Act tried to define a 'relevant abuse' with reference to a particular time-frame, and to what it termed 'gross human rights violations', which included only '(a) the killing, abduction, torture or severe ill-treatment of any person; or (b) any attempt, conspiracy, incitement, instigation, command or procurement to commit [such] an act ...'[13]

Today, Nigel and Duduza still experience serious racial tensions, and blacks are extremely conscious of ongoing structural inequalities. Incidents of racism are remembered clearly and past policies of racial discrimination recalled with deep pain. But stories about the everyday violation of human rights, in relation to education, health, employment, and so on, did not feature at the hearings, as they did not fall directly within the TRC's ambit. While the Commission was interested in exploring the dynamics of race and racism, the focus fell on *gross* violations of human rights, involving overt physical violence.[14]

Furthermore, the definition of a 'relevant abuse' took into account the actions of the perpetrator rather than the consequences for the victim. An act of attempted murder, which may have had very little impact on the life of the intended victim, was included in the TRC's mandate, whereas forced removals, with the attendant loss of property, livelihood, community, and so on, were excluded.

People found it artificial that a 'victim' was defined in a limited way as someone who had been abused for a political motive. The TRC's constant attempt, evident during the public hearings,[15] to unearth the political motive involved in an incident, and thus impose a political narrative on the victim's story, did not always make sense to community members. They did not draw these clear distinctions.

NGO staff had great difficulty explaining the subtle legal differentiations of the Act to victims:

> Part of the problem is the focus on political victims. Many victims do not understand the distinction – why are they not accepted by the TRC? Some feel their suffering has been delegitimised because it is not a gross human rights violation. Some of them may have suffered even more than those who have been recognised. The

type of victimisation does not necessarily match the amount of suffering. Some people who have endured tremendous suffering also managed to bounce back.[16]

Nature and Identity of the Perpetrators

The enabling legislation gave the impression of a strong commitment to exposing the identities of perpetrators. Victims would be allowed to name the perpetrators in public hearings, and the TRC would try to make findings about who was responsible for particular acts.[17]

In practice, there was a legal requirement that the TRC give alleged perpetrators sufficient prior notice that they would be named at a hearing.[18] This notification did not always happen, or happen in time, and victims were consequently often prevented from naming names. Some victims saw this as another of the TRC's attempts to cover up the identities of certain perpetrators. There were suspicions that the Commission was biased or trying to protect local perpetrators, especially when proper explanations for this restriction were not given. The transcript of one victim's testimony at the Duduza hearing provides some insight into these suspicions:

> MR BUTHELEZI: I want to mention the names now. Why did they decide to call me a ...
> CHAIRPERSON: Could you please ...
> MR BUTHELEZI: police informer because ...
> CHAIRPERSON: Could you please listen. We have never stopped you from mentioning those names. If you did not for the time that you were sitting there, do not blame it on this body. We are saying thank you, let us give others a chance.
> MR LEWIN: Did he give us the names?
> DR ALLY: Sorry, where is ...
> CHAIRPERSON: You can still, you can still give us the list of those people.
> MRS SEROKE: Tom, the names are in the statement anyway. We will deal with that later.
> CHAIRPERSON: Thank you for the names, we have the list of those people. Thanks, please, I can literally say, can you please learn to give us the quiet that we need which, I think, you personally need, because you need to understand what is going on and you will appreciate that if you have got remarks to make, please make them, out of here. We would love to give everybody a chance.[19]

Especially when it came to conducting investigations, victims felt that the TRC did not pursue cases unless the perpetrator or the victim was of national status. This concern was also expressed in relation to the amnesty hearings, where amnesty applicants were required to provide full disclosure of their actions. The Amnesty Committee interpreted 'full disclosure' so as to exclude the identity of informers involved in cases of human rights abuse. Victims objected to this interpretation and demanded that such people be named. For the TRC, the main goal of exposing the line of command was to determine who had given the orders. While this was important to victims, it was often just as important, if not more so, to find out which members of their local community had been involved in the abuse.

> At the TRC hearing people expected to hear the truth about a number of key cases. The truth about who informed is central to people, because it had the involvement of local people who still live here. Certain more serious cases were not heard, and many others are also not addressed. People are less concerned about naming the police who were involved. The main concern is the people who were suspected of being informers.[20]

The TRC was also often engaged in allocating institutional rather than personal responsibility. The goal was often to make a finding (in the final report) that a certain political group or state structure should be held responsible for a particular abuse. This allowed the Commission to build a broad picture of the nature, extent and dynamics of abuses during the apartheid era. For victims, such findings generally just confirmed what they and others in the community already knew. Victims often felt the need to hold individual people responsible, to attach a face to the evil. A finding of institutional responsibility did not provide the same sense of justice or catharsis.

Key Victimisation Incidents

The TRC used certain criteria in selecting cases for the public hearings. They chose cases that represented different forms of victimisation (for example, killing, torture); that involved victims of different races and political parties; that were well known in particular communities (for example, massacres); that illustrated particular national patterns of human rights abuses (for example, train killings); and that covered the whole of the mandate period (1960-94).[21]

The Commissioners did not always explain these criteria clearly when a hearing was held, and when they did, community members did not always believe them.[22] One apparent bias that people observed was the selection of cases involving prominent victims. The death or torture of a political leader often seemed to take priority, both in the choice of cases for the public hearings and in the time the TRC invested in further investigations. Victims generally felt that this indicated a lack of concern for ordinary victims.

Victims and other community members were also concerned that what they saw as key local events were not taken seriously by the TRC. Especially where an incident still had important repercussions in the present, and old suspicions continued to divide people, they wanted the Commission to pursue it more vigorously. This was the case, for instance, where an individual who now occupied a prominent position in the community was suspected of involvement in a past incident.

> The TRC should have focused more on specific key cases in Duduza. It focused too much on rather insignificant cases. Certain cases are a crux in terms of understanding the conflict in Duduza. Others are more peripheral. The important cases are: the first killing of a boy during the protest march against the bucket system, the case of Mrs Thobela's family, and the killing of Maki.[23]

The TRC did not consult communities when it prioritised cases for the hearings or for further investigation. In the case of Duduza, the TRC conducted limited further investigations. It focused on corroboration, that is, on confirming that victims were telling the truth, rather than on trying to identify the perpetrator or establish additional facts. The only cases where it did conduct further investigations were the 'zero hand grenade' incident and the killing of Maki Skhosana. Both of these cases were heard at the public hearing, and both had received extensive media attention. These are also the only cases mentioned in the TRC's final report in relation to events in Duduza. None of the dozens of other victims who made statements in Duduza are acknowledged. Some interviewees expressed serious doubts about the TRC's interest in 'common people' and questioned the attention given to more prominent victims:

> The TRC failed to reach real victims. Reconciliation is not about important individuals, but the common people need to reconcile. Prominent people were approached to make statements. Thousands of people who still have birdshot pellets lodged in their skins abound in Duduza. Maybe I do not understand the workings of the TRC.[24]

Conclusion

This case study throws up many questions, both about the nature of local history and about the role of a structure like the TRC in engaging people in a dialogue about the past.

While the TRC had only a brief involvement with Duduza and was limited in its scope, the community viewed the encounter as a critical opportunity to access information and confront official silences. The nature of truth, history and memory in any complex community, especially one that has been fundamentally destabilised by severe conflict, clearly cannot be captured in a single intervention, even by a structure as elaborate and powerful as the TRC. Even if the TRC had tried to engage the community on its own terms, without the broader agenda of constructing a national narrative, it would probably not have been much more successful in satisfying local demands. Truth at the community level is unlikely to be effected by attempts to construct a consensus in the short or medium term. The memory of the past is so caught up in the construction of present relationships and positions of power and status, that the identification of relevant issues, perspectives and narrative styles would have to be revised constantly to accommodate different parties, contexts and time periods.

This is not to argue that the endeavour of engaging with the past is impossible or meaningless. On the contrary, it is deeply meaningful because of its impact on the present and the future of communities. However, it is also an open-ended process. While certain facts can be established beyond any doubt, the relevance of each fact (and each suspicion) will wax and wane as new relationships and social norms are developed. Allowing marginalised voices to participate in such a process is vital in ensuring a more open and honest reflection.

The TRC's brief intervention gave the idea of confronting the past new currency. It brought out various competing views, but did not allow time and space for their resolution. By prioritising a national agenda, it compromised and diminished the truth-recovery goals of certain community members. The complexities of local conflicts were again subjugated to broader concerns about race and national liberation.

The contentiousness of the truth about the local conflict also reflects the shifting nature of conflict. While the conflict in Duduza can be located directly within the struggle over apartheid, the way it plays out in the local community is not simply as a racial or class struggle. Local struggles for resources and power are superimposed on the conflict. The history of violence, and a resultant culture of violence, also undermine the community's ability to deal with conflict among its members, and this complicates the reconciliation process.

It is clear that the promotion of national reconciliation does not automatically produce reconciliation at other levels in the society. Despite political and institutional transformation at the national level, and the creation of peaceful relations between erstwhile political opponents at the community level, the truth (or lack of it) remains a volatile social issue in the local arena. Reconciliation at community level will require extensive further intervention, dealing directly with truth, as well as other concerns, through more open-ended and sustained dialogue, investigation and reflection.

Notes

1. This paper relies largely on research conducted in Duduza during 1997. It also draws extensively on ongoing research and intervention work by the Centre for the Study of Violence and Reconciliation in numerous communities throughout South Africa between 1996 and 2002. The research was made possible partly through funding provided by the United States Institute of Peace for the author's Ph.D. thesis, 'The Truth and Reconciliation Commission and Community Reconciliation: An Analysis of Competing Conceptualisations and Strategies' (George Mason University, Virginia, 1999). The sections of this paper dealing with the TRC's hearing in Duduza were published in the TRC's final report. See Truth and Reconciliation Commission, *Truth and Reconciliation Commission of South Africa Report*, 5 vols (Cape Town, Juta & Co., 1998), vol. 5, ch. 9, para. 130, pp. 423-9.
2. Promotion of National Unity and Reconciliation Act, No. 34 of 1995 (my emphasis).
3. Without arguing that the legislation should have been completely prescriptive, it should be noted that the Act gave the Commission the leeway to take on an enormously broad range of tasks. This created the conditions for much internal disagreement and conflict with the public about what people could legitimately expect from the TRC.
4. For a detailed discussion of the pressures that led to the formulation of the TRC's reconciliation agenda, see H. van der Merwe, P. Dewhirst and B. Hamber, 'Non-Governmental Organisations and the Truth and Reconciliation Commission: An Impact Assessment', *Politikon*, 26:1 (May 1998), pp. 55-79.
5. The numbers of people who watched the weekly television programme *TRC Special Report* are telling: in its first year on air, the programme drew more than one million viewers (G. Theissen, 'The Truth and Reconciliation Commission in South Africa: A Review of Public Opinion Surveys', Centre

for the Study of Violence and Reconciliation, unpublished report (Johannesburg, 1999)).

6. In 'Operation Zero Zero', as it was called officially, two police operatives pretended to be members of Umkhonto we Sizwe, the ANC's military wing, who had come to assist local activists with training. They instructed local youths in the use of hand grenades, and then helped them to plan simultaneous attacks in the townships of Duduza, KwaThema and Tsakane. When the attacks were launched, the booby-trapped grenades exploded prematurely, killing eight youths and severely maiming several others. See *TRC Report*, vol. 3, ch. 6, paras 372-5.
7. Interview with victim, Duduza, 11 June 1997.
8. Ten victims were interviewed individually, and a group of seven additional victims were interviewed informally.
9. Two key local church leaders involved in the TRC consultation process in Duduza were interviewed. The key person in local government responsible for liaising with the TRC confirmed the limited role played by church structures.
10. Interview with church leader, Duduza, 19 August 1997.
11. Interview with victim, Duduza, 2 July 1997.
12. Interview with victim, Duduza, 19 February 1997.
13. Promotion of National Unity and Reconciliation Act, ch. 1, section 1(ix).
14. At times, the Commission was pressured to interpret its mandate more broadly, so as to include forced removals, for instance (Van der Merwe, Dewhirst and Hamber, *op.cit.*). While this attempt and others were turned down, the mandate was sometimes broadened, as in the sectoral hearings.
15. Consider this exchange from the human rights violations hearing in Vosloorus on 7 February 1997:

    DR RANDERA: But why did the links with the IFP ... (indistinct) you say he (Rev Khumalo) was strongly linked to the IFP? I just want us to go away quite clear, was this gang associated with the IFP or was this just because the Reverend's daughter was raped?

    MR NTOMBELA: He was an IFP member, I mean Khumalo.

    MR LEWIN: Could I ask you, I think in following up what Dr Randera has asked, would you describe the conflicts that you have told us about, would you describe it as a political conflict?

    MR NTOMBELA: What was happening had nothing to do with politics but murdering and thugs around.
16. Interview with NGO staff member, 19 June 1997.
17. Section 4 of the Act stipulates: 'The functions of the Commission shall be

to achieve its objectives, and to that end the Commission shall –
(a) facilitate, and where necessary initiate or coordinate, inquiries into –
...
(iii) the identity of all persons, authorities, institutions and organisations involved in such violations ...'

18. This requirement for prior notification resulted from a legal challenge by one of the first perpetrators to be named at a public hearing. Thereafter, the Commission was compelled to give notice to alleged perpetrators of human rights violations before evidence was heard publicly, and to provide them with sufficient information about the allegations against them to enable them to make representation.
19. Transcript of human rights violations hearing, Duduza, 2 February 1997. See www.truth.org.za/hrvtrans/jb_victim .
20. Interview with community leader, Duduza, 19 August 1997.
21. In the report, the criteria of race, age and geographic location are also listed in relation to this selection process.
22. A Commissioner at the Duduza hearing (2 February 1997) spoke about the selection of cases to be heard:

> Now, I know that many people who have made statements become very angry when they are not asked to appear in public hearings and that is, I think, because people may have the wrong idea that those who appear in public hearings are more important than those who do not. That is certainly not the thinking of the Truth Commission. When we select people to come to a public hearing what we try to do is select cases which give us some idea of the nature of the conflict. So we try to use cases to give us some insight or a window into the nature of the conflict. We do not choose people because we think their stories are more important or because they are more important. We also try, we also try to cover the period that the Commission has to look at which is 1960 to 1994.

23. Interview with community leader, Duduza, 15 May 1997.
24. Interview with community leader, Duduza, December 1999.

10

'TELL NO LIES, CLAIM NO EASY VICTORIES'
A Brief Evaluation of South Africa's Truth and Reconciliation Commission[1]

Graeme Simpson

Introduction

It is impossible to understand and evaluate South Africa's Truth and Reconciliation Commission (TRC) properly, or to extract significant lessons from it for other societies in transition to democracy, without analysing the unique political circumstances that gave rise to it. For this reason, the point is frequently made that the history of the South African TRC was inextricably linked to the particular evolution of South Africa's negotiated settlement.[2] However, it is less often acknowledged that this politically fraught frame of reference fundamentally shaped the parameters of the complex truths about the past that were 'recovered' by the TRC.

It is argued in this paper that the TRC's primary mandate to document responsibility for politically motivated violations of human rights in the past and to build reconciliation at a formal political level, shaped and restricted the modes of truth that the TRC was able to extract from its engagement with the history of the apartheid era. A broad deference to historical political orthodoxy – significantly determined by the TRC's legislative mandate – had the effect of politically sanitising versions of the past which offered more complex and less predictable understandings of the magnitude and nature of violence and violation under apartheid. As a consequence, the role of the TRC in building reconciliation and preventing the re-emergence of human rights violations in post-apartheid South Africa has been significantly constrained by a representation of past conflict premised on politically defined cleavages, which are construed as neatly separable analytically from broader patterns of criminal and community violence in South African society. In its extraction of *the* truth about South Africa's past, the TRC's 'privileging' of narrowly defined political violence may therefore do more to mystify than to explain continuity and change in the patterns of violence and violation which continue to pervade this society after apartheid.

The most important aspect of the country's transformation from authoritarianism and racism into a constitutional democracy was that it happened not by revolution or force of arms, but through the compromises of dialogue and political negotiation.

This transition was fundamentally different to that undergone by Nazi Germany after World War II, for example, where the conflict produced a clear victor and where the Allies were able to impose their version of justice on the Nazi regime at Nuremberg. The victors chose prosecution as the primary mode of dealing with the past, not only because they believed it was morally right, but, crucially, because they were able to do so.

The South African transition is also different to that undergone by Chile. When General Augusto Pinochet, the former head of the Chilean junta, agreed to restore power to an elected civilian government, he still commanded sufficient power himself, especially within the politically interventionist military, to ensure that he remained in office as head of the armed forces. As a result of the continued influence of the military, the vulnerable new democratic government was effectively unable, save in a few exceptional circumstances, to bring charges against those responsible for assassinations, torture and disappearances under Pinochet's rule. Although the new government did establish a truth commission that officially investigated, recorded and acknowledged human rights abuses under military rule, those who were responsible remained unpunished.

If post-war Germany represents one extreme of the justice policies pursued in transitional societies, namely prosecution, then Chile represents the other, namely, blanket amnesty for those who committed gross violations of human rights. South Africa, in establishing the TRC, took a position somewhere between these two extremes, in which amnesty was not unconditional, but was rather a *quid pro quo* for full disclosure. At the heart of this hybrid approach was the reliance on a notion of 'truth recovery' as a restorative alternative to punitive justice – through full disclosure by perpetrators (and their supposed shaming) in exchange for amnesty, as well as through voluntary testimony about apartheid's gross human rights violations given by victims (and their supposed healing). Thus, although amnesty for perpetrators was a precondition for the success of the negotiated settlement from the outset, the TRC nonetheless resulted from a last-minute compromise, struck so late in the negotiation process that it had to be tacked onto the end of the interim Constitution, under the heading 'National Unity and Reconciliation', almost as an afterthought. The 'postscript' reads:

> This Constitution provides a historic bridge between the past of a deeply divided society characterised by strife, conflict, untold suffering and injustice, and a future founded on the recognition of human rights, democracy and peaceful co-existence and development opportunities for all South Africans, irrespective of colour, race, class, belief or sex.
>
> The pursuit of national unity, the well being of all South African citizens and peace require reconciliation between the people of South Africa and the reconstruction of society.
>
> The adoption of this Constitution lays the secure foundation for the people of South Africa to transcend the divisions and strife of the past, which generated gross violations of human rights, the transgression of humanitarian principles in violent conflicts and a legacy of hatred, fear, guilt and revenge.
>
> These can now be addressed on the basis that there is a need for understanding but not for vengeance, a need for reparation but not for retaliation, a need for *ubuntu*[3] but not for victimisation.
>
> In order to advance such reconciliation and reconstruction, *amnesty shall be granted* in respect of acts, omissions and offences associated with political objectives and committed in the course of the conflicts of the past. To this end, Parliament under this Constitution shall adopt a law determining a firm cut-off date, which shall be a date after 8 October 1990 and before 6 December 1993, and providing for the mechanisms, criteria and procedures, including tribunals, if any, through which such amnesty shall be dealt with at any time after the law has been passed.
>
> With this Constitution and these commitments we, the people of South Africa, open a new chapter in the history of our country.[4]

After the 1994 elections, the new minister of justice, Dullah Omar, immediately signalled his intention to establish a TRC. Omar was aware that the 'postscript' to the Constitution was binding,[5] and accepted responsibility for enacting legislation that would provide mechanisms and criteria for the granting of amnesty. But, along with a strong, vocal and well-organised human rights sector outside government, he was also concerned that amnesty was a process geared essentially to the interests of perpetrators. If South Africa was to come to terms with its past, build national reconciliation and establish a society based on respect for human rights, the needs of victims would have to be given equal weight.

On this basis, it was argued that any amnesty process that was not accompanied by an attempt to disclose fully the nature of the crimes perpetrated, would have grave implications for the long-term prospects of sustainable democracy. In particular, amnesty would mean that the victims of abuse, on all sides of the political spectrum, would never have access to the information essential to their rehabilitation, let alone any prospect of redress under civil or criminal law. Without public acknowledgement or the possibility of restitution through the courts, there was the risk of widespread resentment and of private retribution – despite the existence of a new democratic dispensation.[6]

The TRC represented a creative response to these concerns. It was decided that the Commission would not only grant amnesty to perpetrators, but would also seek to establish the truth about past human rights violations, provide victims with some form of reparation, and make recommendations to the President about measures the government should take to prevent any future recurrence of abuse. By foregrounding the interests of victims, the TRC would attempt to restore the moral balance to an amnesty agreement born of political compromise. This fusion of amnesty with truth recovery and reparation was without precedent, and its objectives should be borne in mind during any evaluation of the TRC's work. In a sense, truth recovery was viewed not so much as a trade for justice, but as an alternative restorative (rather than punitive) approach to justice. In fact, conversations about the nature and quality of the historical truths recovered by the TRC go to the heart of the Commission's restorative justice aspirations, both in respect of the amnesty process for perpetrators and in respect of the testimonies by survivors.

On this basis, some argue that the focus on the interests of the victims was the TRC's main accomplishment. The newly elected government's only constitutional obligation was to grant amnesty. Instead of settling for this, it arguably transformed a process geared to the interests of perpetrators into one that aimed to restore the dignity of those who had suffered, thereby demonstrating its commitment to fundamental rights and accountability. It is suggested that the government developed a new model for reconciling the often competing and contradictory demands faced by societies in transition.

Of course, there was more to the negotiated settlement in South Africa than compromise on the question of amnesty. This delicate historical process also issued in a new government of national unity that remained dependent on many of the former regime's civil-service institutions and personnel. Of particular significance here were those agencies of state security, including the police, the military and the criminal justice system, that were central to sustaining apartheid. Many of these institutions and personnel had been implicated directly in the torture, execution and disappearance of opponents of the system, or had helped to maintain the legal framework that allowed such abuses to occur. There was a culture of covert, unaccountable activity in government institutions. This had been fostered by a host of legislative measures that actively preserved secrecy and governmental privilege in the name of state security, and thus contributed to widespread corruption and abuse of power.[7] Now these same institutions and people were required to maintain law and order, and to act as guardians of a new Bill of Rights, in a society confronting a potential upward spiral of criminal violence. In addition, many of those who came to power in the new government had been actively involved in armed resistance to apartheid and this had also entailed the violation of human rights, within the country and beyond its borders.

The task of creating or restoring public confidence in state institutions and personnel, and in the rule of law, in a situation where mistrust of these institutions was deeply rooted, was a crucial one. The Parliamentary Committee of the General Council of the Bar of South Africa argued that the concern with political reconciliation should 'be balanced ... by a concern for the administration of justice ... It is apparent that a blurred pursuit of "reconciliation and peaceful solutions" without adequate regard for its impact on policing, the courts, and the control of crime, will do more to threaten social stability.'[8] While the reconstruction of state institutions clearly went well beyond the TRC's limited mandate, the TRC had the potential, in seeking to recover the truth about systematic human rights abuses in these institutions, to make a contribution to their transformation.

Once again, the notion that there was a 'recoverable' and integrated truth about the roles of these institutions (and that the TRC could 'deliver' it) lay at the heart of this more elaborate endeavour – even though institutional transformation was not framed as an explicit part of the TRC's legislative mandate. It could begin the process of promoting transparency in governance and entrenching a human rights culture in South Africa. One could argue that in evaluating the TRC's contribution to reconciliation through truth recovery, the stress should fall on a more critical scrutiny of its limited contributions to this 'forward-looking' agenda of transforming state institutions, rather than on its 'backward-looking' historical exploration of individual cases. Either way, uncontested assumptions about the nature of truth were central to framing all these aspects of the TRC's mandate.

It is imperative that we do not judge the TRC enterprise in isolation from either the constraints imposed by the negotiated settlement or the full range of vehicles designed to promote restorative justice and build national reconciliation, of which it was just one. That would notionally be to set the Commission up to fail before it began its work. More than anything else, reconciliation in post-apartheid South Africa resides in the redress of past inequities, in social and economic justice, which goes far beyond justice in its more narrow legal or punitive forms. The TRC was also confined to dealing with only a small percentage of serious or 'gross' human rights abuses. Few of apartheid's evils can be undone, and not all of them could be addressed by the TRC. Full social justice depends on the establishment and functioning of the Human Rights Commission, to deal with the full spectrum of human rights denials; the Gender Commission, to deal with the legacy of gender inequality; the Land Claims Court, to deal with the history of dispossession; the Youth Commission, to deal with the ongoing marginalisation of young people, which the shift from confrontation to negotiation arguably compounded, etc.

The TRC was set a near-impossible task from the outset. In a large country with many rural inhabitants, merely documenting a purely narrative history of all the gross violations of human rights that occurred under apartheid, and providing space for the victims to recount their stories, was impossible in just two years. When we judge the TRC against its own ambitious mandate, as set out in the Promotion of National Unity and Reconciliation Act,[9] we are therefore measuring it against an ideal. However, it remains possible and is crucially important to evaluate the TRC critically in relation to some of its own stated objectives, and particularly to scrutinise its operations and assess its processes through the eyes of victims themselves. This is all the more essential considering that the South African TRC is widely – and often uncritically – regarded as a model for other countries in transition.

'Home Truths': Political Compromise – A Double-Edged Sword

At the risk of stating the obvious, the fact that the TRC was established in the first place was a significant victory for the negotiation process. Instead of pursuing the convenient, politically expedient path of collective amnesia, the opposing parties were able to agree that public space should be made available to victims and survivors, and to the country as a whole, to look back on the past and recount the horrors of the apartheid system. The amnesty provisions in the TRC legislation, which set certain conditions for the granting of amnesty,[10] have remained controversial. However, it could be argued that this was a creative way of ensuring that the amnesty clause previously inserted in the 'postscript' to the interim Constitution would at least remain conditional upon full disclosure – and that this better facilitated reconciliation, through balancing perpetrators' interests in amnesty against victims' interests in the recovery of the truth. In so doing, the TRC process placed truth recovery – with all the assumptions about the ability to balance forensic with other more contradictory versions of the truth – at the heart of a victim-centred reconciliation endeavour, which was framed as an elaborate exercise in restorative justice.

Nonetheless, the TRC clearly reflected elements of the compromise and expediency that were intrinsic to the negotiated settlement. The Commission was largely defined by the fact that it was a statutory product of this delicate political process, and was implemented during a period of social transition, when the embryonic South African democracy appeared extremely vulnerable. It has been argued that many of the concessions that were made, especially with regard to amnesty, were necessary not only to keep the negotiations moving forward, but also to sustain the tenuous commitment to democracy made by the inherited military and police establishments. In many ways, this very delicate political context continued to plague the TRC and to undermine its successes.

One significant aspect of this context was the brief and uncomfortable existence of the government of national unity, which contained representatives of the previously warring factions. Although the fortunes of the government of national unity were bound up with many other factors, it is nonetheless noteworthy that this political vehicle, having served the purpose of shaping the objectives and legislative framework of the TRC, disintegrated shortly after the Commissioners had been appointed and the Commission finally established. The circumstances in which the TRC had been defined and irrevocably set upon a path therefore changed dramatically shortly after its birth. This shift influenced the complicated nature of the TRC's activities in the following two years, as it sought to be a vehicle of reconciliation and healing within an increasingly robust and combative political environment. The result was a politically contested approach to versions of the past, which eventually played itself out most strikingly in the widespread political criticism of the TRC's interim report, released in October 1998 – but which also plagued the internal operations of the TRC throughout its investigations.

Consequently, the TRC was hardly free from political tension, both internally and in relation to the wider society. It was probably inevitable that the Commission would generate political conflict and be used as a political football by competing parties. Clearly the notion of *sufficient consensus,* which shaped the agreements between political parties at the negotiation table, was no longer a functional vehicle for generating a shared vision or a collective verdict on the past. Arguably, one of the TRC's greatest failures was its inevitable propensity for pandering to these hostile political groupings, in a bid to keep them committed to the process.

From the outset, the National Party and other right-wing groupings, clearly concerned that they would be damaged by the Commission's investigation of past deeds, claimed that it was likely to be a witch-hunt rather than a forum for reconciliation. The National Party, and the Inkatha Freedom Party, continually accused the TRC of bias. Once the National Party left the government of national unity, and was no longer subject to the political constraints that had played so great a role in shaping the TRC, it frequently went to court to inhibit the Commission's work, and eventually refused angrily to cooperate at all. The reason given was that the TRC was violating the terms of the Act, which required it to operate without bias in considering gross violations of human rights on all sides of the political conflict. The most telling episode in this saga came when the National Party, having failed to make any substantial apology for its own role in the creation and implementation of apartheid, actually demanded an apology from the TRC instead! This was a rather transparent political stroke, designed to shift the focus of public attention from the National Party's complicity in gross violations of human rights to the alleged indiscretions of the TRC, and it would not have appeared nearly so masterly had the TRC acted more firmly in its dealings with the former government and other right-wing interests during the preceding year.

When the Commission was being set up, steps were taken to assuage doubts about political bias and avert political manoeuvring. In addition to its legislative mandate to investigate violations on all sides of the political conflicts of the past, the composition of the Commission itself was also meant to ensure evenhandedness. But when the Commissioners were selected, rather than simply considering the human rights track record of each candidate, an effort was made to represent as broad a range of political interest groups as possible, in an attempt to demonstrate impartiality. While the importance of securing public perceptions of objectivity cannot be dismissed glibly, and the Commissioners themselves clearly cannot be held responsible for this inclusive approach, there is little doubt that the TRC subsequently grappled with its consequences, many of which its architects may not have foreseen. Political conflicts within the TRC, fuelled by the vastly different political backgrounds and beliefs of the Commissioners and their staff, unquestionably had a negative effect on the operational efficiency of some of its Committees. The tense political climate was also one of the reasons why the Commission found it difficult to accept constructive intervention from outside or to incorporate non-governmental organisations (NGOs) and specialised historians into its operations.

The TRC was consequently under constant pressure to demonstrate its even-handedness, and this had an enduring impact on the ways in which it extracted its truths about the past, the profile given to particular cases and experiences, and its machinations in producing an aggregated version of past conflicts in its interim report. In its effort to appear impartial and build reconciliation, it was sometimes overly tentative. For instance, the Commission proved reluctant to make full use of its substantial powers of search, seizure and subpoena. Faced with vocal right-wing opposition, and eager to secure the support of right-wing political parties, the Commission resisted opportunities to acquire information assertively, and instead sought to win over its opponents more delicately. This undoubtedly impacted on the quality of information extracted by the Commission. In particular, the reliance on voluntary disclosure proved problematic both for the purposes of verifying information received, and for an amnesty process that was controversial precisely because of the understandable reluctance of perpetrators to come forward voluntarily.

A flood of applications for amnesty did occur towards the end of 1996, as the cut-off date of 15 December loomed (this was subsequently extended by the state president at the TRC's request). But it is arguable that the rush had less to do with the cut-off date than with the successful prosecution of Eugene de Kock, the notorious apartheid assassin (dubbed 'Prime Evil' by the media), who provided extensive information during his trial about other senior state operatives involved in gross human rights abuses. This suggests that the threat of prosecution, far from being incompatible with a truth-recovery process linked to a conditional amnesty, in fact contributed significantly to its eventual partial success.

Some victims expressed legitimate frustrations at the fact that the amnesty process would prevent them from obtaining full justice, while it also could not guarantee that it would add any new information to what they already knew about the murder of their loved ones. A constitutional challenge to the amnesty process was brought by the Azanian People's Organisation (AZAPO), as well as the relatives of prominent murdered activists Steve Biko, Griffiths and Victoria Mxenge, and Dr Fabian Ribeiro. Rather than viewing these actions as legitimate and understandable, at the time some TRC Commissioners presented them as hostile to the Commission and its quest for reconciliation. Although most of these tensions were tackled more sensitively by the TRC in the last year of its operation, they did damage the Commission's image, especially considering the early failures of the process of voluntary disclosure before the Amnesty Committee.

A BRIEF EVALUATION

The Human Rights Violations Committee was less subject to the controversies that plagued the amnesty process, despite the sometimes highly subjective representations of the past proffered by victims who testified before the Committee. The operations of this Committee, which needed to draw no moral or political distinctions between the experiences of victims from all sides of the conflict, proved to be the great strength of the TRC. The Committee gave little impression of overt or covert bias, and served the objective of impartiality well. The result was a uniquely powerful process, in which a full spectrum of people whose human rights had been violated in the past testified before the Committee and the South African public. The social impact of this public testimony was one of the greatest achievements of the TRC (notwithstanding the reservations expressed by Simpson and Posel in the introduction to this volume), and will undoubtedly continue to have a pervasive influence on South African society.

The political successes and failures of the TRC, as well as its ability to extract reliable information, must also be viewed more broadly in the context of the state institutions inherited by the new government as a consequence of the 'sunset clause', which was provided for in the politically negotiated settlement and protected the incumbency of state bureaucrats. It was obviously impossible to create credible, trustworthy institutions overnight, or to transform their culture and capacity to deliver instantaneously. Established bureaucrats were often reluctant to implement the programmes of the new political leadership, while many of the new senior functionaries installed by the incoming government lacked the technical expertise and experience to run state departments effectively. There was a consequent growing gap between the new government's visionary policies and its capacity to translate policy into practice. The TRC, as a product of precisely this innovative policy-making approach, was affected directly. The Commission relied on institutions such as the South African Police Service and the Office of the Attorney-General to facilitate its work. The inefficiency and apparently wilful obstructionism of some state functionaries are, by their nature, difficult to document, but they undoubtedly affected the Commission, its political profile, and the credibility of the versions of the past that it sought to extract.

These 'hidden liabilities' of South Africa's negotiated settlement illustrate well that, for all its undisputed achievements, the political compromises built into the CODESA negotiations were a double-edged sword. Nowhere was this more apparent than in the amnesty agreement and the associated suspension of civil and criminal justice which underpinned much of the negotiations process – particularly the assumption that amnesty could be made conditional on the requirement for truth recovery based on full disclosure by those who perpetrated gross violations of human rights under apartheid.

'The Whole Truth and Nothing but the Truth': Debating Criminal Law and Restorative Justice

In extracting lessons from the South African TRC that may be of value to other transitional societies, it is useful to consider some of the debates that have arisen over the requirement for truth recovery and its relationship to reconciliation and justice.

To start with, some have suggested that there is an inherent contradiction between truth recovery linked to amnesty on the one hand, and punitive criminal justice on the other. This has often been stated as a stark choice between reconciliation and justice, as if the two were inherently incompatible. By contrast, many frustrated victims of apartheid have argued simply that there can be no reconciliation without full justice. In practice, the Commission unintentionally demonstrated that truth recovery and prosecution can work effectively in tandem, and that a conditional amnesty based on full disclosure may be anything but incompatible with prosecution in some instances. As already suggested above, the threat of prosecution was probably more important than the prospect of amnesty in driving at least partial disclosure by perpetrators appearing before the Amnesty Committee.[11] Their revelations, along with the testimonies of victims before the Human Rights Violations Committee, provided a powerful and graphic cumulative picture of the dehumanising effects of apartheid. One might argue that, in the final analysis, some form of 'truth recovery' of the kind undertaken by truth commissions, however limited and whether accompanied by criminal prosecutions or not, is always better – and more likely to foster reconciliation in the long term – than collective amnesia about gross human rights violations.

Nonetheless, some of the most striking lessons to be learned from the South African TRC concern the fundamental clumsiness of criminal law as a means of doing substantive justice, of achieving reconciliation, and of meeting the needs of victims and survivors of human rights abuses for information and acknowledgement. This raises important questions about the punitive justice paradigm and the extent to which it supposedly offers better prospects of serving victims' needs, based as it is on a formal notion of truth necessary to secure a conviction and punish the perpetrator. In this regard, there is a more meaningful debate to be held on the differences between punitive and restorative systems of justice and the assumed roles of truth recovery within them, than on the supposed incompatibility of 'justice' and 'reconciliation' approaches in general. Nowhere was this debate more explicitly engaged than in the Constitutional Court of South Africa, the highest court in the land.

In one of its most far-reaching and earliest cases, the validity of the amnesty provisions, which had been entrenched in South Africa's interim Constitution, was challenged before the newly established Constitutional Court. This constitutional challenge to the Promotion of National Unity and Reconciliation Act was brought by the Biko, Mxenge and Ribeiro families – and the prominence of the victims alone makes the case notable. It is not possible to consider all aspects of the Constitutional Court's decision here, but a few key points will be highlighted.

There is a certain irony in asking a court to rule on the validity of an agreement without which the court itself would probably not exist. This is precisely what the Constitutional Court was doing in evaluating the constitutionality of the amnesty provisions in the Act. Constitutional courts are typically required to safeguard both democracy and the fundamental rights of individuals. In this particular matter, the potential tension between these two imperatives was also thrown into sharp relief. In their papers before the Court in the matter of *AZAPO and Others* vs. *The President of the Republic of South Africa and Others*, the applicants argued that section 20(7) of the Promotion of National Unity and Reconciliation Act was unconstitutional. The pertinent part of section 20(7) provides that:

> No person who has been granted amnesty in respect of an act, omission or offence shall be criminally or civilly liable in respect of such act, omission or offence and no body or organisation or the State shall be liable, and no person shall be vicariously liable, for any such act, omission or offence.

The applicants' central contention was that this provision violated the right of access to court enshrined in section 22 of the Bill of Rights, which provides that:

> Every person shall have the right to have justiciable disputes settled by a court of law or, where appropriate, another independent or impartial forum.[12]

The applicants argued that by extinguishing the criminal liability of perpetrators to whom amnesty has been granted and preventing victims from bringing civil claims against those who have abused them, section 20(7) violated an individual's right of access to justice.

The Constitutional Court held that extinguishing criminal and civil liability was constitutional in this case, and advanced two main reasons. First, it cited the 'postscript' to the interim Constitution. In the interests of a peaceful transition to democracy, and with due regard for the difficult balance that had to be struck between justice and reconciliation, the Court found that the interim Constitution had explicitly chosen reparation over retaliation, and *ubuntu* over victimisation. Further, the Court argued that 'amnesty' had no fixed meaning, and that the term could be defined broadly or narrowly, depending on the circumstances, to include the extinguishing of civil liability, or to exclude it. In the case of South Africa, the offer of amnesty would only act as a genuine incentive for perpetrators to make a full disclosure of their crimes, if it entailed extinguishing both civil and criminal liability. Few people would come forward if they knew this would expose them to damages claims in civil suits. If perpetrators did not come forward, the Court argued, victims would never know the truth and the process of reconciliation would be impeded. On this basis, the Court held that it was permissible to extinguish civil liability in respect of acts for which amnesty had been granted. A particular – and arguably naive – notion of *full disclosure* of the truth therefore lay at the heart of the Constitutional Court's rationale in upholding the conditional amnesty in the Act as constitutional.

Second, the Court held that in most instances the right to prosecute those who have committed gross violations of human rights is, in any event, an 'abstract right'.[13] This is because the evidence necessary to obtain convictions, or even to sustain civil claims, does not usually exist or has been deliberately destroyed.[14] In this context, the Court argued that one of the only ways in which victims could obtain the truth about past abuses was if perpetrators were provided with an incentive to come forward and make full disclosure, and the removal of criminal liability was precisely such an incentive. In addition, this would encourage perpetrators to confront their past and help society to understand its history. The Court held that these were important elements of reconciliation, to which the interim Constitution was committed, and implicitly this view was premised on assumptions about the nature and impact of such disclosure or truth recovery.

The Court could have substantiated its argument that the right to prosecute is really 'an abstract' one by referring to the state of South Africa's criminal justice system. Even if the evidence to prosecute perpetrators existed, the criminal justice system would be incapable of processing a large number of prosecutions (of which there might be thousands) or of securing convictions. The initiative to rebuild public confidence in the legal system and the rule of law would be harmed immeasurably if such prosecutions failed, allowing perpetrators who had been acquitted to deny their involvement in human rights abuses. A culture of impunity would be perpetuated, eroding any residual faith in the rule of law, and possibly leading to even greater anger and cynicism on the part of victims and survivors. Indeed, it is arguable that these were the precise consequences of the failed attempts to prosecute the former Minister of Defence, General Magnus Malan, as well as the more recent failed prosecution of the head of apartheid South Africa's chemical weapons programme, Dr Wouter Basson.

Even the newly established International Criminal Court (ICC) might run similar risks. If the 'strike rates' of the Bosnian and Rwandan War Crimes Tribunals are anything to go by, there is limited point in pursuing punitive justice if it is not effectively enforceable, whether nationally or internationally. Significant, but largely symbolic trials (such as that of Serbia's Slobodan Milosevic) might play a vital role in restoring international legal principles and in demonstrating that even the most senior leaders of state are not above the law, but arguably do little to foster the integrity of the rule of law at grass-roots level or bolster public confidence in institutions of criminal and civil justice for ordinary victims who enjoy no remedy.

Furthermore, even when prosecutions do take place, the extent to which they satisfy the needs and expectations of victims and survivors is debatable. In South African jurisprudence, a criminal conviction does not automatically found a civil claim for compensation on the part of the injured party. There are relatively few cases of gross human rights violations which hold out good prospects of a successful prosecution owing to the lack of evidence; and, in most of them, civil justice will also remain out of reach for the simple reason that it is unaffordable. Until these jurisprudential anomalies are eliminated, or the South African justice system is substantially transformed, the Constitutional Court may be right: there is only an abstract right of access to justice for the majority of the victims of apartheid's gross violations.

The punitive justice model is therefore all too easily misrepresented as being in the best interests of victims. Yet this discussion has revealed the clumsiness of punitive criminal law as a means of securing some form of direct compensation or reparation for the victims. The discussion has also sounded a warning about the danger of trying to speak on behalf of victims and survivors by presuming that they have an inherent interest in punitive justice, instead of rendering their own complex voices and needs audible more directly. The harsh reality is that the vast majority of apartheid's victims probably stood to gain more from the opportunity to tell their stories (coupled with the meagre reparations promised by the TRC) than from the criminal justice system. This is not to deny the devastating loss that the compromise on amnesty entailed for those few exceptions, such as the Biko and Mxenge families, who stood an excellent chance of succeeding through the criminal and civil courts. While it may be scant consolation to them, their sacrifice is the bitter pill that arguably had to be swallowed for the general good.

The Constitutional Court's rulings in the case brought by AZAPO contain important comments on the relationship between national jurisdiction and international law, which may be significant for the future workings of the ICC. In evaluating South Africa's obligations under international law,[15] the Court made a cursory survey of three countries in South America, namely, Chile, Argentina and El Salvador, and concluded that all three had accepted the principle that amnesty should be granted to violators of human rights in order to consolidate emerging democracies. On this basis, it suggested that there is no single or uniform practice in international law regarding the granting of amnesty.

There are a number of problems with this stance. First, the Court failed to consider any of the instances where emerging democracies have chosen to punish rather than pardon those who have committed gross violations of human rights. In two of the most recent instances in Africa, both the Rwandan and the Ethiopian governments chose to prosecute offenders.[16] Second, the Court is on shaky ground when it asserts that there was a principled acceptance, in the three countries canvassed, of the need to grant amnesty in order to consolidate democracy. In both Chile and Argentina, the amnesties had much more to do with powerful, interventionist militaries, which either blocked the transition to democracy or threatened the new democracy with a coup unless their conditions were met.[17] It is unfortunate that the Court extracted a principle about consolidating democracy from circumstances in which certain forces insisted upon amnesty to escape the consequences of their criminal actions. The Court is correct, albeit for the wrong reasons, that there is no standard practice among states on the granting of amnesty. However, this assertion is not helpful in itself, and could just as well be used to support the contention that prosecutions are not obligatory, as to support the proposition that they are permissible and appropriate.

After the parochialism, chauvinism and outright hostility to international law shown by South African courts under apartheid, one would expect the new Constitutional Court to have devoted more time and rigorous thought to this topic. This neglect is all the more disappointing if one considers the various other judgements that the Court handed down in the period preceding the TRC case, almost all of which referred to international law and regarded it as persuasive. The strength of international law derives in part from the fact that it is accepted by the community of nations and applied in their courts. The struggle for democracy in South Africa (an ironic example, in this context) was given extra impetus by the fact that apartheid could be condemned, locally and internationally, as a violation of international law. By adopting such a narrow and uncreative approach to the status of international law within our domestic legal system, concerning a matter that will be scrutinised by other countries and courts in similar situations, our Constitutional Court has eroded the moral and legal force of international law at home and abroad.

It would clearly have been preferable for the Court to have conducted a thorough and rigorous survey of international law on the subject before coming to the conclusion that it did. Although there is considerable debate on the issue, it is arguable that such a survey could still have supported the conclusion that the amnesty provisions articulated in the Act do not violate international law. Space does not permit an exhaustive treatment of this issue,[18] but two brief points should suffice to demonstrate that the argument could be made. First, the amnesty in South Africa is not unconditional, nor was it granted by an outgoing government to itself. It is activated only by the voluntary, full disclosure of perpetrators themselves, and should only be granted if the criteria defining a political crime are satisfied and if the means chosen to achieve the political objective were proportionate. One might also stretch a point and say that there is a punitive element in the 'shaming' associated with public amnesty hearings and the publication of the names of those who are granted amnesty in the Government Gazette. Second, it is generally accepted in international law that a nation does not have to 'commit political suicide' in fulfilling its obligation to punish those responsible for gross violations of human rights. Even commentators who have gone to great lengths to demonstrate that there is a duty to punish certain crimes under international law, concede that this obligation should be tempered by other considerations if fulfilling it would plunge a country into violence or destroy an embryonic democracy.[19]

Cachalia adopts this position in considering South Africa. He argues that the 'moral imperative' does not always yield a conclusive answer as to whether states are obliged to prosecute gross violations of human rights, and that other needs and objectives may demand a different approach. In particular, he refers to the need for national reconciliation and the need to secure the compliance of strategically located elites, which might otherwise threaten the process of democratisation. Although international law imposes an obligation on states to investigate and prosecute gross human rights violations, Cachalia argues that states have a discretion in the exercise of this obligation. However, it is generally agreed, he continues, that all governments have an obligation to establish *the facts*, at least, so that *the truth* becomes publicly known and officially part of a nation's history. This obligation remains even where 'clemency' is the best policy option in a particular state at a particular time.[20]

However, whether by reference to Cachalia's approach or to the more constrained analysis of the Constitutional Court, vast assumptions are made –

in the name of legal principle – about the quality and quantity of truth likely to be delivered by the TRC. While constant reference is made to the notion of full disclosure as a requirement for amnesty-seeking perpetrators, at no point are criteria or standards set for the kind of adequate disclosure necessary to satisfy the requirement of *the truth*, which in turn (in Cachalia's terms) will provide for a cumulative and 'official' version of a nation's history.

In practice, the TRC's Amnesty Committees constantly grappled with how the full disclosure requirement was to be met, perfectly illustrating the competing notions of what constituted truth recovery.[21] Indeed, it may be argued that from one amnesty decision to another, there was such pervasive inconsistency in the interpretation of what was expected for full disclosure as to suggest that the requirement was never consistently satisfied. This is best illustrated by the finding reached in one amnesty judgement in which amnesty was granted, but where it was concluded not that the applicant had dispensed with the requirement of full disclosure, but that *it could not be said that he hadn't done so*.

Debates continue to rage about the extent to which well-orchestrated and coordinated versions of events were presented by groups of applicants to ensure consistency in their individual amnesty applications. There was also inconsistency on whether information about other participants or chains of command should be demanded to satisfy the requirement of full disclosure, or whether individuals' versions of their own actions could be deemed enough. These differences were most powerfully illustrated in the case of the Boipatong massacre, where only seventeen applicants sought and were granted amnesty, although no further information was provided about the nearly three hundred other perpetrators involved in this brutal event, other than those who had subsequently died. Similarly, substantial evidence of police complicity in the event was simply never confirmed or denied. In other cases, the strong suggestion that police informers were involved could never be properly tested. In one such case, involving the murder of youth activist Sicelo Dlomo by his comrades on the suspicion that he was an informer (but where it was suggested that one of the murderers seeking amnesty may himself have been a police spy), a TRC investigator concluded that although it was known who killed Dlomo, the motive could not be established clearly. Elsewhere in this volume, Pigou makes the point that given the inadequate investigative capacity of the TRC, the quality of information gleaned in any particular case largely depended on the presence or calibre of the legal counsel for victims affected by particular amnesty applications. Furthermore, competing versions of whether specific acts were criminally or politically motivated, whether they were undertaken for personal reasons, such as revenge or pecuniary gain, or in the name of a known political organisation, were seldom conclusively or consistently adjudicated by the Amnesty Committees.

These are just a few among many examples of the practical failure of the amnesty process to recover the uncontested truth about the past, in the way imagined by the Constitutional Court. It can be concluded that while the criterion of full disclosure may work to justify a conditional amnesty as a matter of legal principle, in practice it was virtually meaningless, as there was no consistent notion of what full disclosure constituted in any particular case. Rather than resolving the question, as mooted by the Constitutional Court, the operations of the Amnesty Committees simply generated more debate on what might constitute an adequate quality or quantity of truth to justify the granting of amnesty. At best, full disclosure as a *quid pro quo* for amnesty, based as it was on the moral imperative of truth recovery that lay at the heart of the Constitutional Court's decision in the AZAPO case, is rendered as ill-defined in legal principle as it ultimately was in the investigative practices of the Amnesty Committees of the TRC itself.

'Beyond a Reasonable Doubt': Legal Truth or Psychosocial Truth?

Despite the extent and significance of the debates on legal and constitutional principles described above, the major legal challenges to the TRC did not come from frustrated victims but from threatened perpetrators. It is one of the richest ironies of the establishment of constitutional democracy in South Africa that the very people who formerly perpetrated gross violations of human rights proved to be most adept at resorting to their constitutional entitlements to protect themselves against exposure. The National Party's attempts to undermine the work of the TRC through the courts, on the grounds that it was biased, have already been mentioned. Alleged perpetrators used a wide range of procedural points in a similar way, threatening defamation suits, demanding prior notice if they were to be implicated, insisting on amnesty hearings being held in camera, and so on. Ultimately, it was those who had most to hide who astutely sought constitutional protection, almost crippling the TRC by wrapping it up in costly and time-consuming litigation.

However, most of the legal and jurisprudential dilemmas faced by the TRC were actually rooted in its own dual role as a fact-finding, quasi-judicial enterprise obsessed with forensic truth and verifiable information on the one hand, and a psychologically sensitive mechanism for victim storytelling and 'healing' on the other. This duality was manifest in the different approaches and roles of its various committees. The Amnesty Committee operated more along quasi-judicial lines, constrained substantially by the demands of due process. By contrast, the Human Rights Violations Committee, in its public hearings, grappled constantly with two competing needs, namely, to give victims space to tell their stories in an uncensored manner, and to verify information. The results were mixed: sometimes the fact-finding objective was sacrificed totally in the name of psychological sensitivity towards the testifying victim; at other times, sharp cross-examination by Commissioners seemed to negate the 'storytelling' objective completely.

At the procedural level, most of the legal challenges to the Commission revolved around prior notification of those mentioned in the testimonies of others, and centred on the argument that those named or implicated as perpetrators should be given due notice and enjoy the constitutionally enshrined right to defend themselves. This exacerbated tensions in the Human Rights Violations Committee, by thrusting it on the path towards adversarial and procedure-bound fact-finding, or by encouraging self-censorship on the part of victims, who were concerned about potential defamation suits. These legal challenges clearly had a negative effect on the 'culture' of the hearings. They also raised the spectre of the earlier Goldstone Commission of Inquiry, which had become bogged down procedurally for over three years, investigating just eleven incidents of public violence. Needless to say, the Human Rights Violations Committee simply could not afford such a legally-oriented approach, especially considering its obligation to hear in public or take statements from over 20 000 victims. The very objective of the truth-recovery process – to produce public knowledge – would have been compromised.

It may be that the two processes – quasi-judicial fact-finding versus victim-centred storytelling – were fundamentally irreconcilable, and for a simple reason: different kinds of truth were at stake. The 'formal' truth sought through legal process is a testimony constrained by the legal rights of others, subject to strict criteria of verification, and often deliberately shaped by an agreed universe of facts or information (for example, in plea-bargaining exercises or where defence and prosecution teams jointly establish an 'agreed statement of facts'). Such formal truth recovery for the purposes of establishing criminal liability is ostensibly based on objective criteria ('beyond a reasonable doubt'), and excludes any contextual information that cannot be demonstrated to have had a direct impact on the experience or activities of the individual testifying or being tried. The substantive truth associated with sociological, psychological or historical investigation, however, while it may contain or be reduced to empirical information, also engages with and accommodates contradiction, recognises the validity of the subjective, and exists only in the wider universe of experience which contextualises the actions and motivations of the protagonists. Whereas legal examination presumes that competing interpretations may be 'judged' by an objective standard and definitively resolved, historical or psychological investigation presumes no such resolution, but rather recognises that there is no single, easily integrated truth, only competing versions. If the processes of social and psychological healing can take place at all through the recounting of past abuses and trauma, then they certainly cannot take their proper course if constantly subject to the constraints of formal judicial process.

Any attempt to recover a suppressed and unwritten history shaped by past conflicts (which in many respects endure at a local and personal level throughout the lengthy process of transition to democracy, rather than simply evaporating in the course of the national negotiations), will inevitably have to engage with these tensions and contradictions. Creative attempts to provide previously silenced victims with a voice and to acknowledge their suffering publicly will often seem to be at odds with another fundamental objective of the transition, which is to restore the popular credibility of procedural justice. For this reason, it is imperative that victims and survivors are well organised and that their voices are rendered audible directly, rather than allowing politicians and policy-makers to speak on their behalf and to cultivate collective truths about forgiveness, reconciliation, reparation and retribution, which are actually quite remote from victims' realities, and frequently not even present in their testimonies.

One of the most important lessons to be learned from the TRC is that a grave disservice is done to victims by those who thus claim to speak on their behalf, whether in the name of punitive justice or in the name of reconciliation. In the process, the victims themselves are effectively silenced.

Much has already been said about the failure of punitive justice to serve victims as well as is often presumed. It should not be assumed that a truth commission could necessarily achieve more through 'reconciliation' (itself a contested term). In both instances, the needs of victims are at risk of being treated as uniform and static. By generalising and conveniently summarising the expectations of victims, their complex, inconsistent human identities are diminished, and the extent to which needs vary from victim to victim and change over time is ignored. Generalised claims that victims are willing to forgive perpetrators who confess, or that they are merely seeking acknowledgement and symbolic reparation, are no more reliable than similarly broad claims that victims need or demand punitive justice.[22]

The discourse of 'forgiveness' embroidered much of the Commission's work, informing the predominantly Christian religious character of its proceedings and permeating media reports on the public hearings. The onerous expectation was consequently created that reconciliation depended on the victims' ability to forgive. In truth, the TRC was no more about forgiveness on the part of victims than it was about contrition on the part of perpetrators seeking amnesty. If the Commission did offer an opportunity for dealing with the wounds of the past and for healing, then expressions of anger and the desire for revenge (rather than forgiveness) might in fact have done more to effect the sort of recovery that enables 'victims' to redefine themselves as 'survivors'. It is equally arguable that true reconciliation in South Africa will more likely be achieved by integrating the anger, sorrow, unresolved trauma and other complex feelings of victims, rather than by subtly suppressing them.

A proper evaluation of the TRC reveals that the victims' needs were complex, in keeping with the complex human identity, and shaped by the enduring and complicated impact of trauma. What some craved more than anything else was the basic information about disappeared relatives, while others sought widespread acknowledgement of their torture. Some sought direct confrontation or a mediated encounter with the perpetrators responsible for their suffering, while others only wanted to know about the systems and the chain of command that led to the abuse. Some rejected the TRC enterprise entirely and demanded full justice, others were magnanimous in their ability to forgive the perpetrators and move on. The needs of some were intensely personal and private, whereas others needed to be acknowledged by their community or vindicated politically.

The needs of individual victims also changed over time. When they first testified, many sought no more than acknowledgement and symbolic reparation, but once a perpetrator had confessed to killing their loved ones, or sometimes merely through the passage of time, some of these needs understandably changed. Similarly, as the prospects of material reparations became more real, so some victims began to demand monetary compensation. In many other instances, when the TRC failed to uncover the facts, make proper investigations, or add new knowledge to what was already known, some victims became embittered and disillusioned. All of these needs are legitimate, necessary and integral – rather than contrary – to building reconciliation in a historically traumatised society.

One central lesson from all this concerns the importance of support structures for victims and organisations to speak on their behalf, especially as the architects of the commission and the commission itself may be too willing to make political compromises. In Argentina and Chile, survivors only found an organisational voice once the findings of their truth commissions had left them dissatisfied and angry. In South Africa, by contrast, some support groups and other civil organs were organised early on, and so were able to articulate the needs and demands of victims during the life of the Commission and shape the process as it unfolded.

These support structures played a critical role in complementing the TRC's own initiatives to provide direct emotional support for victims who relived their traumas through their testimony. While the Commission's psychological support to victims may have been limited, the mere recognition of the need for an integrated victim aid and empowerment component was significant.[23]

However, there is a trite and convenient truth proffered by many observers of the TRC about the relationship between victim testimony and healing, which also demands greater critical scrutiny. It should be acknowledged that simply testifying or telling the story does not necessarily entail psychological healing or reconciliation.[24] The frequent assumptions that publicly shed tears – usually framed by the television cameras that take in the backdrop of the TRC's banner stating that 'Healing is Revealing' – are necessarily accompanied by some sort of *catharsis* on the part of testifying victims, also need to be debunked. Survivor testimony was frequently associated with high expectations, which reached beyond merely seeking the acknowledgement of an official truth-finding body. Many survivors came before the TRC expecting to gain additional information or have their own versions and understandings of events actively confirmed. The three survivor stories of Duma Khumalo, Thandi Shezi and Sylvia Dlomo-Jele recounted in this volume all illustrate the potentially devastating impact of the failure to deliver on these expectations – whether through half-truths recovered, contrary versions uncovered, or the subjective reality simply being covered up. The unresolved trauma brought out in this process may in fact lead to destructive and damaging responses rather than cathartic healing, making it all the more important that sustained psychological services are offered to victims who testify, once they are out of the glare of the television cameras and beyond the reach of popular voyeurism.

The TRC's provisions for reparations were particularly important as far as victims' expectations were concerned. The question of what survivors wanted and needed was hotly debated, although the views of the victims themselves were not often heard. Not surprisingly, victims' needs and expectations in this regard were particularly complex and often contradictory, rather than neat and consistent, as was often suggested. Some victims simply expressed a desire for symbolic reparations, such as a tombstone to commemorate the death of a loved one, while others demanded financial assistance to compensate for the loss of a breadwinner. Some sought scholarships for the dependants of those who were killed or had disappeared, but others rejected any form of reparation as an inadequate substitute for punishment of the perpetrators.

In whatever form, the idea of state-sponsored reparation was implicitly and explicitly central to the constitutional status of the TRC. Notionally, the constitutionality of the Commission's amnesty provisions rested on the idea that the state would provide reparation to survivors in lieu of the compensation or damages they could otherwise have been entitled to claim from perpetrators, but which the granting of amnesty had denied them. This was also explicit in the judgement of Justice Didcott in the AZAPO case. The TRC was committed to providing reparations, although these would obviously fall far short of the potential monetary compensation payable from any successful civil claims. However, unlike the Amnesty Committee, whose decisions were subject to review by a court of law only, the Reparation and Rehabilitation Committee was only empowered to make recommendations or set policy guidelines, which remained dependent on the political will and financial capacity of government to implement. In theory, reparations would not just take the form of monetary compensation for individual victims, but would focus primarily on collective and often symbolic measures. Another priority would be services and counselling for those who testified.

Given the magnitude of historical oppression in South Africa, the new democratic state could easily be bankrupted if it tried to meet these obligations in respect of all victims of abuses perpetrated in the name of its apartheid predecessor. However, an exclusive focus on monetary compensation for the 22 000 victims who appeared before the TRC would equally present serious moral and political dilemmas, based upon a selective engagement with the past. That aside, the state of the social welfare services illustrates the grave difficulties the new government faces in translating any creative or visionary reparations policy into meaningful services and benefits. The limited 'reach' of the state suggests a vital need to transform inherited governmental welfare services along with the institutions of the criminal justice system, as already discussed. Government is highly unlikely to satisfy the recommendations of the TRC in respect of reparative measures for victims, and to date has failed to produce even a policy on the implementation of reparative measures – ostensibly because the TRC has not finished its final report.

Government's inertia on this matter undoubtedly raises questions about the soundness of the Constitutional Court's perspective. Not only can questions be asked about whether or not the criterion of full disclosure has been satisfied in the course of the TRC process, but when this is set alongside the failure of any governmental delivery mechanisms for reparations, then the two main grounds upon which the Constitutional Court held the amnesty provisions to be constitutional appear to be very shaky. There is reason to be apprehensive. In response to a request from some victims for urgent assistance, the Reparation

Committee tabled a draft policy on urgent interim reparations as early as March 1997. Only eighteen months later, just weeks before the publication of the TRC's interim report, did government finally deliver some limited formal assistance of this sort to a relatively small group of victims.

It must be said that the question of reparation is extremely complex, especially in a country like South Africa, which has competing developmental concerns and severely limited financial resources. It is also an intractable problem, considering that the TRC relies on government to implement any proposals it makes on reparation. There is an unresolved tension between individual needs and demands on the TRC on the one hand, and the economic and political rationale that underpins communal reparation on the other. To put it another way, there is tension between reparation for individual victims of gross violations of human rights as defined in the Act, and the new government's concern to redress historically entrenched inequities more generally. In this regard, the TRC has also been criticised for not confronting the economic beneficiaries of apartheid adequately, at least partially as a consequence of the Commission's mandate and preoccupation with establishing political responsibility for past violations, and despite the fact that the TRC did hold special hearings on the role of the business community under apartheid.

The issue of material compensation or reparation for victims raises countless difficulties that are also embedded in the subjective experiences and expectations of various survivors. Some victims resent the fact that they need to prove they qualify for reparation at all, or that their suffering may be quantified monetarily. Yet different victims may require different reparation packages. The complex questions of how to differentiate between them without compromising the even-handedness of the Commission, or of how to compensate thousands of people with different needs, most of whom are impoverished, but without placing an untenable burden on the state, have not been answered by the TRC. Victims' needs for reparation are expressed individually, but the more individualised the process becomes, the more difficult the debates to which it gives rise and the more complex the task of implementation. However, strictly collective or symbolic reparations, such as monuments or memorials, do not adequately address many individual needs.

The TRC tended to underestimate the expectations of victims for monetary compensation, often because of the selective representation of victims as willing to 'forgive' or to accept purely symbolic reparation. In fact, the TRC did not adequately monitor the changing needs and expectations of many victims, who will certainly not be satisfied with symbols, and are extremely sceptical of the government's commitment to providing direct compensation.

Conclusions

If the South African TRC may be viewed as an innovative exercise in restorative justice that sought to place victims at the heart of the negotiated transition, then it did so on the basis of a perspective on the past that effectively selected a specific category of victims and perpetrators of violence who were deemed to be political. Indeed, the controversy that continues to rage about reparations revolves around the concern that this category of victims may be 'privileged' relative to the wider communities that suffered the structural violence, the denial of opportunity, and the daily violations and displaced violence of apartheid.

It is striking how the amnesty process, because of its exclusive concern with violent acts committed for a political motive, confronted the blurred dividing line between 'political' and other forms of violence under apartheid, in seeking to determine who was eligible for amnesty and who was not. The Human Rights Violations Committee did briefly confront the sponsored involvement of criminal gangs in political assassinations, and thus the blurring of the boundary between political and criminal violence. Yet the Amnesty Committee daily took decisions that sought to sustain this boundary as a clear demarcation bisecting South Africa's orthodox political history.

Thus, in the case of the Boipatong massacre, an Inkatha Freedom Party member was granted amnesty for the killing of an eight-month-old baby along with its mother. In answering questions about this during the hearing, the applicant proffered by way of explanation the argument that 'a snake gives birth to a snake', suggesting that if the mother was a political enemy, then so too was the baby. There are even more significant illustrations of the dilemmas that confronted the Amnesty Committees in their adjudication of which acts were deemed to be political and which not. In some cases involving 'necklace' murders and mob violence, amnesty was granted on the basis of the 'implied authority' of political parties; yet in others, such as the assassination of ANC and SACP leader Chris Hani by two white right-wingers, no political authority was found to exist, and so amnesty was refused. In some cases, amnesty was refused on the grounds that money had been paid to the assassins of political opponents, suggesting financial motives that were personal, whereas in other cases it was held that financial bonuses paid to state agents for their acts of violence did not supersede their political motives.

Perhaps the most important contradiction that played itself out in the findings of the Amnesty Committees concerned the question of race or racism as a political motive for gross violations of human rights. In some instances, racial motivation was deemed to be 'political' or held in the name of a known political organisation, while in others it was not, with the result that some were granted amnesty for such actions whereas others were denied it. The issue here is not whether the individual findings were 'fair' or not, but rather to point out that by 'privileging' acts of political violence, the ironic effect was to denigrate and mask such factors as race, class or gender as relevant and *self-explanatory* categories in understanding the dominant patterns and experiences of gross violence under apartheid.

At best, these amnesty decisions were unpredictable and arbitrary. At worst, they entailed an unconscious selection process that sanitised the apartheid past of its uncomfortable lack of political orthodoxy. Historical patterns of conflict were represented in a way that effectively denied the presence of violent social movements that would never find a comfortable place in the orthodox lexicons. These were movements that were chillingly antisocial, yet were equally the product of the damage done by apartheid's seismic dislocation, dispossession and industrialisation. Perhaps the most disturbing of these movements were those that adopted the discourses and practices of social banditry – precisely because they migrated so easily across the boundaries of crime and politics, between aspirations to social equality and antisocial violence.[25]

The simple political narrative that remains is striking in the way it cleanses both liberation politics and state violence – associated as they were with the fortunes of particular political parties and movements – of the criminal pathologies of South Africa's particular social dislocation. The prevalent violence of everyday social life finds little complex expression in this version of the past, which simply ignores the extent to which the apartheid system that criminalised politics simultaneously politicised crime.

In this context, it is simplistic to describe South Africa as a 'post-conflict' society in the wake of the TRC. Instead, the real challenge lies in grappling with and monitoring continuity and change in the patterns of social conflict that continue to dominate the democratic South Africa, and the easy slide between political and criminal violence that has always complicated analysis of South African life, but which may have been shrouded rather than exposed by the TRC. In seeking to meet this challenge, this paper points to some of the (perhaps inevitable) limitations of the TRC as a *restorative justice* mechanism in the true sense of the term, because of its historical imperative and its explicit mandate to deal with the issues of violence and reconciliation exclusively by reference to political responsibility, narrowly defined.

Proper evaluation of the efficacy of *transitional justice* mechanisms such as the TRC must therefore be situated within the specific context of transmuting patterns of violence. This perspective demands a shift in the debates on transitional justice, from an exclusively retrospective scrutiny of past injustices, important as this is, to a strategic and proactive engagement with the challenges that face justice institutions in newly emerging democracies, where patterns of violence and social conflict change, rather than simply being brought to an end by political settlements, and where the lines of social cleavage at the heart of such historical violence are redefined rather than simply staying the same. Such an approach demands an engagement both with the past and with the future, and insists not only on a scrutiny of justice in transition, but of violence in transition as well.

This analysis has profound implications for how we understand the roles and challenges of transitional justice interventions, including the South African TRC. In particular, it suggests the need for a less simplistic or theoretical understanding of the dangers of impunity in society, as opposed to one simply premised on the need for compliance with the principles of public international law (vital though this is).

In the final analysis, it remains difficult to draw clear-cut conclusions about the TRC, although evidently it has not made quite the contribution to reconciliation claimed by its most ardent supporters and assumed by international audiences from a distance. Certainly, it would be a grave mistake to judge the whole TRC by the obvious shortcomings of its final report, which simply cannot hope (and does not pretend) to reflect the full complexity of thirty-five years of history. The great value of the TRC lay in the process rather than the published end product.

We should also guard against a 'sanitised public transcript' which suggests that anger, vengeance, or violent conflict are absent from post-apartheid South Africa. There is a grave risk that out of the testimonies and confessions of a few, a truth will be constructed that disguises the way in which black South Africans, who were systematically oppressed and exploited under apartheid, continue to be excluded and marginalised in the present. The sustained or growing levels of violent crime and antisocial violence, which appear to be new phenomena associated with the transition to democracy, are in fact rooted in the very same experiences of social marginalisation, political exclusion and economic exploitation that previously gave rise to the more 'functional' violence of resistance politics. The fundamentals of social and economic justice were untouched by the TRC.

One of the stated aims of the TRC was to ensure that gross violations of human rights do not occur again in South Africa. In evaluating its achievements in this regard, we must not assume that social conflict will play itself out along the same political and racial lines as in the past. On the contrary, it might express itself through new forms of violence.

Indeed, there is a real possibility that the TRC, by granting amnesty to confessed killers, may actually have contributed to the sense of impunity that fuels the burgeoning rate of violent crime.[26] This phenomenon is not unique to South Africa: violent crime has flared in many countries after the transition to democracy, and in many newly deregulated and emerging economies once 'political' violence has decreased. In fact, this phenomenon might contain the most fundamental lessons we can learn about the nature of societies in transition from autocracy to democracy.

Indirectly, violent crime now poses the gravest threat to an embryonic human rights culture in South Africa. Understandable popular hysteria and moral panic about the levels of violence have begun to generate a backlash against human rights, which are perceived as serving the perpetrators at the expense of the victims. The possibility that this backlash might thwart efforts to change the institutional culture of the criminal justice system is nowhere clearer than in the sustained levels of police brutality, torture and deaths in police custody – forms of violence that reflect unfortunate continuities amidst all the changes taking place in South Africa.[27]

There are undoubtedly times when countries may have to sacrifice legal principles in the name of political pragmatism, in order to end war or achieve peace. However, when amnesty is granted with scant regard for its impact on the credibility of the criminal justice system and its processes, we breathe life into the sense of impunity at the heart of criminal behaviour. At some point, someone will have to bear the moral responsibility, not only for the 'political' violence of the past, but for the 'criminal' violence of the present. Ultimately, if the rhetoric of reconciliation is to be translated into reality in South Africa, we will have to go beyond formal political and constitutional change to tackle the deep-seated social imbalances that underlie the culture of violence at the most fundamental, structural level.

Notes

1. This paper is based on an earlier version written in October 1998, immediately prior to the publication of the TRC's interim report.
2. See A. Boraine, 'Reining in Impunity for International Crimes', in C.C. Joyner and M. Cherif Bassiouni (eds), *Reining in Impunity for International Crimes and Serious Violations of Fundamental Human Rights: Proceedings of the Siracusa Conference, 17-21 September 1998* (Siracusa, 1998), pp. 221-4; G. Simpson, 'Proposed Legislation on Amnesty/Indemnity and the Establishment of a Truth and Reconciliation Commission', Submission to the Minister of Justice for South Africa (Johannesburg, 1994); G. Simpson and P. van Zyl, 'South

Africa's Truth and Reconciliation Commission', *Temps Moderne*, 585 (1995); G. Simpson and P. van Zyl, 'Witch-hunt or Whitewash? Problems of Justice in Transition in South Africa', Centre for the Study of Violence and Reconciliation (CSVR) Occasional Paper (Johannesburg, 1997).

3. *Ubuntu* is the mainspring of the African humanist world-view, an attitude of tolerance and empathy grounded in the interdependence of the individual and the collective. It is conveyed in the expression: *'Motho ke motho ka batho babang'* – 'A person is a person through other people.'
4. My emphasis. Section 251, Constitution of the Republic of South Africa Act, No. 200 of 1993.
5. Section 232(4) of the Act makes the 'postscript' a binding part of the interim Constitution.
6. See G. Simpson, 'Blanket Amnesty Poses a Threat to Reconciliation', *Business Day*, 22 December 1993.
7. For a brief discussion of the broadly based definitions of 'state security' in South African legislation under apartheid, and for a partial description of the range of this legislation, see S. Africa, 'An Assessment of National Security Legislation in South Africa', Military Research Group (unpublished, 1992). Also see R. Williams, 'Covert Action and Democracy: General Considerations and Concepts', Military Research Group (unpublished, 1991).
8. Memorandum by the Parliamentary Committee of the General Council of the Bar of South Africa, October 1992, pp. 1-2.
9. No. 34 of 1995.
10. To qualify for amnesty a person had to satisfy two basic requirements. In terms of section 20(1)(c) of the Promotion of National Unity and Reconciliation Act, the person had to fully disclose all acts for which amnesty was being sought. Full disclosure might entail providing evidence on the activities of co-conspirators or those who gave the orders for the offences in question. Further, the offence had to meet the criteria prescribed in the Act. Sections 20(2)(a)-(f) specified four broad categories of person who could apply for amnesty:
    1. A member of a publicly known political organisation or liberation movement who waged a struggle against the state or any former state (referring specifically to former 'homelands' or 'Bantustans') or another publicly known political organisation or liberation movement.
    2. An employee or member of the 'security forces' of the state, or any former state, who attempted to counter or resist a struggle being waged by a member of a publicly known political organisation or liberation movement.

3. An employee or member of the security forces of the state who engaged in a political struggle against a former state or vice versa.
4. Any person involved in a *coup d'état* or attempted *coup d'état* against a former state.

In terms of section 20(3), the Amnesty Committee had to consider all of the following criteria in order to make its determination:
1. The motive of the person who committed the act.
2. The context in which it occurred.
3. The legal and factual nature of the offence, including its gravity.
4. Whether the person was following orders.
5. The relationship between the act and the objective pursued.
6. The proportionality of the act to the objective pursued.

Anyone who acted for personal gain (section 20(3)(i)) or out of personal malice, ill will or spite (section 20(3)(ii)) would not be granted amnesty.

11. Since contrition was not a requirement for receiving amnesty, one commentator noted dryly that most perpetrators came forward not because they had 'seen the light' but because they 'felt the heat'.
12. Constitution of the Republic of South Africa Act, No. 200 of 1993.
13. By 'abstract', the Court did not imply that the rights were purely theoretical or could not be claimed against the state, but rather that they were largely impossible to exercise in practice. The same might be said of civil claims, which may be severely impaired in practice because South African rules of prescription dictate that such claims prescribe after three years.
14. In South Africa, the four-year negotiation period allowed for the systematic destruction of incriminating documents. Evidence suggests that the National Intelligence Service was still destroying files in 1996, two years after the first democratic elections. See G. Simpson, 'Truth Recovery or McCarthyism Revisited? An Evaluation of the Stasi Records Act of 1991 with Reference to the South African Experience', CSVR Occasional Paper (Johannesburg, 1994).
15. The following paragraphs draw extensively on Simpson and Van Zyl, 'Witch-hunt or Whitewash?'
16. See L. Huyse, 'To Punish or Pardon: A Devil's Choice', in Joyner and Bassiouni (eds), *Reining in Impunity*, pp. 79-90; and G. Wakjira, 'National Prosecution: The Ethiopian Experience', in Joyner and Bassiouni (eds), *Reining in Impunity*, pp. 189-92.
17. The case in which a Spanish court sought to extradite Pinochet from Britain demonstrates the failure of blanket amnesties, and once again reveals

limitations in the Constitutional Court's assessment of the importance of international law in relation to domestic amnesty arrangements.
18. For greater insight into the debates in international law, see D. Orentlicker, 'Settling Accounts: The Duty to Prosecute Human Rights Violations of a Prior Regime', *Yale Law Journal*, C (1991), pp. 2537-615; and N. Roht-Arriaza, 'State Responsibility to Investigate and Prosecute Gross Human Rights Violations in International Law', *California Law Review*, 78:2 (1990), pp. 449-513. For an examination of the debate in the South African context, see F. Cachalia, 'Human Rights in Transitional Situations: Towards a Policy Framework', Centre for Applied Legal Studies, unpublished paper (Johannesburg, 1992); and contrast this with 'South Africa: Accounting for the Past: Lessons from Latin America', *Africa Watch*, IV (1992).
19. See Orentlicker, 'Settling Accounts'.
20. Cachalia, 'Human Rights in Transitional Situations', pp. 1-2.
21. It is a matter of considerable debate as to how (or whether) the Amnesty Committee applied the criterion of 'full disclosure'. Saino has argued that it was inconsistently applied, at best, and occasionally quite arbitrarily defined. See M. Saino, ' "Gone Fishing": An Initial Evaluation of the South African TRC's Amnesty Process', CSVR Occasional Paper (Johannesburg, 1998). Also see the TRC website at www.truth.org.za/amnesty for details of amnesty decisions.
22. On this and the perspectives that follow, see Centre for the Study of Violence and Reconciliation and Khulumani Support Group, *Submission to the TRC: Survivors' Perceptions of the TRC and Suggestions for the Final Report* (1998). This report is based on eleven reconciliation and rehabilitation workshops undertaken by the CSVR between 7 August 1997 and 1 February 1998. The CSVR also produced two documentary videos, detailing victims' expectations of the TRC at the beginning of the process and re-evaluating them one year later. See H. Han and L. Segal, *Khulumani – Speak Out!*, CSVR video (Johannesburg, 1995); and L. Segal, B. Hamber and H. Han, *SisaKhuluma: We Are Still Speaking*, CSVR video (Johannesburg, 1997).
23. B. Hamber, 'The Burdens of Truth: An Evaluation of the Psychological Support Services and Initiatives Undertaken by the South African TRC', *American Image*, LV (1997).
24. See B. Hamber, 'Dealing with the Past and the Psychology of Reconciliation: The TRC – A Psychological Perspective', paper presented to the 4th International Symposium on 'The Contributions of Psychology to Peace', Cape Town, 1995; B. Hamber, 'Do Sleeping Dogs Lie? The Psychological Implications of the TRC in South Africa', CSVR Occasional Paper

(Johannesburg, 1997); B. Hamber and S. Lewis, 'An Overview of the Consequences of Violence and Trauma in South Africa', CSVR Occasional Paper (Johannesburg, 1997).
25. See G. Simpson, 'Shock Troops and Bandits: Youth Crime and Politics', in J. Steinberg (ed.), *Crime Wave* (Johannesburg, Wits University Press, 2001).
26. See G. Simpson, 'A Culture of Impunity', *Star*, 24 January 1998.
27. There were 737 reported deaths in police custody or as a result of police action during the twelve-month period from April 1997 to March 1998. A total of 429 deaths were reported in the six months from January to June 1998. D. Bruce, I. Liebenberg and R. Atkins, 'Towards a Strategy for Prevention: The Occurrence of Deaths in Police Custody or as a Result of Police Action', Report for the Independent Complaints Directorate (1998).

INDEX

A

Abduction 70
abstract right 232
Act
  see Promotion of National Unity
    and Reconciliation Act
African National Congress (ANC)
  29, 31, 46
  abuses committed by 53
  action in Zimbabwe against the 33
  archive records of the 30
  blanket amnesty to 39
  bombing of London office 21
  conflict with IFP 26, 152, 174, 176,
    179, 184
  engagement with Duduza
    207-209, 211
  in Kathorus 182, 185, 190-197
  involvement with Sicelo Dlomo
    case 108-109, 111-113, 115
  Thandi Shezi's involvement with
    124, 125
Africa Watch 19, 29
Alberton Town Council 183-184
Alexandra 192
American Association for the
  Advancement of Science 68
amnesty 3, 40-41, 242
  blanket 39
  dealing with, under Constitution 223
  granting of 2, 38, 226, 234, 247
  in Boipatong massacre case 244
  in Sicelo Dlomo case 114-115
  opposition to 98
  unconditional 221
amnesty applications/applicants
  3-4, 54-55, 173-174, 228, 236
  by security forces 55-57
  by self-defence units 59
  cross-border attacks 53
  cut-off dates for 41, 47, 55-57,
    147, 222
  from convicted prisoners 43-44
  investigated by Amnesty
    Committee 50
  Kasinga raid 32
  Khumalo gang 193
  legal aid to 44
  Sicelo Dlomo case 32, 39, 105-108
  testimony of 39
Amnesty Committee 4, 28, 32, 39-41,
  54-55, 230, 237, 242, 244
  applications to 47-48
  independence of 27
  interpretation of 'full disclosure'
    214, 236
  refused to hear cases 43

Sicelo Dlomo case 98, 110-115
Thandi Shezi case 1127
work done by 47-50
amnesty hearings 6, 27, 34, 49, 147, 193
  in camera 237
  in Duduza 205
  of Ngema tavern case 196
  of Sicelo Dlomo case 109
  of Thandi Shezi case 127
Amnesty International 19, 29, 136
amnesty investigations/investigators
  58-59
amnesty process 38-41, 59
  after 1994 elections 222-223
  failure of 237
  Investigation Unit's role in 51
ANC
  see African National Congress
ANC Youth League 193, 196
Angola 30, 32
Anti-Apartheid Movements 19, 136
apartheid 6, 38, 84, 141-142, 153, 156,
  175, 180, 220, 224
  black South Africans under 246
  in TRC Report 162-166
  historiography of 164
  gross violence under 245
APLA
  see Azanian People's Liberation
    Army
archives 29-31
Argentina 234, 240
Attorney-General's Office
  facilitation of TRC work 229
  relationship with Investigation
    Unit 54-56
audi alteram partem rule 6
Azanian People's Liberation Army
  (APLA) 82, 134
Azanian People's Organisation
  (AZAPO) 41, 103, 228, 234, 237
AZAPO
  see Azanian People's Organisation
*AZAPO and Others vs The President of
  the Republic of South Africa and
  Others* 231-232, 242

B

Basson, Dr Wouter 20, 56, 233
Beech, Robert 31
Berry, David 31
Biko family 40, 231, 233
Biko, Steve 228
Bill of Rights 224, 231
Bisho killings 78, 194
blanket amnesty 39
Boipatong massacre 193-195, 236, 244

Bopape, Stanza 49
Bophuthatswana 53
Bosnian War Crimes Tribunal 233
BOSS
  see Bureau of State Security
Botha, Pik 194
Botha, PW 6, 27, 49, 137
Botswana 32-33
Bureau of State Security (BOSS) 51
Buthelezi, Chief Mangosuthu 26, 46

C

Calendar time 73, 78, 82, 84
CAST
  see Civic Associations of the
    Southern Transvaal
CBS, interview with Sicelo Dlomo 102
CCB
  see Civil Cooperation Bureau
Centre for the Study of Violence
  and Reconciliation 104, 125
Children under Apartheid 102
Chile 234, 240
  National Commission for Truth
    and Reconciliation (Chile) 22, 24
  transition in 221
Christians/Christian theology 9, 26, 239
Church Street bomb 78
Ciskei 33, 162
Civic Associations of the Southern
  Transvaal (CAST) 192
Civil Cooperation Bureau (CCB)
  27, 33, 57
CODESA
  see Convention for a Democratic
    South Africa
Coetzee, Cobie 137
Coetzee, Dirk 110
commissioners 3, 5, 26, 28, 163, 167,
  226-227
  allegations against 38
  mandate interpretation by 18
community hearings 205-206
community relations 208
  conflict 206-208
Congress of South African Students
  (COSA) 181
Congress of South African Trade
  Unions (COSATU) 21, 182, 184-185
Conservative Party 207
Constitution 222
Constitutional Court 41, 230-237
constitutional problems 40-41
controlled vocabulary 69-70, 80-81
  see also language/terminology
Convention for a Democratic South
  Africa (CODESA) 173, 194, 229

INDEX

corroboration 54, 58
COSA
   see Congress of South African Students
COSATU
   see Congress of South African Trade Unions
criminal law 230
   and restorative justice 230-237
Criminal Procedure Act 100
Cronje, Brig Jack 53, 55
cross-border raids 29-30, 50, 53
Crossroads 183, 185-186, 190, 194
cut-off dates 41, 47, 56-57, 147, 222

D

Data sources 37-60
Daveyton 192
DCC
   see Directorate of Covert Collection
death row 136-137
death sentence 135-137
declarative memories 77
definitions, development of 21
De Goede, Nico 188
De Klerk, FW 6, 137, 195
De Kock, Eugene 27, 33, 53-55, 57, 228
democracy 246
   constitutional 221
Department of Public Prosecutions 56
Detainees' Parents Support Committee (DPSC) 101-102, 111-112
'dialogue' truth 154
Diepkloof Prison
   see Sun City
Directorate of Covert Collection (DCC) 31
Directorate of Security Legislation 58
Directorate of Special Tasks (DST) 30
Dlamini, Jacob K 133, 135, 142
Dlomo-Jele, Sylvia 99-115, 241
Dlomo, Sicelo 39, 59, 98-115, 236
DPSC
   see Detainees' Parents Support Committee
DST
   see Directorate of Special Tasks
Dolodlo, Theophilus 32
Dube, John (Silver)
   combat cells 108
   involvement in Sicelo Dlomo case 107-112, 115
   involvement in Thandi Shezi case 118-119
Duduza 24
   background to conflict 206-208
   churches in 208-209
   community hearings in 205-206
   conflict in Duduza 206-208, 216
   hostels in 208
   human rights abuses in 204

tensions between TRC and 204-217
   TRC's involvement in 208-209
Duduza Civic Association 206-208
Duduza Town Council 206, 208
Dumakude, Lester 109, 113
Du Toit, Andrè 68

E

East Rand 173-198
elections 5, 10, 84
El Salvador 234
Engelbrect, Major Gen Krappies 56
ethnic cleansing 189, 191, 197
ethnography 158

F

Factual truth 47, 154-155, 164, 174
forensic truth 6, 11, 154, 165, 174-175
forgive and forget 39, 239-240
full disclosure 214, 232, 237
funding/financing 179
Further Indemnity Act 48

G

Gazankulu 32
Gender Commission 225
gender inequality 166, 225
Germany, transition in 221
Germiston 181, 191
Germiston and District Taxi Association 181-182
global truth 68-69
Goldstone Commission of Inquiry 31, 55-56, 192-193, 195, 238
Government of National Unity 226
Greater Nigel Council 207
gross human rights violations
   see human rights violations
Grosskopf, Hein 109, 113
Guguletu Seven 23

H

Hani, Chris 196-197, 244
Harms Commission 57
healing 151, 240-241
Healing is Revealing 12
healing truth 154-155, 174
historical inquiry 153
historical memory/truth 68-87, 224
   official and unofficial 75-77
historiography 164-165
history 167
   and causation 10, 166, 175, 177
   and TRC 19-20, 23-25
   versus law 22-25
Holomisa Park 186, 190, 194
homelands 32, 33
hostel dwellers 182-187, 190-191, 197
Human Rights Commission 225

human rights violations 3-4, 11-12, 58, 67-68, 98, 151, 156-157
   and apartheid 162-166
   cross-border raids 1529
   cut-off dates 41, 47, 56-57, 147, 222
   definition according to Act 42-43
   definition of 71, 153
   documentation of 84
   during mandate period 19, 40
   hearings on 20
   in Duduza 204-217
   in post-apartheid South Africa 220
   Investigation Unit's role 51
   involving minority groups 45
   on the East Rand 174-176
   TRC report coverage 32, 150, 159
Human Rights Violations Committee 3-4, 40, 49-50, 59-60, 229-230, 238, 244
   corroboration 54
   Sicelo Dlomo case 98, 105, 109
   Sylvia Dlomo-Jele's testimony to 105
   time pressure 41
   work done by 44-47

I

IBI
   see Independent Board of Inquiry
ICC
   see International Criminal Court
IFP
   see Inkatha Freedom Party
impartiality, achieved by TRC 150-151
impimpi 118-119
Indemnity Act 48
Independent Board of Inquiry (IBI) 110, 188
in-depth investigations 52-53
information access, to Investigation Unit 56-58
information gathering 21, 31, 42, 74-75
   by Investigation Unit 52
   data sources 37-60
   state-controlled information 57-58
information management system 34, 67-72, 74-75
   cognitive landscape of the 69-72
   documentation 84-86
   victims' narratives 80-81
information organisation 31-32
information sharing 31-32
Inkatha Freedom Party (IFP) 120, 125, 244
   and the TRC 227-228
   conflict with ANC 26, 152, 174, 176, 179, 184
   engagement with Duduza 206, 209
   in Kathorus 177, 182, 185, 187-197
   political prisoners 134
   statements submitted to TRC 46
Institute of Race Relations 20
Interim Constitution 5, 222, 226, 231-232

International Criminal Court (ICC) 233-234
international law 234-235, 246
interpretation, problems of 18-20
Investigation Unit 26, 31, 48, 77, 85
  access to information 56-58
  corroboration 54
  decentralisation of 51
  in-depth investigations 52-53
  problems encountered by 52-53
  relationship with Attorney-General's Office 54-56
  Sicelo Dlomo case 109, 115
  verifying information 72-75
  work done by 50-52
investigators 31, 38, 50-54
Ismail, Aboobaker 27

J

JMCs
  see Joint Management Centres
Joe Slovo squatter camp 194
John Vorster Square 118-119, 122, 127
Joint Management Centres (JMCs) 52
Joubert, Brig Joep 53
judicial problems, faced by TRC 40-41
justice 140-143, 233
  amnesty to criminal justice system 224-225
  and reconciliation 230
  social 226

K

Kagiso 185
Kairos 19
KAPTA taxis 194
Kassinga raid 30, 32
Katlehong 24, 191
  hostels in 189, 197
  self-defence units in 59
  taxi-violence in 181-182, 194
  violence by hostel-dwellers in 190
  violence by squatters in 186
  violence in 179
Katlehong Taxi Organisation (KATO) 181
Kathorus 197
  migrants 180, 187
  the case of 173-198
KATO
  see Katlehong Taxi Organisation
Khalanyoni hostel 183-186, 190
Khanyile, Sochs 195-196
Khulumani Support Group 131-132
  Duma Khumalo's involvement with 131, 138-140, 144
  in Duduza 208
  Sicelo Dlomo case 104-106
  Thandi Shezi case 125-126, 129
Khumalo, Duma 131-144, 241
Khumalo gang 193-194

Khumalo, Mbhekiseni 193-194, 196
Khuthatha hostel 186
Krugersdorp 185
KwaMadala hostel 194
KwaMakhutha massacre 53
KwaNdebele 32-33, 53
KwaThema 208-209
KwaThema hostel 186
KwaZulu 33, 54, 152, 195
  Kathorus migrants 180-181, 187
  police investigations 58
  statements made to TRC in 46
Kwesine hostel 191, 194
Kwesine railway line 197-198

L

Language/terminology 19, 22
  see also controlled vocabulary
  statement-taking 79
  terminology 54, 58
Lands Claim Court 225
law
  history versus 22-25
lawyers 6
Lebowa 32-33, 53
Legal Aid Board 44, 137
legal representation/representatives 6, 43-44, 49, 98
legal truth 5-6, 237-243
Le Roux, Lt Gen Johan 56
Lesotho 30, 32-33
Light of God Church of Zion 193
Lindela hostel 186, 188
local community level, reconciliation at 216-217
local truths 68-69
  versus national narratives 204-217
Lubowski, Anton 32

M

Makhubu, Clive
  combat cells 108
  involvement in Sicelo Dlomo case 107-108, 114
Malan, Magnus 49, 58, 233
Mamasela, Joe 56, 110
Mamdani, Mahmood 66
mandate of TRC 5, 12, 43, 149-150, 153, 156-157, 220
  challenge of TRC mandate 18-20
  completeness 151-153
  complexities of 148
  in Kathorus 174-179
  pursuit of social truth 174-179
  tensions in 12, 137-141
mandate period
  violations committed during 45, 98
Mandela, Nelson 9
Mandela United Football Club 101
Mandela View camp 191, 194
massacres 214

Boipatong 193-195, 236, 244
  KwaMakhutha 53
  St James' Church 78, 82-83
mass media 7-9
Mazibuko hostel 194
Meadowlands 192
memory, types of 75-77
methodological pluralism 158, 168
methodology
  problems of 18-20
  TRC report 17-18, 34
Meyer, Roelf 194
Mhambi, Prince 196
micro-politics 85
migrants 191-192
  from Kathorus 180
  from KwaZulu 187
Military Intelligence 30, 57, 162, 195
Minyuku, Dr Biki 68
MK
  see Umkhonto we Sizwe
Mokati, Edward (Prof) 118
Motherwell 55
motives 159, 162, 164, 189, 190, 197
Mozambique 30, 32
Mshayazafe hostel 197
Mthembu, Sipho 118
Mthimkulu, Siphiwe 41
Mxenge family 40, 231, 233
Mxenge, Victoria 228

N

Namibia 32
Nancefield 192
narratives 10, 159
  competing narratives 209-215
  of victims 77-80
narrative truth 154, 159, 174-175
National Commission for Truth and Reconciliation (Chile) 22, 24
National Intelligence Agency 57
national narratives
  versus local truths 204-217
National Party (NP) 48, 99, 194, 207-209
  and the TRC 227-228, 237
National Peace Accord 193
National Security Management System (NSMS) 45, 52-53
National Unity and Reconciliation 222
nation-building 10-11
nationhood 9
natural history 81-83, 151
Ndwandwe, Phila Portia 32
Nigel 206-207, 209, 212
Ngema tavern 196
NGOs
  see non-governmental organisations
non-governmental organisations (NGOs) 51, 212, 228
NP
  see National Party
NSMS

INDEX

see National Security Management System
Ntuli, Sam 179, 192-194
Nyada, Siphiwe 27
Nyawose, Petros and Jabulile 32

O

Objectivity 86, 156
   achieved by TRC 150-151
Octopus Effect 31-32
official historical memory 75-77
Operation Protea 30
organisational problems
   with writing of TRC report 27-32

P

Perpetrators 3, 6, 8, 10, 21, 44, 156, 166, 168, 221, 232, 237, 239
   amnesty-seeking 236, 240
   nature and identity of 213-214
personal truth 154, 174
Phola Park 176, 183-186, 190-191, 197
   self-defence units 192, 196
police files 57
political acts 245
   definition according to Act 42
political parties 10
political prisoners 134
politicisation 188
positivism 5, 22, 156
Power Park 192
Pretoria High Court 135-136
Prof
   see Mokati, Edward
Project Coast 31
Promotion of National Unity and Reconciliation Act 5-6, 18-19, 25-26, 39-40, 60, 68, 70, 78, 205
UF Act
   amnesty provisions in 231-232, 235
   constitutional challenges to 230-231
   definition of human rights violations 42-43, 79
   definition of political act 43
   definition of relevant abuse 212-213
   judge TRC against 225
   parliamentary amendments to 47
   reparation right defined in 243
protocol 21, 70
   and statement-taking 78-80
psychosocial truth 237-243
public hearings 3, 7, 48, 54, 78, 209, 214, 235, 238
punitive justice model 233, 239

Q

Qwa Qwa 32

R

Race 212, 214

racism 43, 165, 210, 212
   and apartheid 162-166
   in post-apartheid South Africa 221
rape 120-121, 124, 126-127, 129-130
   UF sexual abuse
Ratanda 208-209
recollection 78
reconciliation 40, 149-150, 215, 239
   and justice 230
   and truth 39
   conflicting imperatives of 25-27
reconstruction 81
Record of Understanding 195
rehabilitation 84
relevant abuses 212-213
remuneration 98
reparation 11, 18, 46, 84, 139, 240-244
Reparation and Rehabilitation Committee 242
report
   see TRC Report
research, limits of 20-22
Research Department 4, 17-35, 149, 163-165
researchers 29, 31, 42
   mandate interpretation 18-20
researching
   of truth from inside Research Department 17-35
resources, available to TRC 42
restorative justice 10-12, 244-245
   and criminal law 230-237
restorative truth 154, 174
Ribeiro, Dr Fabian 228
Ribeiro family 40, 231
right-wing political parties 227-228
Riot Squad 133
Robben Island 134
rural areas 32, 70
Rwandan War Crimes Tribunal 233

S

SACC
   see South African Council of Churches
SADF
   see South African Defence Force
SCC
   see State Security Council
SDUs
   see self-defence units
Sebokeng 184-185, 187, 190, 195
security concerns 29-31
security force/security force members 20, 22, 29, 43, 53, 55, 190, 195, 209
   legal representation for 49
   rape by 120
security police 58
   Duma Khumalo case 134, 142
   Sicelo Dlomo case 114
   Thandi Shezi case 122

self-defence units (SDUs) 59, 191, 195-196
   in Kathorus 197
   in Phola Park 192-193
self-protection units (SPUs) 195
Seven Day War 29
severe ill-treatment 21, 70
sexual abuse
   see rape
Sharpeville 78, 133, 162
Sharpeville Six 131, 133, 143
   Bishop Desmond Tutu's involvement with 138
   death sentence 135-137
   TRC hearing 139
Shezi, Thandi 117-130, 241
Silver
   see Dube, John
simultaneity 82
Sithole Committee 192-193
Skhosana, Maki 207, 209, 215
Smit, Lt Gen Basie 56
social contextualisation, of victimisation 209-212
social truth 154-155, 174
   the case of Kathorus 173-198
SOSCO
   see Soweto Students Congress
source material 22
South African Council of Churches (SACC) 101
   Bishop Desmond Tutu's involvement with 138
   protests against Sharpeville Six death sentence 136
South African Defence Force (SADF) 26, 30, 32-33, 53, 127, 162
South African National Defence Force (SANDF) 26, 32
   archive records of the 30
   information access 57
South African Police Service 176
   facilitate TRC work 229
   information access 57
South West African People's Organisation (SWAPO) 30, 33, 127
Soweto Special Branch 110
Soweto Students Congress (SOSCO) 99, 103
Soweto uprising 46, 74, 78, 83, 99-100, 176, 206
Soweto Youth Congress (SOYCO) 125
SOYCO
   see Soweto Youth Congress
space constraints, in writing of TRC report 28-29
spatial coordinates 78, 82, 84
SPUs
   see self-protection units
squatter camps 31, 191-192, 194
state agencies, amnesty to 224-225
statement-taking 21, 45, 71

and protocol 78-80, 177-178
State Security Council (SCC) 29, 52
Steyn, Gen Pierre 55
Steyn Report 20, 55
St James' Church massacre 78, 82-83
sufficient consensus 226-227
Sun City 121, 124-125, 134
  UF Diepkloof Prison
support structures 240-241
SWAPO
  see South West African People's Organisation
Swaziland 32-33

T

Taxi permits 180
taxi war/violence 179-182, 188, 194, 197-198, 209
television 7-9
television programmes 34, 102
tensions, between TRC and Duduza 204-217
Terrorism Act 133
The Story I Am About to Tell 126
Third Force 191
Thokoza 59, 179, 181-182, 186, 189-191, 195, 197
Thokoza Hostel Dwellers Association 192
Thokoza Youth Congress 184
time-frame, of the TRC 41-42
time pressures 179
  with writing of TRC report 27-28
torture 50, 70, 100, 119-122, 135-136, 214
train attacks 50, 190-192, 194-195, 214
transition
  in Chile 221
  in Germany 221
  to democracy 220-221, 246
transitional justice 150, 245
Transkei 33
transparency, of governance 224
TRC
  see Truth and Reconciliation Commission (TRC)
TRC Report 17-35, 147-169
  covering apartheid 162-166
  findings 161-162
  foreword in 148, 167
  language/terminology 22
  motives and causes 159-160
  nature of 147
  political successes/failures 229
  political tension caused by 227
  problems with writing of 27-32, 187
  space constraints 28-29
  time pressures 27-28
  types of truths 154-157, 174
  use of window cases 158, 176-177
  weaknesses 25, 27, 32, 160-161, 177
TRC Special Report 34
Tripartite Alliance 191

Trojan Horse incident 78
truth 12-13, 40, 66-68, 149-150, 235-236
  complexity of 154
  conflicting imperatives of 25-27
  legal truth 237-243
  psychosocial truth 237-243
  relationship with reconciliation 39
  researching of 17-35
  types of 154-157, 174
Truth and Reconciliation Commission (TRC) 2, 66
  amnesty arrangement 48-50
  brief evaluation of 220-247
  constitutional problems faced by 40-41
  Duma Khumalo case 138, 143-144
  everyday practices of the 67-87
  in context 1-13
  Investigation Unit 50-52
  judicial problems faced by 40-41
  political tension in 229
  Research Department 4, 17-35
  resources available to 42
  successes/failures/achievements 37-60, 166-169, 229
  Thandi Shezi case 128
  time-frame of the 41-42
truth commissions 1-2, 5, 19, 22, 25, 34, 66, 230
truth production 66-87
truth recovery 230, 232
truth researching, inside Research Department 17-35
Truth Talk 58
Tsakane 208-209
Tshabala, Sipho 107-108, 112, 114
Tutu, Bishop Desmond 9
  chairman of TRC 138
  foreword in TRC Report 148, 167

U

Ubuntu 149, 222, 232
UDF
  see United Democratic Front
Umkhonto we Sizwe (MK) 53, 195
  political prisoners 134
  Sicelo Dlomo's involvement 101, 107-109, 111
  Thandi Shezi's involvement 118
United Democratic Front (UDF) 27, 33, 99, 184
United Workers' Union of South Africa (UWUSA) 182
unofficial historical memory 75-77
UWUSA
  see United Workers' Union of South Africa

V

Vaal Administration Board 142
Vaal Triangle uprising 46, 133

Van Heerden, Andries 119, 127
Venda 32-33
Verryn, Bishop Paul 132
victims 3, 10, 133, 156, 166, 168
  deconstruction of narratives 80-81
  exclusion of 'victims' 69-72
  hearings 34
  public hearings 213-215
  reconstruction of narratives 80-81
  reframing narratives in time and space 77-80
  stories of 3, 8, 97-144, 209-212
victimisation 213, 222, 232
  key incidents of 214-215
  social contextualisation of 209-212
violations
  see human rights violations
violence 188-189, 192
  threat to new South Africa 246-247
Vlakplaas 33, 55-56, 110
Vlok, Adriaan 27
vocabulary 21
  see also controlled vocabulary
Vosloorus 179, 183, 185, 187, 195
Vosloorus hostel 186

W

Wadeville taxi rank 197
Weberian social science 158-160
Wessels, Albert 31
Williams, Craig 27
window cases 23, 158, 176-177
women 166
World Council of Churches 136

X

Xhosas 182-186, 190-191

Y

Youth 101
Youth Commission 225

Z

Zambia 32
Zimbabwe 30-33, 129
Zonkesizwe 190-191, 194
Zulus 182-186, 190-192
Zungu, Precious 107-108
Zwane, Pule 110